BRITISH WOMEN COMPOSERS AND INSTRUMENTAL CHAMBER MUSIC IN THE EARLY TWENTIETH CENTURY

British Women Composers and Instrumental Chamber Music in the Early Twentieth Century

LAURA SEDDON

LONDON AND NEW YORK

First published 2013 by Ashgate Publisher

2 Park Square, Milton Park, Abingdon, Oxon OX14 4RN
711 Third Avenue, New York, NY 10017, USA

Routledge is an imprint of the Taylor & Francis Group, an informa business

First issued in paperback 2016

British Library Cataloguing in Publication Data
A catalogue record for this book is available from the British Library

The Library of Congress has cataloged the printed edition as follows:
Seddon, Laura.
British women composers and instrumental chamber music in the early twentieth century / by Laura Seddon.
pages cm
Includes bibliographical references and index.
ISBN 978-1-4094-3945-5 (hardcover : alk. paper)
1. Music by women composers--Great Britain--20th century--History and criticism. 2. Chamber music--Great Britain--20th century--History and criticism. 3. Women composers--Great Britain. I. Title.
ML82.S43 2013
785.0092'520941--dc23

2013002718

ISBN 978-1-4094-3945-5 (hbk)
ISBN 978-1-138-24963-9 (pbk)

Contents

List of Figures

List of Tables

List of Music Examples

List of Abbreviations

cl	Clarinet
db	Double bass
eng hn	English horn
fl	Flute
GSM	Guildhall School of Music
hn	Horn
NGDDMM	New Grove Dictionary of Music and Musicians (2001)
NGDWC	New Grove Dictionary of Women Composers
NUWSS	National Union of Women's Suffrage Societies
OLMS	Oxford Ladies Musical Society
pf	Pianoforte
pf qnt	Piano quintet
pf qrt	Piano quartet
qnt	Quintet
qrt	Quartet
RAM	Royal Academy of Music
RCM	Royal College of Music
S	Soprano
str qrt	String Quartet
SWM	Society of Women Musicians
TNG	The New Grove (1980)
va	Viola
vc	Violoncello
vn	violin
WI	Women's Institute
WSPU	Women's Social and Political Union

Preface

During an undergraduate course I took on women composers, the Society of Women Musicians (SWM) was mentioned in a footnote in lecture notes on Ethel Smyth (1858–1944). After discovering and devouring Smyth's volumes of memoirs, which did not contain detailed information on the SWM, or indeed other women composers, at that time I was unable to find any other sources which referred to them further. Later research on the 1908 American tour of French composer Cécile Chaminade (1857–1944) further stimulated my interest in the activities of women musicians in the early twentieth century. Yet, I was frustrated in attempts to find chamber works by British women for recitals. Thus, I hoped an exploration of the SWM archive at the Royal College and the archives at the Wigmore Hall would bring to light information on the composers involved in the Society especially those who had written instrumental music.

From many months spent in the archives, the names and activities of an extraordinary group of women emerged; some of these were active members of the SWM and others were composers who distanced themselves from it. Many of the names remain elusive and scores of much of the music mentioned in programmes no longer exist. Some documents and music by a small group of women (including the founders of the Society and active composer members) have however survived. These have allowed a very overdue, in-depth study of the activities, and in particular the instrumental music, of women composers in early twentieth-century Britain.

Laura Seddon, August 2012

Acknowledgements

I would like to thank the following for their invaluable help during this research: Rhian Samuel, Derek Scott and Christopher Wiley.

Peter Horton and staff at the Royal College of Music Library, London; Bridget Palmer, Janet Snowman, Ian Brearley and staff at the Royal Academy of Music Library, London; Julie Anne Lambert and staff at the Bodleian Library, Oxford; Alison Smith at Cardiff University Library; Rory Lalwan at Westminster Archives; and staff at the British Library, the National Library of Wales, Westminster Music Library, the Barbican Music Library and Morley College Library.

Paula Best, Publications and Archive Manager at the Wigmore Hall, and Jackie Cowdrey, Archivist at the Royal Albert Hall. Heidi Bishop, Laura Macy and staff at Ashgate.

Merryn and Colum Howell, Cara Lancaster, Pamela Blevins, Barbara Englesberg, Holly Ingleton and City University Gender Group for discussing my work.

Special thanks to Jill Seddon, Peter Seddon, Chloe Seddon, Claire Harrop and staff at Victoria Learning Centre and Carlos Duque.

Introduction

Any assessment of women's music and its reception requires consideration of their role in musical society. Early twentieth-century Britain offered women composers a very particular set of circumstances, both social and musical, in which to create their works. The main purpose of this book is to uncover some neglected works and place them in the context of early twentieth-century British music. This exercise builds on the pioneering work of Derek Scott, Derek Hyde, Sophie Fuller and Paula Gillett.[1] The general focus of these studies and other works in this area, however, has been the necessary collection of biographical material, the presentation of cultural context and, more specifically, the promotion of songs and piano works by women. This study, therefore, is part of a second wave of musicological investigation into British women's music. In this spirit it will consider some aspects of women's history and feminist criticism as well as feminist musicology.

Chapter 1 begins by situating the subjects of the book first as women and then, in the next chapter, as composers, within the prescient era that led into the First World War and out of it again. One of the most significant areas of research, presented in chapter 3, has been an investigation of the formation of the Society of Women Musicians (SWM) in London in 1911 and the responses of women composers to it. Lastly, in chapters 4 and 5 there is an investigation of the music of some of these women, situating it, too, within or in opposition to the traditions of the day.

The study focuses on women's instrumental chamber music for a number of reasons, most importantly because of its prevalence in their catalogues of works. Women who were primarily and often highly commercially successful vocal composers appeared to be expanding their repertoire in these years by writing instrumental trios, quartets or quintets. Conversely, women who had written large orchestral works, such as Ethel Smyth (1858–1944) and Edith Swepstone (1885–1930), also chose to write chamber music in these years. In addition, contemporary commentators, such as SWM member Katherine Eggar (1874–1961), philanthropist Walter Willson Cobbett (1847–1937) and composer Thomas Dunhill (1877–1946), were advocating instrumental chamber music as a means for British music to progress and compete with that produced in other European

---

[1] Derek Scott, *The Singing Bourgeois: Songs of the Victorian Drawing Room and Parlour* (London, 1989), Derek Hyde, *New Found Voices: Women in Nineteenth Century English Music* (Ash, 1991), Sophie Fuller, 'Women Composers During the British Musical Renaissance 1880–1918' (upub. PhD Diss. Kings College University of London, 1998) and Paula Gillett, *Musical Women in England, 1870–1914: Encroaching on all Man's Privileges* (Basingstoke, 2000).

countries. In comparison to their other compositions, the chamber works of women often show a particular stylistic adventurousness. One of the parameters of this study is that it will consider only instrumental music for ensemble, thus excluding music for solo piano and vocal music in any combination; genres which had been associated with women composers since the nineteenth century.

At the beginning of the twentieth century, despite the formal digressions in some of the works of late Romantics such as Liszt and Wagner and the impressionist Debussy, sonata form held sway in much European music. In Britain, Elgar, Parry, Stanford and Mackenzie, as well as theorists such as Donald F. Tovey and Ebenezer Prout, were influential in their use and advocacy of the form. Thus sonata form loomed large in the legacy of women composers. How they responded to this in the composition of their chamber works offers considerable insight into their attitudes towards the canon itself. A high proportion of chamber works by women were phantasies, supposedly free-form compositions. Many were written as entries for the Cobbett competitions instigated in 1905. Each composer's relationship to sonata form and the possibility of an emerging female aesthetic are explored.

In addition, in the case studies in chapters 4 and 5, works by Adela Maddison (1866–1929), Ethel Smyth, Morfydd Owen (1891–1918), Ethel Barns (1873–1948), Alice Verne-Bredt (1868–1958) and Susan Spain-Dunk (1880–1962), including three phantasies, are analysed.[2] One of the phantasies was written as a competition entry, another was a commission and the status of the other is unclear. The works in total represent a range of instrumental combinations: two string quartets, one piano quintet and three trios. Some of the works were published, had multiple early performances and a number of recent concert revivals, while others remain in manuscript form. The above women represent three generations of composers active at the beginning of the twentieth century, attaining widely differing levels of public recognition and private 'success'.

These British composers were all actively composing in London at different periods in their lives, although they were not necessarily born there.[3] Some had close links with the London music colleges, and studied composition as part of their education; some studied privately and others such as Alice Verne-Bredt were

---

[2] Many secondary sources give Ethel Barns's date of birth as 1880 but her birth certificate specifies 1873. See also Barbara Englesberg, 'The Life and Works of Ethel Barns: British Violinist Composer 1873–1948' (unpub. PhD Thesis, Boston University, 1987), pp. 1 and 3.

[3] Ethel Barns, b. London, d. Maidenhead, spent most of her life living in central London; Alice Verne-Bredt was born in Southampton but moved to London in childhood and spent most of her life living in London; Susan Spain-Dunk, b. Folkestone, d. London, spent most of her life in central London; Morfydd Owen, b. Treforest, Wales, d. Oystermouth (on holiday), moved to London after completing her studies in Cardiff in 1912; Ethel Smyth, b. London, d. Woking, spent her life based in the south of England but travelled a great deal; Adela Maddison, b. Ireland, d. Ealing, lived in London, Paris and Berlin. See Sophie Fuller, 'Women Composers', pp. 300–301.

taught informally by family members. While it cannot be claimed that they reflect every woman composer's life in Britain, as a group their works are representative of women composers and they highlight many of the issues facing women in musical society.

In this investigation, 1920 represents the end of an era. This was the point at which the SWM started to campaign for the rights of women performers and became less concerned with the work of women composers. The phantasy competitions became less prevalent in the 1920s as Cobbett's financial support of composers diminished. Instead, he concentrated on instigating other competitions and providing support for students and performers. A new generation of women composers then emerged, including Elizabeth Maconchy (1907–1994), Elisabeth Lutyens (1906–1983), Dorothy Gow (1893–1982) and Grace Williams (1906–1977).[4]

Consideration of women composers as a separate entity from their male counterparts is a necessary division for this analysis. This is not to argue that women did not face many of the same challenges as male composers, rather that the range of barriers facing creative women and the female experience of interacting within a 'patriarchal' musical society warrant further investigation. At the same time, while many of the initial feminist musicological studies have taken for granted dichotomies such as male/female, public/private and equality/difference, this book's methodology aims to investigate and deconstruct such binary relationships within the context of early twentieth-century music. This discussion therefore raises a number of important questions, which may usefully be addressed at the outset and are considered throughout the text:

Why Focus on 'Women'?

Is there something that binds 'women' as a group or is the category of 'women' maintained because it is the basis of feminism as a construct and without it the discipline would not exist? This is a much-debated issue, as Judith Butler argues, in her influential book, *Gender Trouble*:

> [T]here is the political problem that feminism encounters in the assumption that the term *women* denotes a common identity. Rather than a stable signifier that commands the assent of those whom it purports to describe and represent, *women*, even of the plural, has become a troublesome term, a site of contest, a cause for anxiety.[5]

[4] For further information on Lutyens, Maconchy and Williams see Rhiannon Mathias, *Lutyens, Maconchy, Williams and Twentieth-century British Music: A Blest Trio of Sirens* (Farnham, 2012); Elisabeth Lutyens, *A Goldfish Bowl* (London, 1972) and Malcolm Boyd, *Grace Williams* (Cardiff, 1980).

[5] Judith Butler, *Gender Trouble: Feminism and the Subversion of Identity* (London, New York, 1990), p. 3.

This is more than just a semantic issue; many writers have highlighted their concern that the term 'women' is always defined in relation to 'men'. In the 1950s one of the first to investigate this in terms of 'women' as 'Other' was Simone de Beauvoir who argued that the relationship between the terms 'man' and 'woman' was not an equal binary:

> In actuality the relation of the sexes is not quite like that of two electrical poles, for man represents both the positive and the neutral, as is indicated by the common use of *man* to designate human beings in general; whereas *woman* represents only the negative, defined by limiting criteria, without reciprocity.[6]

More pertinently for this study, the assumption that there are enough similarities between 'women' of differing age, class, race and historical period to justify the category 'women' as a useful distinction has also been contested. Is the only thing that binds women the oppression that they have experienced, or is there something more to the female experience of being? As de Beauvoir argues, the fact that women's oppression is based on biological differences rather than a specific historical event has made the oppression far more difficult to detect and deconstruct.

> When a man makes of woman the *Other*, he may, then, expect to manifest deep-seated tendencies toward complicity. Thus woman may fail to lay claim to the status of subject because she lacks definite resources, because she feels the necessary bond that ties her to man regardless of reciprocity, and because she is often very well pleased with her role as the *Other.*[7]

Germaine Greer asserts that the concepts of the 'sisterhood' of women, with common ideals and even politics, is a dangerous one: 'even more questionable than the suggestion that sisterhood unites women across class and ethnic lines is the claim that sisterhood binds women of different generations. Sisters, by definition, belong to an age set.'[8] Greer, however, does advocate a 'female' experience and she is convinced that '[f]eminism exists outside the realm of political instrumentality, as an idea'.[9]

The definition of 'woman' within a male domain has repercussions for those involved in academic research. Beverly Thiele expands on Artemis March's three forms of invisibility of women; 'exclusion, pseudo-inclusion and alienation'.[10] Thiele indicates that even academic work that includes women does not 'speak

---

6 Simone de Beauvoir, *The Second Sex*, ed. H.M. Parshley (Harmondsworth, 1972), p. 15.

7 Ibid., p. 21.

8 Germaine Greer, *The Whole Woman* (London, 2000), p. 292.

9 Ibid., p. 11.

10 Beverly Thiele, 'Vanishing Acts in Social and Political Thought: Tricks of the Trade', in *Defining Women Social Institutions and Gender Distortions*, ed. Linda McDowell and Rosemary Pringle (Cambridge, 1992), p. 28.

of the parameters of women's lives without distortion. Women's experience is interpreted through male categories because the methodology and values of the theorists remain androcentric'.[11] This has particular relevance for how musicologists structure their analyses of women's music, as it may be that certain methods of analysis will not yield considered and fruitful results. Thiele goes on to advocate a greater development of gynocentric themes before a universal political theory can emerge. She writes 'As Mary O'Brien's theorizing in *The Politics of Reproduction* (1981) illustrates so well, gynocentric theory is more than a mere counterbalance … it is the turn of a spiral, not a flip of a coin'.[12]

Yet this area of feminist theory merely sets up yet another binary of gynocentric versus androcentric analyses. Here six women composers are considered within the context of the musical society in which they were working including interaction and comparison with male composers. As Susan McClary argues:

> [T]he women who have composed music throughout Western history have coexisted within the same cultural contexts as their better-known male counterparts. Thus, if we are to understand how they might have operated differently within the same stylistic and syntactical procedures as men, we have to begin unpicking what and how those apparently neutral procedures themselves signify.[13]

This study, therefore, attempts to avoid simplistic categorisation of 'woman'; the women themselves did not consider themselves a group, but an analysis that has allowed for issues of gender and sexuality has been deliberately constructed, to build on previous biographical research and work on the canon.

How does the Relationship between Sex and Gender affect this Book?

The dichotomy of sex and gender has implications for this book in relation to the 'female' experience. De Beauvoir commented:

> It would appear, then, that every female human being is not necessarily a woman; to be considered so she must share in that mysterious and threatened reality known as femininity – Is this attribute something secreted by the ovaries? Or is it a platonic essence, a product of the philosophical imagination? Is a rustling petticoat enough to bring it down to earth?[14]

---

11 Ibid.

12 Ibid., p. 33.

13 Susan McClary, 'Reshaping a Discipline: Musicology and Feminism in the 1990s', *Feminist Studies*, 19/2 (Summer, 1993): p. 409.

14 De Beavoir, *The Second Sex*, p. 13.

In the increasing amount of work in this area, the prominent idea that sex was biologically determined and that inescapably led to a particular gender for that body, thus leading to a desire for the opposite sex, has been questioned primarily by Judith Butler. She argues for a more fluid approach towards gender and desire, so that the dichotomies of male/female and masculine/feminine are no longer bound together. She asserts that certain gendered behaviours or 'performances' have become so dominant that they have been especially detrimental to women.

> When feminist theorists claim that gender is the cultural interpretation of sex or that gender is culturally constructed, what is the manner of mechanism of this construction? If gender is constructed, could it be constructed differently, or does its constructedness imply some form of social determinism, foreclosing the possibility of agency and transformation? Does "construction" suggest that certain laws generate gender differences along universal axes of sexual difference?[15]

A decade later Greer goes as far as to argue that: '[f]emininity has nothing to do with sex. Men can do femininity better than women can because femaleness conflicts with femininity as maleness does not.'[16] These late twentieth-century explorations of gender have implications for the analysis of the women in this study, who experienced the conflict between late nineteenth/early twentieth-century ideas of [female] femininity and the choice to represent themselves as composers. Applied to a musical context, it can be argued that it was often 'easier' for male rather than female composers to maintain some notion of femininity in their music and their lives.

Are Public and Private Mutually Exclusive?

This book examines the assumptions that women's works were more suited to private performance and that 'salons' and 'At Homes' were exclusively the preserve of women. It suggests that it was possible as a woman composer to move between public and private spheres and in fact there were many links between the two. Feminist theorists have again questioned the idea that women are inclined to be closer to 'nature' and therefore the family and the private sphere, whereas men are somehow connected to culture and the public arena. Sherry Ortner describes this dichotomy:

> The family (and hence women) represents lower-level, socially fragmenting, particularistic sorts of concerns, as opposed to interfamilial relations representing higher-level, integrative, universalistic sorts of concerns. Since men lack a 'natural' basis (nursing, generalised to childcare) for a familial orientation, their

[15] Butler, *Gender Trouble*, p. 7.

[16] Greer, *The Whole Woman*, p. 87.

> sphere of activity is defined at the level of interfamilial relations. And hence, so the cultural reasoning seems to go, men are the "natural" proprietors of religion, ritual, politics, and other realms of cultural thought and action in which universalistic statements of spiritual and social synthesis are made.[17]

However, as Alison Jaggar argues, 'we cannot say that "biology determines society" because we cannot identify a clear nonsocial sense of "biology" nor a clear, nonbiological sense of "society"'.[18] It is therefore nonsensical to suggest that woman is closer to nature or that activities traditionally associated with women are somehow more 'natural'.[19] This is not to suggest that beliefs surrounding 'private' and 'public' were not pervasive in early twentieth-century musical society, as has been explored in relation to women composers by Sophie Fuller, but rather that the level of complexity and movement between the two, for differing purposes, deserves further consideration.[20]

How Might the 'Equality Versus Difference' Debate Apply to Early Twentieth-century Women Composers?

This question has been extremely important in evaluating how to assess the musical ideologies of individual women composers and the SWM. Linda MacDowell and Rosemary Pringle define different periods of feminist thought by 'shifts in emphasis' on equality and difference, but go on to argue that 'Increasingly, feminists have realised the importance of avoiding the either/or; both forms may be regarded as male-identified. Whether women are defined as the same as men, or different from them, men remain the reference point, the ungendered 'norm' against which women are compared'.[21]

Being compared to this 'ungendered norm' has not been beneficial to women and it can be argued that the supposed 'choice' between equality and difference has made the exploration of women's place in society more difficult. While difference can lead to ghettoisation, Greer argues against equality:

---

[17] Sherry B. Ortner, 'Is Female to Male as Nature is to Culture?', in *Key Concepts in Critical Theory*, ed.. Carol C. Gould (Atlantic Highlands New Jersey, 1997), p. 21.

[18] Alison M. Jaggar, 'Human Biology in Feminist Theory: Sexual Equality reconsidered', in *Key Concepts in Critical Theory*, ed. Carol C. Gould (Atlantic Highlands New Jersey, 1997), p. 51.

[19] Ibid., p. 53.

[20] Fuller, 'Women Composers During the British Musical Rennaissance'.

[21] Linda McDowell and Rosemary Pringle, 'Introduction', in *Defining Women Social Institutions and Gender Divisions*, eds Linda McDowell and Rosemary Pringle (Cambridge, 1992), p. 13.

> It is virtually impossible to separate the idea of equality from the idea of similarity. If we accept that men are not free, and that masculinity is as partial an account of maleness as femininity is of femaleness, then equality must be seen to be a poor substitute for liberation … The denial of real difference can be as cruel as forcing different-sized feet into a single-sized shoe.[22]

The deconstruction of the binary relationship between equality and difference has been much considered but the difficulty in finding a solution is apparent. Joan W. Scott has attempted this through poststructuralist theory:

> The only alternative, it seems to me, is to refuse to oppose equality to difference and insist continually on differences – differences as the condition of individual and collective identities, differences as the constant challenge to the fixing of those identities, history as the repeated illustration of the play of differences, differences as the very meaning of equality itself.[23]

While this book examines 'women' composers, it will attempt not to place them in a homogeneous grouping and will analyze the differences between their approaches to composition, their sense of identity as composers and their interaction with a patriarchal musical world.

What Considerations should be Taken into Account when Applying Modern Feminist Theory to Historical Situations?

Although consideration of contemporary feminist thought is essential when developing an appropriate methodology for examining works by women, merely transferring modern ideas of sex and gender to a specific historical period would lead to a flawed representation. Wendy Cealy Harrison and John Hood Williams write of Denise Riley's consideration of the historical nature of these categories:

> Like Ann Oakley, she describes what she calls historical 'loops' by means of which women cycle between a refusal to inhabit the femininities that are thrust upon them and an assertion of an alternative, but no less compelling, account of a female nature, which, as she says, an older feminism had always sought to shred to bits.[24]

---

22 Greer, *The Whole Woman*, pp. 395–6.

23 Joan W. Scott 'Deconstructing Equality-versus-Difference: or, The Uses of Post-Structuralist Theory for Feminism', in *Defining Women Social Institutions and Gender Divisions*, eds Linda McDowell and Rosemary Pringle (Cambridge, 1992), p. 262.

24 Cealy Harrison and John Hood-Williams, *Beyond Sex and Gender* (London, Thousand Oaks, New Delhi, 2002), p. 215.

Pertinent to this study, Riley finds that investigations into the relationship between the individual and the historical collective aspects of being a woman is important in understanding that 'Being a woman' has differing periodicities which are not only phenomenological, played out moment by moment for the individual, but are also historical – collectivities and characterisations of "women" are established in a myriad historical-discursive formations'.[25]

Historical context is also important to this investigation as this first era of feminism had a much greater focus on political rights than the sexual/psychological basis of second and third wave feminism. Thus, as shall be discussed later, the interaction between sex and gender in the early twentieth century is, in many ways, very different from that found in contemporary discussions.

Historical differences are not always easy to ascertain, because as Leonore Davidoff argues, historical source material can often reflect assumed dichotomies, especially that of public versus private, mainly due to methods of data collection.[26] In order to present as complete a narrative as possible of the woman composer's role in society, this research utilises a variety of historical sources from the personal (diaries, letters) to the collective (minutes, membership lists, speeches, student records) to the public (publicity, concert programmes, scores, musical criticism).

How has Feminism Influenced Musicology?

The consideration of feminist theory as a tool for musicologists happened somewhat later than in other arts criticism, especially literature and art history. There has been some concern that feminist musicologists have actually been detrimental to the 'cause' of women composers; indeed many contemporary women composers have disassociated themselves from 'feminist views'. The composer Vivian Fine, who had studied with Ruth Crawford Seeger, stated in an interview 'I never thought of myself as a woman composer, and of course, Ruth was a woman composer, so that was something very fundamental that I got from her'.[27] Although Fine dealt with themes of equality and women's suffrage in works such as *Meeting for Equal Rights* (1976), the above statement highlights the complexities of identity as a woman and a composer.[28]

Historically, women composers may have been wary of claiming a distinguishing female 'voice' within their work; this – what Gilbert and Gubar have classified as the 'female affiliation complex' – has also been the case within literature. Women

---

[25] Denise Riley, 'Does Sex Have a History? "Women" and Feminism' *New Formations*, 1 (Spring 1987): p.38.

[26] McDowell and Pringle, *Defining Women*, p. 16. see also Leonore Davidoff, *World's Between: Historical Perspectives on Gender and Class* (Cambridge: Polity Press, 1995).

[27] Leslie Jones, 'Seventy Years of Composing: an Interview with Vivian Fine', CMR, 16/1 (1997): p. 23.

[28] Ibid., p. 25.

composers' position in the late twentieth century has become more radical and female identity has started to be seen as beneficial: '"Sounding like a woman" is taking on other connotations now however, at least among women. To quite a few of the people I talk with it implies that vague term, a sense of the wholeness of the work and a strongly centred work. A positive term.'[29]

Rhian Samuel addresses this issue with regard to music in her foreword to the *New Grove Dictionary of Women Composers*, citing early twentieth-century composers Mabel Wheeler Daniels (1877–1971) and Helen Hopekirk (1856–1945) who 'eschewed the labels "feminist" and even "woman composer", yet worked for women's suffrage'.[30] Although Samuel feels that, in general, women composers in more recent years have engaged with the concept of a female voice in music, there is still some resistance; successful women composers from the late Priaulx Rainier to the living Kaija Saariaho informed her that they did/do not wish to be called women composers. Furthermore, Samuel relates that some women would only appear on a BBC radio programme Samuel made in the process of publicising the dictionary in 1995 if the interview were restricted to 'the music' and did not raise gender issues.[31]

This is a phenomena that Sally Macarthur has also considered:

> I have also noted that many female composers reject the notion of the 'feminine' in their work and with identifying themselves as women composers: they consider themselves as composers not women composers. When composers disavow the 'feminine' it could be that they reject the essentialising of their own bodies as marginal and different.[32]

As will be discussed, however, there were exceptions to the general reluctance to identify the female 'voice' in the first decades of the twentieth century.

While some may argue that feminism has hindered the absorption of historical women composers into the canon, it is extremely unlikely that, without feminist writings on music, this could ever be achieved. Marcia Citron claims that feminism is actually allowing a more critical approach to develop: 'Feminism, a relative newcomer, has influenced discursive practices such that work on historical

---

29 Annea Lockwood et al. 'In Response', *Perspectives of New Music*, 20/1 and 2 (Autumn 1981–Summer 1982): p. 305 also cited in Marcia Citron, *Gender and the Musical Canon* (Cambridge, 1993), p. 162 and Rhian Samuel, 'Women's Music: A Twentieth-Century Perspective', Preface 2 to *The New Grove Dictionary of Women Composers*, eds Julie A. Sadie and Rhian Samuel (London, 1994), p. xv.

30 Samuel, 'Women's Music', p. xiv.

31 Discussion with Rhian Samuel, City University, 2008.

32 Sally Macarthur, *Towards a Twenty-first-century Feminist Politics of Music* (Farnham, 2010), pp. 124–5.

women, including newly discovered figures need not focus solely on documentary recuperation but can utilise more critical approaches as well.'[33]

Paula Higgins feels that feminist musicology and especially Susan McClary's work has only scratched the surface when investigating the social reasons for the difficulties historical, and indeed contemporary, women composers have faced. This project will consider further what Higgins describes as 'assumptions':

> McClary and feminist musicology in general have yet to interrogate a whole series of assumptions that have served to explain the invisibility of women in music such as: (1) their exclusion from institutional training; (2) their failure to publish (and hence to act as agents of influence); (3) their lack of versatility, in confining themselves largely to 'minor' works; (4) their lack of professional status; and (5) their lack of originality.[34]

Along with other feminist arts criticism, feminist musicology has debated the nature of the canon, reflecting not only on the lack of female representation but the gender-divide of genre. Women novelists, for example, have historically considerably outnumbered their male counterparts. Indeed the novel is still seen as a primarily female form, especially in terms of its consumption: 'Reading groups, readings, breakdowns of book sales all tell the same story: when women stop reading the novel will be dead.'[35] This female preponderance can be seen to a lesser extent with the musical ballad in the late nineteenth and early twentieth centuries, whose composers, performers and audience were predominantly female.[36]

The literary critic, Mary Eagleton, sees dangers in the creation of a female literary canon:

> Rather than disrupting the individualistic values by which the mainstream canon has been created, feminist critics sometimes merely replace a male first eleven with a female one: so you study Aphra Behn instead of Dryden, Edith Wharton instead of Henry James, Dorothy Wordsworth instead of William.[37]

The literary and film critic, Viviane Forrester, however, anticipates the argument that there are no women in the canon because their work is not good enough by asserting that 'considering quality is to miss the point':

---

33 Marcia Citron, *Gender and the Musical Canon* (Illinois, 2000), p. 4.

34 Paula Higgins, 'Women in Music, Feminist Criticism, and Guerilla Musicology: Reflections on Recent Polemics', *19th Century Music*, 27/2 (Fall, 1993): p. 189.

35 Ian McEwan, 'Hello Would You Like a Free Book?' *The Guardian Online*, 19 September 2005 <www.guardian.co.uk/books/2005/sep/20/fiction.features11> [accessed 18 October 2009].

36 See Derek Scott, *The Singing Bourgeois* and Derek Hyde, *New Found Voices*.

37 Mary Eagleton, 'Introduction' in *Feminist Literary Theory: A Reader*, ed. by Mary Eagleton (Oxford, 1986), pp. 3–4.

> The quality of vision is not the point – in the hierarchical sense – it is not better (how absurd to speak of a 'better' vision), it is not more efficient, more immediate (certain women will assert that it is, but that's not the point), but it is lacking. And this deficiency is suicidal.[38]

This view is indeed applicable to the musical canon in its present condition and highlights the dangers of just giving selected women honoured places in music history. Samuel discusses this issue in relation to women composers and the attitudes of those evaluating musical quality:

> Some critics assert that women's music has not survived because it is simply not good enough. The issue of 'quality' in music can provide a convenient means of dismissing women's music, both heard and unheard, particularly when the critic overlooks such vital issues as the fact that aesthetic judgments are never absolute and that criteria for musical quality are inextricably linked to the established repertoire in a spiral that constantly bypasses women composers.[39]

Perhaps one of the most influential works on the position of women in the canon has been Marcia Citron's *Gender and the Musical Canon.*[40] Here Citron looks comprehensively at the different manifestations of women composers' exclusion from the Western musical canon. She acknowledges the potential criticism for analyzing 'women' in isolation: 'For women we must draw distinctions between a woman as a specific individual and women in general and realise that one flirts with essentialism and its potentially negative connotations when discussing the latter.'[41]

Later feminist musicological studies such as *Gendering Musical Modernism* by Ellie Hisama and Joanna Bailey's article, 'Gender as style: Feminist Aesthetics and Postmodernism', deal with the classification of 'women' and the notion of a female musical aesthetic in greater depth.[42] Hisama claims:

---

[38] Viviane Forrester, 'What Women's Eyes See' in *Feminist Literary Theory: A Reader*, p. 35. Work on the canon in literature and film in relation to women was far in advance of musicology. Forrester and Eagleton were both addressing this issue twenty years before Marcia Citron published Gender and the Musical Canon.

[39] Samuel, 'Women's Music', pp. xiii–xiv.

[40] Citron, *Gender and the Musical Canon.*

[41] Marcia Citron, 'Feminist Approaches to Musicology', in Cecilia Reclaimed*: Feminist Perspectives on Gender and Music*, eds Susan C. Cook and Judy S. Tsou (Illinois, 1994), p. 25.

[42] Ellie Hisama, *Gendering Musical Modernism: The Music of Ruth Crawford, Marion Bauer, and Miriam Gideon* (Cambridge, 2001) and Joanna Bailey, 'Gender as Style: Feminist Aesthetics and Postmodernism', *Contemporary Music Review*, 17/2 (1998): 105–113.

> I shall not seek to argue that specific compositions share some sort of commonality because they were written by women who were working within a specific idiom and historical moment … I offer analyses of their music that are informed by the conditions of gender and politics within which they exist.[43]

Hisama asserts that each analysis is work-specific and that her conclusions are not universal.[44] While in agreement with much of Hisama's methodology, by including a larger group of women, this study aims to balance acknowledgement of differences in approach, as discussed earlier, with an exploration of the possibility of an emerging female aesthetic.

Macarthur also attempts to address the problem of reinforcing dichotomies:

> In order to overcome the difficulty which emerges wherever I find myself almost inevitably wanting to construct a dichotomy, I attempt to slip into the intersices that separate men's music from women's. I want to think about women's music as being part of a continuum encompassing men's music while at the same time, as contradictory as the idea may seem, separating it from men's music.[45]

It is inevitable then, that women's music in the early twentieth century shares many features in common with men's music and this is dependent on the conditions of composition, for example, pieces composed for competitions. However, as Macarthur goes on to argue, the question is 'whether there are more differences between men's and women's styles than there are within each of them'.[46]

Writing about music by women is an emotive issue and the writer's gender inevitably informs the discussion; for example Jane Bowers and Judith Tick write, 'We are "looking after" women's music and women musicians themselves – remembering them through the methods historians apply in their attempts to objectify the past.'[47] This can lead to either over-laudatory uncritical assessment or, as Shoshana Felman believes, a retrograde stance:

> What is 'to speak *in the name* of' the woman? What in a general manner, does 'speech in the name of' mean? Is it not the precise repetition of the oppressive gesture of *representation* by means of which, throughout history of logos, man

---

43 Hisama, *Gendering Musical Modernism*, p. 2.

44 Ibid., p. 10.

45 Sally Macarthur, *Feminist Aesthetics in Music* (Westport, Connecticut, London, 2002), p. 3.

46 Ibid., p. 20.

47 Jane Bowers and Judith Tick (eds), *Women Making Music The Western Art Tradition 1150–1950* (Urbana, 1986), p. 3.

> has reduced the woman to the status of the silent and subordinate object, to something inherently spoken for.[48]

Although being a woman does not entitle the writer to speak 'in the name of women', it allows her to write with a declared sympathy for her topic, and a sense of objectivity whose limitations are openly acknowledged. Susan McClary has advocated this position, arguing that scientific attitudes need not always be applied to musicology.[49] The fact that a woman's composing is an emotive and often difficult issue to write about should not, therefore, be used as justification for simply opting out of the debate. Sociologist Tia DeNora has some reservations, however, in applying sociological theories to musicology, although she is, in general, positive about the possible connections: 'McClary [in *Feminine Endings*] tends to sideline issues relating to (1) how situated listeners other than herself make sense of music, (2) how semiotic codes are far from totalizing … and (3) how codes exist in plural (sometimes contradicting each other) …'.[50]

McClary has argued against accusations that specifically feminists, but also female musicologists in general, are turning music into a political issue. She feels this notion has been used to discredit and further marginalise work on women's music. McClary argues that the fact that specific groups claim ownership of different categories of music has already made music political in nature.[51] Thus, the white, 'middle class' male has been perceived to own the Western classical tradition.[52] Concentrating on women's music, therefore, merely brings its political 'nature' into focus, rather than *making* it political. This attitude, however, does not just involve ownership but also promotion; the historian as advocate simply reveals another layer of political meaning. But of course, no historian's ordering of events, or her/his narrative style, is ever neutral. Feminism, therefore, cannot – and need not – deny its involvement in the politicizing of music and music history.

Accepting, as Catherine Hall does, that history is 'always about investigating the past through the concerns of the present, and always to do with interpretation', this book, will therefore, attempt to apply aspects of feminist theory with a sensitivity to historical context, especially when considering ideas of gender roles and behaviour.[53]

---

48 Shoshana Feldman, 'Women and Madness: The Critical Phallacy', in *Feminist Literary Theory: A Reader*, ed. Mary Eagleton (Oxford, 1986), p. 36.

49 Susan McClary, *Feminine Endings Music, Gender, Sexuality* (Minneapolis, 1991), pp. 21–22.

50 Tia DeNora, 'Review of Feminine Endings', *Contemporary Sociology*, 22/1 (1993): p. 117.

51 McClary, *Feminine Endings*, p. 25–26.

52 The term 'middle class' itself is of course, absurdly generalizing, as the six case studies in this study will show.

53 Catherine Hall, *White, Male and Middle Class: Explorations in Feminism and History* (Cambridge, 1992), p. 1.

What is Happening in Feminist Musicology Now?

The initial flush of musicological research that could be classified as 'feminist' in the 1990s has receded considerably, with many of those who contributed ground-breaking texts moving on to other areas of interest. Yet an EBSCO search in January 2012 for 'feminism and music' shows 15 results between 1990 and 1994, remaining fairly constant with 12 results between 1995 and 1999, and 10 results between 2000 and 2004. Between 2005 and 2011, however, there was a rise of 19 results. The same search on the British Library's main catalogue shows 21 results between 1991 and 1998, 41 results between 1998 and 2003, and an increase to 88 results between 2003 and 2011. While a significant number of the publications deal with popular music studies and gender, it is certainly not the case that there is no work being done on women's music in a feminist context.

Although vital work is continuing to be done on the social contexts of women's music, Macarthur and Hisama are part of only a small group of musicologists who have addressed issues of feminist analysis in recent years. It can be argued that the initial explorations in analysing both women's music and men's music from a feminist perspective, such as McClary's seminal analysis of Beethoven and Citron's on Chaminade, have not been built upon by others. Thus to some extent the momentum was lost.

Chapter 1

Contexts: The Lives of Women Composers

The early twentieth century witnessed immense change in British society, especially the emancipation of woman's place within it. The death of Queen Victoria in 1901 and the coronation of Edward VII ushered in a new era characterised by developing technology, a shifting class structure and social unrest. The British Empire, while diminishing, still included a quarter of the world's population.[1] 1910 then marked a transition not only with the coronation of George V but the increasing disintegration of Liberalism, the rising intensity of the suffrage campaign, the issue of Irish home rule and strikes in a number of industries.[2] As Historian Kate Caffrey notes, 'For all its hindsight atmosphere of tranquil sunset glory, the Edwardian period was jumpy with disaster'.[3] What aspects of society and politics, therefore, affected the lives of women musicians in general and more specifically women composers? This chapter considers the issues of generation, class, education, career and patronage, sexuality, marriage and motherhood, politics and war, and how they would have impacted on a woman in her development as a composer.

From birth, a woman musician's generation, as defined below, along with her social and financial position, generally delineated her opportunities, including her education and freedom in her choice of personal relationships and career. In the latter, it even defined the level of professionalism to which she could aspire. Women actively composing in this period spanned three generations: roughly, women born before 1870, those born in approximately the next 20 years, and those born post-1890, many of whom were still students. As far as British composers were concerned the first generation included Ethel Smyth (1859–1944), Liza Lehmann (1862–1918), Dora Bright (1863–1951) and Adela Maddison (1866–1929); the second, Katherine Eggar (1874–1961), Marion Scott (1877–1953), Ethel Barns (1873–1948), Susan Spain-Dunk (1880–1962) and Rebecca Clarke (1886–1979); and the third, Morfydd Owen (1891– 1918) and Dorothy Howell (1898–1982).[4]

This last period provided the cradle for composers such as Freda Swain (1902–1985), Elisabeth Lutyens (1906–1983), Grace Williams (1906–1977) and Elizabeth Maconchy (1907–1994) whose careers not only flourished for the next half century but who have also enjoyed enthusiastic revivals of their music during

---

[1] David Thomson, *England in the Twentieth Century: (1914–79)*, rev. Geoffrey Warner (Harmondsworth, 1981), p. 23.

[2] Ibid., p. 32.

[3] Kate Caffrey, *The Edwardian Lady: Edwardian High Society 1900–1914* (London, 1979), p. 13.

[4] See Appendix 1 for more information on Bright, Clarke, Howell and Lehmann.

their centenary years. It might be argued that these younger women benefited the most from the activities of the generations to be examined in this book.

The first generation described above was more likely to have studied privately or to have undertaken instrumental studies – but not composition – at the music conservatoires in London. Emanating from the aristocracy and upper-(middle)-classes, these women generally remained within these circles rather than moving in musical society. The second generation can be defined as the 'political' generation who, in the early twentieth century, were most active in setting up organisations such as the Society of Women Musicians (SWM), putting on concerts of women's music and generally promoting women's issues. Most received their musical education at the Royal Academy of Music (RAM), or the Royal College of Music (RCM), usually studying piano or violin as their first instrument, though some, such as Ethel Barns, also studied composition. The composers of the youngest generation were considerably freer than their predecessors, often living independently in London while studying. Composition tended to be their principal study, but they joined women's societies less frequently.

Many of the women composers and musicians of the older generation were still chaperoned before marriage and were supervised continually; this is illustrated by the case of the singer Elsie Swinton (née Ebsworth, 1874–1966). David Greer recounts that she was born in Russia and came from a wealthy, but not aristocratic, background.[5] She completed her education at a finishing school near St. Leonard's-on-Sea on the south coast of England and by the age of 18 was living in London with her mother. Her activities were closely monitored, even to the extent of her reading materials being censored:

> But it irked her that she was not allowed to go about freely on her own. These were still days of chaperonage, and while it was in order for her to walk alone near home, in the Sloane Street area, any expeditions further afield – to Piccadilly or Bond Street – required the attendance of her maid, Miss Richardson.[6]

The youngest generation can be seen to have considerably more freedom even while still students in London. Even though Dorothy Howell was from a conservative Catholic family from Birmingham and lodged at a Catholic boarding house during her studies at the RAM, she was allowed to take trains by herself: 'having carefully selected a carriage containing two females I steamed back safely to Harrow.'[7] It was necessary, however, for Richard (Dick) Sampson, the brother of her sister's fiancé, to escort her to dinners and concerts in the evenings. Equally, the pianist Myra Hess (1890–1965), who was from a Jewish family and was brought up in a middle-class home in St John's Wood, was allowed to travel back

[5] The following information about Elsie Swinton is taken from David Greer, *A Numerous and Fashionable Audience: The Story of Elsie Swinton* (London, 1977).

[6] Ibid. p. 25.

[7] Letter from Dorothy Howell to her mother, 1914, uncatalogued, Dorothy Howell Trust.

and forth from the Academy in the company of her friend, Irene Scharrer, and was able to socialise with friends, without supervision.[8]

As discussed in the introduction, there was not a single experience of being a 'woman'. The class structure was one of the main factors to influence how both men and women were expected to function in society, but it affected their lives very differently. This research focuses on the educated and/or generally more wealthy, who inhabited the 'middle' and 'upper' classes, as the women composers under discussion came primarily from these levels of society. How a woman composer was treated very much depended on her socio-economic background. As discussed earlier with regard to geographic background, the women composers focused on in chapters 4 and 5 came from a variety of socio-economic backgrounds within the middle and upper-middle classes. Adela Maddison and Ethel Smyth both came from families with military backgrounds and as composers they moved in aristocratic/bohemian social circles. Ethel Barns's father was a zinc merchant and then owned an iron foundry in Holloway, while Susan Spain-Dunk's father was listed as a builder on her RAM student record.[9] Morfydd Owen's family were shopkeepers and Alice Verne-Bredt came from a family of German immigrants who were professional musicians/teachers.[10]

While the lifestyles of those in different classes varied considerably, class-structure was apparently less rigid than in the Victorian era and it was possible to elevate yourself with money. '[T]he uppermost class, characterised by its wealth, status and above all political power, was an amalgam of top business and professional men and the landed aristocracy.'[11] Indeed, A.N. Wilson argues, 'Money was not merely important in Edwardian England, it was paramount. Lord Bryce, British ambassador to the United States from 1907 to 1912, believed Britain was more money-obsessed than America, and in that sense less class-bound'.[12] Yet this mobility was still not as easily obtainable for wealthy independent women as for men.

Women from the more privileged parts of society found some greater independence and even, occasionally, entry into higher education. Women could take degrees at provincial universities but, despite having women-only colleges, Oxford did not allow women to take degrees until 1919 and Cambridge not until after the Second World War.[13] Women's entry into the professions depended greatly on whether they were responsible for their household: 'It is perhaps less

---

8 See Appendix 1 for more information on Hess and Scharrer.

9 Englesberg, 'The Life and Works of Ethel Barns', pp. 1–3 and Susan Spain-Dunk Student Record, RAM Archives, London.

10 See chapters 4 and 5 for further biographical information.

11 Arthur Marwick, *The Deluge British Society and the First World War* (New York, 1965), p. 22.

12 A.N. Wilson, *After the Victorians: 1901–1953* (London, 2005), p. 54.

13 Arthur Marwick, *Women at War 1914–1918* (London, 1977), p. 18 and Wilson, *After the Victorians*, pp. 265–6. Women were admitted to the RAM and the RCM in the nineteenth century and in certain disciplines out-numbered male students.

commonly recognised that running an upper-middle-class household could also prove most difficult and time consuming. For, although servants were there to save housewives from unladylike drudgery, they were unable to relieve them of the burden of overall responsibility.'[14]

In reality, women who did not have to work for a living and had limited domestic responsibilities had vast amounts of time to fill but considerable restrictions on acceptable activities. Even in c. 1905, a correspondent in the women's magazine, *The Lady's Realm*, describes the boredom imposed on her:

> I do a lot of fancy work and read a number of library books; but even these delights are apt to cloy upon over indulgence in them. Sometimes I am tempted to envy girls I see going off on their bicycles to golf or hockey; or the others who write books, lecture, and earn their living in some way or another. At least they do not endure continually the half-contemptuous pity of their relatives; they do not feel themselves to be hopeless failures.[15]

By the end of the nineteenth century, given the fact that musical education for women was increasingly established at public institutions, piano teaching as an industry flourished. The start of a woman composer's musical education was very often the private piano lesson. The industry provided a very necessary income for unmarried women, though the repertoire was mainly 'salon' music and the teaching quality was sometimes poor. As one young lady put it, 'The arch-crime cannot be laid at the door of any unfortunate individual old maid, such as the one into whose clutches I was at a tender age delivered. It was the crime of a class, of a social organisation'.[16]

The importance of music, especially the piano, in the lives of Edwardian women should not be underestimated. This instrument (or the pianola) was present in every respectable home and was a necessary part of a woman's general education and attributes.[17] Ruth Solie observes, 'It has been suggested by more than one writer that for nineteenth-century girls and women the piano was closely related to the diary itself in its status as a confidante and source of emotional release'.[18] She argues that the musically proficient woman was a marriageable commodity, not least because her playing offered entertainment for fathers and brothers after a

[14] Jane Lewis, *Women in England 1870–1950: Sexual Divisions and Social Change* (Brighton, 1984), p. 113 cited in John Benson, *The Rise of Consumer Society in Britain 1880–1980* (London, New York, 1994), p. 181.

[15] n.a., 'The Truth About Man' in *The Lady's Realm A Selection from the Monthly Issues: November 1904 to April 1905* (London, 1972), p. 81.

[16] Charlotte Haldane, *Music My Love! One Listener's Autobiography* (London, 1936), pp. 19–20.

[17] Ruth A. Solie, *Music in Other Words: Victorian Conversations* (Berkeley, 2004).

[18] Ibid., p. 110.

day at work. It also structured the young woman's time.[19] The range of instruments acceptable for women was also increasing, so that different sounds were becoming part of women's daily lives.[20] In this period there were still some resonances of eighteenth-century attitudes, as Richard Leppert explains: 'Overriding questions of ability or interest, the culture demanded music as an appropriate mark of both femininity itself and female class status. As such music was routinely viewed by parents as an asset to their daughters' future matrimonial stock.'[21]

Despite the difficulties faced by women composers, composition often held an important place in their lives. It was no longer merely an acceptable activity to fill time periods during the daily lives of women, but a creative process.[22] However, composition was not often viewed as 'useful' or productive in a child's development. The pianist Harriet Cohen (1895–1967) describes composition and improvisation when she was a child: 'At home I got endless scoldings because I would not get on with practising, but spent hours composing, with Dad's help. Both Olga [her sister] and I much preferred this form of music to working on our chosen instruments.'[23]

When reaching higher levels of musical education those who progressed to UK institutions almost exclusively came to London, and most of them spent the majority of their careers in the city. London was the centre of British musical society, attracting audiences and performers from Europe and America to its concert halls. There was a substantial amount of public as well as private music-making in the frenetic years before the First World War, culminating in London's hosting of the International Musical Congress, 29 May to 3 June, 1911.[24] Muriel Draper, an American living in London, describes the sense of inclusiveness within London's musical society thus:

> London, was indeed, one of the perfect cities to live in during the epochal era that disappeared from the face of the world in August, 1914. In no capital of Europe could prime ministers be made so easily at dinner-tables, yet perhaps in no capital of Europe could dinner tables become so small. The engagement of Russian dancers was discussed with due solemnity in the galleries of the House

[19] Ibid., pp. 95 and 103.

[20] For a discussion on women instrumentalists in America in this period see Judith Tick, 'Passed away is the Piano Girl: Changes in American Musical Life, 1870–1900', in *Women Making Music The Western Art Tradition, 1150–1950*, eds Jane Bowers and Judith Tick (London, Basingstoke, 1986).

[21] Richard Leppert, *Music and Image: Domesticity, Ideology and Socio-cultural Formation in Eighteenth-century England* (Cambridge, 1988), p. 29.

[22] Leppert, *Music and Image*, p. 28.

[23] Harriet Cohen, *A Bundle of Time: The Memoirs of Harriet Cohen* (London, 1969), p. 23. See Appendix 1 for more information on Harriet Cohen.

[24] This was the 4th Congress of the International Musical Society, following Leipzig in 1904, Basle in 1906 and Vienna in 1909.

> of Parliament, and M.P.s clamoured for boxes when the engagement thus settled was due to open.[25]

Most of the women musicians in this study were centred in two areas of London: South Kensington/Notting Hill and Hampstead/St John's Wood. Many of the musicians and composers who had studied at the RCM lived and performed in the former area, although Marion Scott lived near Paddington. There were certain streets in Kensington that between 1901 and 1920 attracted several composers, such as Bedford Gardens where Katherine Eggar, younger composer Ruby Holland (dates unknown), Amanda Aldridge (1866–1956) and Frank Bridge (1879–1941) all lived.[26] Further towards the RAM in Marylebone (and nearer the latter area) were the majority of music publishing houses and concert halls including the Æolian Hall, the Queen's Hall and Bechstein Hall.

In Hampstead and St John's Wood a number of musical families from different backgrounds lived within a large population of artists and writers. These included the Welsh composer Morfydd Owen who lived for a time in Heath Street in Hampstead and Myra Hess who, as mentioned previously, grew up in St John's Wood. The family of the composer Arnold Bax (1883–1953) moved to Hampstead in 1896: 'they were much struck at once by the contrast with South London. "Here," said the wife of a famous bookseller to Bax's mother, "we are not fashionable, only literary and artistic".'[27]

Advanced musical training, as with higher education in general for women in the early part of the century, was extremely varied. For example, as early as 1895, a certain Florence Higgins was awarded a Mus. Bac. from the University of London, but Oxford University, despite allowing women to study music to degree level, did not award music degrees to women until 1921.[28] The most popular institutions at which women studied music were London's conservatoires. These included the RAM, which opened in 1823, the RCM (1883), and the Guildhall School of Music (GSM), which admitted amateurs in 1880 and professionals in

---

25 Muriel Draper, *Music at Midnight* (London, 1929), p. 136.

26 There is a blue National Trust plaque to Frank Bridge in Bedford Gardens but no mention of Eggar, Holland or Aldridge (see Appendix 1 for more information on Aldridge, Bridge and Holland). The Aldridge family lived there from 1901–1932, Frank Bridge moved there in 1914 and Eggar and Holland are listed as living there in the 1920 British Music Society Composer directory.

27 Marian C. McKenna, *Myra Hess: A Portrait* (London, 1976), p. 7. See Appendix 1 for more information on Bax.

28 Percy Scholes. *The Mirror of Music 1844–1944: A Century of Musical Life in Britain as Reflected in the Musical Times* (London, 1947), pp. 666 and 682 cited in Sophie Fuller, 'Women Composers', p. 51. As discussed previously, women were offered other subjects at Oxford from as early as 1919. For more information on this issue, see Vera Brittain, *The Women at Oxford: A Fragment of History* (New York, 1960) also online at http://www.archive.org/details/womenatoxfordafr013166mbp.

Figure 1.1 Katherine Eggar's house, Bedford Gardens, London

Figure 1.2 Marion Scott's house, 92 Westbourne Terrace, London

1910. There were also smaller institutions such as Morley College, where students learnt composition under Gustav Holst (1874–1934) – female composition student Marie Arrigoni won prizes for her part-songs in 1911 – and had access to the Morley College orchestra and choir.[29]

Female students certainly outnumbered males in singing and piano from the nineteenth century, while later, the numbers of string students increased and a few female wind students appeared. Composition as a first study was available to women of the third generation under discussion; Morfydd Owen took this option – as a postgraduate – at the RAM as did Dorothy Howell.[30] The 1912 RAM prospectus shows a class composition option for those who did not take composition as a first study. This comprised a weekly class lesson of an hour, but was only available to those who had obtained the necessary grade in harmony and counterpoint. As women were less likely to have studied these subjects prior to attending the RAM they were also probably less likely to achieve the required grade than their male counterparts.

Maude Valerie White (1855–1937) was unusual for a woman of the older generation in that she studied composition with George Macfarren (1813–1887) and Frank Davenport (dates unknown) at the RAM from 1876.[31] She was a prolific song composer and travelled widely throughout her life especially in Italy and Sicily. She mixed with the highest tiers of society and the support of a variety of patrons allowed her to disseminate her music widely. Composition was a natural process for her; she describes the pleasure of experimentation:

> One afternoon – an unforgettable one for me – I was sitting alone in the drawing room when something compelled me to go to the piano and sing Byron's 'farewell, if ever fondest prayer'. I knew the poem well, and improvised the music to the words without the slightest difficulty. It is the way I have composed the melody of almost every song I have ever written, naturally working up the accompaniment and adding many little details after-wards. I was so surprised – so utterly taken aback with the rapidity with which the whole song had taken shape, that I thought it could only be a mere coincidence which would never be repeated.[32]

White, however, appears to have needed considerable encouragement from her mother and teachers at the RAM to consider composition as a profession. She was self-effacing in the extreme, but like many of her generation this was an attractive quality that was encouraged in a young woman. White remained aware of her

---

29 See *Morley College Magazine*, 1910–1920, Morley College Library Archive, London.

30 See Rhian Davies, 'A Refined and Beautiful Talent: Morfydd Owen (1891–1918)' (unpub. PhD thesis, University of Wales, Bangor, 1999) and the Dorothy Howell papers in the Dorothy Howell Archive, Dorothy Howell Trust.

31 See Appendix 1 for more information on White and Macfarren.

32 White, *Friends and Memories*, p. 105.

own (self-imposed) limitations, however, and these limitations were a cause of frustration to her teachers:

> He [Macfarren] lost his temper with me, but I must say it was only for a few seconds. He thought it was a pity that I devoted myself to vocal music, and advised me try my hand at something instrumental. Unfortunately he suggested a concerto. I was in despair. I told him I was positively certain I was incapable of such a thing, but he insisted on it, and I went home to do my worst.[33]

Given this unsuccessful experiment, Macfarren did not encourage White to compose any more instrumental works. Years later in Vienna, White tried and failed again to write instrumental music. It is perhaps a reflection of her education, experience and the expectations placed on her as a woman that she considered herself lacking the skills to write in this genre. 'This time my failure was accompanied by such appalling depression that I felt as if I wanted to wipe music right out of my life.'[34]

Liza Lehmann (1862–1918) was a composer who was of the same generation and a close friend of White. Lehmann is perhaps more typical of her generation in that she did not study composition at a conservatoire but privately in Rome, Wiesbaden and London.[35] But as with White and Harriet Cohen, composition was important to her: 'I sang in public for nine whole years – and how intensely I often wish that *most* of those years had been spent in the more profound study of composition in its manifold branches.'[36]

The RAM and the RCM, the most highly regarded conservatoires in London, differed considerably in terms of their composition provision. According to William Weber, in the 1880s, the RAM presented many more student compositions in concert than the RCM, which also programmed fewer works by staff (programmes from the early twentieth century suggest that the RAM continued to promote student composers).[37] Even when student composers performed their own works in the late nineteenth century, the RCM appears not to have encouraged its female students in this:

> There were occasional performances of student compositions for piano, either solo or ensemble, more often than not with the composer as pianist. This was, however, an essentially male pursuit: despite the predominance of women

[33] Ibid., p. 143.

[34] Ibid., p. 264.

[35] Her composition teachers were Raunkilde, Wilhelm Freudenberg and Hamish MacCunn.

[36] Liza Lehmann, *The Life of Liza Lehmann* (London, 1919), p. 179.

[37] William Weber, 'Concerts at Four Conservatoires in the 1880s: A Comparative Analysis' in *Musical Education in Europe 1770–1914*, eds Michael Fend and Michel Noiray (2 vols, Berlin, 2005), vol. 2, pp. 331–50.

> pianists, and the presence of women among the composition pupils, no women pianists performed works of their own composition[.][38]

This attitude, prevalent at the RCM, may also explain why, even as late as the 1910s, first-study women composers tended to enrol at the RAM. Those composers at the RCM such as Marion Scott did so in combination with an instrumental first study. Although Rebecca Clarke was the first woman to study composition with Stanford in 1907 she was something of an anomaly.[39]

While studying composition and piano at the RAM, younger-generation composer Dorothy Howell displayed a confidence that is in sharp contrast to the crippling self-doubt of many women composers of this period. In a letter to her mother in 1915 she relayed, 'My pieces seemed to have caused quite a sensation last Sat and I'm told that Corder and the Principal were both *very* favourably impressed'.[40] Howell, along with Morfydd Owen, revelled in the atmosphere of the RAM and developed her compositional skills as well as her piano performance.

Ethel Smyth was convinced that women of all generations were adversely affected by the quality of the musical education provided for them, although it should be remembered that she chose not to continue with her conservatoire training in Leipzig and studied privately instead:

> Face this truth; that because of what has been our position hitherto in the world of music, there is not at this present moment (1933) one single middle-aged woman alive who has had the musical education that has fallen to men as a matter of course, without any effort on their part, ever since music was.[41]

After completing their education and trying to establish a reputation as a composer many women found that while individuals were supportive, musical society in general did not have an inclusive attitude towards them. Although some such as Walter Willson Cobbett and Henry Wood (1869–1944) were willing to programme their works, by 1920, the proceedings of the Musical Association published a paper claiming women had failed to prove themselves:

---

38 Janet Ritterman, 'The Royal College of Music 1883–1899 Pianists and their Contribution to the Forming of a National Conservatory' in *Musical Education in Europe 1770–1914*, eds Michael Fend and Michel Noiray (2 vols, Berlin, 2005), vol. 2, p. 364.

39 Clarke had previously studied the violin at the RAM but left in 1905 when her harmony teacher, Percy Miles proposed to her. See Appendix 1 for more information on Charles Stanford.

40 Letter from Dorothy Howell to her mother, 23 June 1915, uncatalogued, Dorothy Howell Trust.

41 Ethel Smyth, *Female Pipings in Eden* (Edinburgh, 1933), p. 12.

> The idea that this so-called emancipation of women will develop all sorts of new abilities in future is quite absurd. 20 or 30 years is quite enough to see what women can do, and they have had more than that.[42]

This is in contrast to a paper given to the Musical Association in 1883, where Stephen Stratton, while expressing the opinion that there had not yet been a great woman composer, argued that 'there is no reasonable ground for assuming that she cannot excel in any art under the like conditions [with men]'.[43] He goes on to list hundreds of women composers in an appendix, as evidence that even in unfavourable conditions such as lack of education, women had been active in composition.

Securing patronage was a fundamental aspect of the life of a professional composer at this time. Particularly for the first generation of women composers under discussion, support from wealthy female friends could be vital for performance opportunities and publication costs. Smyth is one such case: her aristocratic friends significantly helped further her career. She presented her music to Queen Victoria and received financial support from Empress Eugenie and the wealthy American heiress to the Singer fortune, the Princesse de Polignac (1865–1943).[44] Adela Maddison was also patronised by the Princesse. Her friend, Mabel Batten (1856–1916), who was a singer and the lover of the writer, Radclyffe Hall (1880–1943), was asked to provide financial support for Maddison when she had to return destitute to England from Germany at the beginning of the First World War.[45] Even though both Smyth and Maddison were from fairly wealthy backgrounds, their careers probably would not have flourished without the support of such women.

Financial patronage of composers continued to flourish, though an increasing number of alternatives gradually emerged. Walter Willson Cobbett, for example, chose to fund composition competitions and publications on music rather than personally-chosen individuals. Also a few groups like the SWM provided performers and performance opportunities for composer-members. Because women in general received far fewer commissions than men, it could be argued that such patronage was more important to them. Yet, all composers, relying on others, whether it be a patron, a competition, or a commission, had to maintain social acceptability; women, much more than men, had to tread a fine line between being creative, eccentric and even exotic, and trespassing beyond the bounds of polite society.

---

[42] J. Swinburne, 'Women and Music', *Proceedings of the Musical Association, 46th Session, 1919–1920* (January 1920), p. 24. See Appendix 1 for more information on Henry Wood.

[43] Stephen S. Stratton, 'Woman in Relation to Musical Art', *Proceedings of the Musical Association, 9th Session, 1882–1883* (May 1882), p. 115.

[44] See Appendix 1 for more information on the Princesse de Polignac.

[45] See correspondence between Adela Maddison and Mabel Batten, Mabel Batten and Cara Lancaster, Lancaster Family Collection, London. This issue is discussed in more detail in Chapter 4. See Appendix 1 for more information on Batten and Hall.

The upper classes themselves often did not revel in the arts and patrons also had to be cautious. Frances, Countess of Warwick (1861–1938) who was part of the elite Marlborough House set (although she later distanced herself from them), recalled the 'bright young things' of the early twentieth century, who had money as well as political connections.[46] They were, however, fearful of the radical nature of art: 'Art meant Bohemianism, and they only had the haziest idea what Bohemianism meant, they assumed it was sinister and immoral.'[47]

Similarly to educated aristocratic women, numbers of women composers from wealthy backgrounds managed to travel abroad, often staying with friends all over Europe. Those women, who spent some time away from London and obtained performances of their work in other countries, increased their standing within British musical society, which in turn led to more promotion of their work abroad. Adela Maddison, who lived for periods in Paris and Berlin, and Ethel Smyth, who had studied in Germany and travelled all over Europe, were able to secure performances in Leipzig as well as Paris and, in the case of Smyth, in Venice and Prague. Similarly Maude Valerie White, who travelled a great deal in Italy and Sicily, secured performances of her works as she travelled.[48]

Along with the financial and social position of these women, the roles expected of them were also very much dependent on their domestic position (whether or not they were married). The concept of the 'new woman' was considered dangerous not only by men but also by many older women. 'Unlike the odd woman, celibate, sexually repressed, and easily pitied or patronised as the flotsam and jetsam of the matrimonial tide, the sexually independent New Woman criticised society's insistence on marriage as women's only option for a fulfilling life.'[49]

The sense of sexuality of many unmarried and indeed married women composers is not known. The unmarried are evenly distributed between the three generations of women under discussion; they include Ethel Smyth, Katherine Eggar, Marion Scott, Dorothy Howell and Maude Valerie White and range from women who had lesbian relationships, or intense non-sexual relationships with women, to those who had sexual relationships with men (or combinations of the three). While some, such as Ethel Smyth and Adela Maddison, had lesbian identities, others, such as Katherine Eggar and Marion Scott, had close relationships with each other, which were quite possibly non-sexual.[50] Despite differing levels of intimacy –

---

46 See Appendix 1 for more information on the Countess of Warwick.

47 Frances Countess of Warwick, *Afterthoughts* (London, 1931), p. 79.

48 Maude Valerie White wrote two volumes of autobiography recounting her experiences travelling: *Friends and Memories* (London, 1914) and *My Indian Summer* (London, 1932).

49 Elaine Showalter, *Sexual Anarchy Gender and Culture at the Fin de Siècle* (London, 1991), p. 38.

50 Ethel Smyth, earlier in her life, had an enduring relationship with her librettist Henry Brewster, but its exact nature is not clear.

Maude Valerie White and Myra Hess both had intense relationships with women – it would be dangerous to assume lesbian identities or outlooks for such women.

While the same level of hysteria did not apply to lesbians as to homosexual males, lesbian women had to be cautious and sometimes chose to appear less conspicuous by marrying. But a lesbian identity had some advantages for a composer: she could be supported by lesbian or pro-lesbian patrons, including the Princesse de Polignac, Mabel Batten and Frank Schuster, and move in what Sophie Fuller terms the 'lesbian fin de siècle' circle.[51] Also, she would generally have been free of the pressures of having children and running a large household.

There were increasingly discussions in the press about women's sexuality, especially in relation to the new discipline of psychoanalysis. As Michael Mason observes, this led to an increased public conjecture as to a woman's ideal situation.[52] Celibacy was still seen as the preferable option for single women; perhaps surprisingly, the suffrage movement did not challenge such an opinion. As Mason notes, 'There is thus a considerable irony in the fact that many women suffragists at the end of the nineteenth century were vehemently opposed to any relaxing of sexual standards, and actually urged greater continence'.[53] The idea that, instead of damaging a woman, a life of chastity could lead to increased concentration and energy in other fields was applied not only to religious, temperance and feminist work, but also to women's musical activities.[54]

The public debate on gender and specifically the nature of femininity was even more important for the woman composer than that of sexuality. Derek Scott suggests: 'As more and more women took to composition, nineteenth-century criticism moved away from the metaphysical use of "masculine" and "feminine" in describing music and, instead, began to use these terms as an aesthetic confirmation of sexual difference.'[55]

Yet *pace* Scott, the terms, 'masculine' and 'feminine' continued to define the range of the compositional styles of men. Katharine Ellis argues that, while Beethoven was acknowledged to possess both feminine and masculine qualities, certain groups of composers were classified as feminine:

> At different times during the century, other repertories came to be gendered feminine as well. Baroque music, Haydn, Mozart, and even Hummel were drawn into a stereotypically feminine world of decorative and sweetly plaintive

---

[51] For information on Frank Schuster and Mabel Batten, see Sophie Fuller, 'Devoted Attention: Looking for Lesbian Musicians in Fin-de-Siècle Britain', *Queer Episodes in Music and Modern Identity*, eds Sophie Fuller and Lloyd Whitesell (Urbana, 2002), pp. 79–101. See Appendix 1 for more information on Frank Schuster.

[52] Michael Mason, *The Making of Victorian Sexuality* (Oxford, 1994).

[53] Ibid., p. 3.

[54] Ibid., p. 225.

[55] Derek B. Scott, *From the Erotic to the Demonic: On Critical Musicology* (New York, 2003), p. 25.

> expression, contrasting with the gigantic outbursts of Beethoven or the dazzling virtuosity of Liszt and Thalberg.[56]

Although, as Ellis observes, these classifications shifted in different historical periods, in early twentieth-century Britain women could not please: using either style, they were always encroaching on male preserves. In a perpetual 'double-bind', they were discouraged from writing 'masculine' music while at the same time were criticised for presenting overtly 'feminine' music. The use of the term 'feminine' to describe music certainly had different connotations for male and female composers:

> [femininity] when applied to men's music, generally serves to indicate an emotional breadth (the composer can be both masculine and feminine) … [However], the term 'feminine' applied to a woman's music (as in 'feminine productions') may simply serve to remind us of the composer's sex – and therefore her artistic status.[57]

Although through this period it was becoming increasingly acceptable to compose on a more professional and perhaps 'male' platform, it was an unacceptable and seemingly frightening prospect for a woman composer to lose her femininity. It was something that few women were prepared to countenance, whether they tried to compete on male terms or whether they promoted a female aesthetic.[58] Ethel Smyth, with her pipe and tweeds, therefore, was quite a phenomenon, even in the 1920s and 1930s.

This set of double standards for the reception of works by men and women is undoubtedly related to the concept of 'genius'. Christine Battersby has identified five usages of the word genius: personality-type i.e. an outsider or near to madness; a 'specific mode of consciousness' i.e. passion, intuition, instinct; energy i.e. 'sublimated sexual energy; quantification of talent through scientific methods'; and lastly, it is a word whereby a 'person's cultural achievement is evaluated and assessed against an appropriate background of artistic genres and traditions'.[59] She argues that only the last meaning of the term could be applied to a feminist reading to define a female genius. It seems early twentieth-century philosophers and psychologists considered the female genius to be an impossibility. Otto Weininger published his thesis, *Sex and Character*, in 1903, which was translated in 1906 and was read throughout Europe. 'Whilst there are people who are anatomically men and psychically women, there is no such thing as a person who is physically

[56] Katharine Ellis, 'Female Pianists and Their Male Critics in Nineteenth-Century Paris', *Journal of the American Musicological Society*, 50/2–3 (1997): p. 364.

[57] Samuel, 'Women's Music', pp. xiv–xv.

[58] For more detailed discussion see Chapter 5.

[59] Christine Battersby, *Gender and Genius: Towards a Feminist Aesthetics* (London, 1989), pp. 156–7.

female and psychically male not withstanding the extreme maleness of their outward appearance and the unwomanliness of their expression.'[60]

Few women composers, however, were prepared to reveal male qualities in their physical appearance and their compositional style. Ethel Smyth was something of an exception; Richard Specht describes her appearance and manner:

> But one day, before I had had time to examine the score, the door-bell rang, and ere my servant – visibly astonished at the appearance of the visitor – could prevent it, in came a woman, hair rather untidy, hat of no known form, a jacket and mantle upon which wind and storm had done its worst, the colour being no longer recognisable. A firm hand grasped mine, and with a rather mischievous smile that lends a gentle and comradely expression to a face that is not at all 'pretty' that life somewhat sternly modelled, she said: 'You see, after all, I have come myself', and then she begins to talk, very cleverly, with incredible vitality and impulsiveness, thanks me for my interest in her work, raves about Mahler and also the work of Prince Edmond de Polignac, whom she considers one of the great musicians, and so on and so on.[61]

Of the women actively composing in the early twentieth century, approximately half were married. Many, however, fell foul of the expectations placed upon them within marriage. When Ethel Barns' marriage broke down in 1913 after her husband – the singer Charles Phillips – had a series of affairs with his singing students, she was virtually ostracised from the upper-class circles in which she moved and also ceased to be a member of the SWM.[62] Ethel Smyth became so infatuated with the Princesse de Polignac that the latter severed links with her for a time, though she actually continued her advocacy of Smyth's music in secret.[63] The reputation of the singer, Elsie Swinton, was shattered after the rumour broke that she had had an affair with the conductor and composer, Hamilton Harty (1879–1941) – although probably not sexual – and the Swintons moved to Scotland with her parents.[64] It is unclear whether it was her husband or Elsie herself who decided to end her musical career, but it appears the unsuitable nature of a career on the stage in combination with personal scandal was considered unacceptable for a woman of her generation and position in society.

---

60 Battersby Ibid. p.115.

61 Richard Specht, 'Dr Ethel Smyth' *MT*, 53/829 (March, 1912): p. 168.

62 See Englesberg, 'The Life and Works of Ethel Barns'. One of Phillip's pupils, a Mrs Bowman (Madame Gertrude Allin) joined the SWM in 1913 the last year of Barns's membership and after the scandal broke Barns may not have wished to have contact with his pupils there. See Appendix 1 for more information on Charles Phillips.

63 Sylvia Kahan, *Music's Modern Muse: A Life of Winnaretta Singer, Princesse de Polignac* (Rochester, 2003), p. 155.

64 Greer, *A Numerous and Fashionable Audience*, pp. 111–15.

Figure 1.3 Ethel Smyth

Many married women composers had professional or amateur musician husbands, although husbands as composers of greater professional standing were rare indeed.[65] Both Susan Spain-Dunk's and Liza Lehmann's composer-husbands were less successful than their wives, and combined their composing with other activities. Indeed some women whose husbands supported a continuation of musical activities actually increased their compositional activity and decreased their performing work after marriage because it was more compatible with increased time in the home. Indeed, in Lehmann's case, it was her marriage to the artist and musician, Herbert Bedford (1867–1945), that allowed her to give up her performance career and to compose consistently.[66]

Lehmann is an example of a woman who found support in a marriage that aided her development as a composer. Of this she said, 'I may say here that his

[65] This could be related to the fact that women composers who married successful men composers tended to stop writing when they married. The most famous example of this is the American, Ruth Crawford Seeger. See Rhian Samuel, 'Women's Music', p.xvii.

[66] See Appendix 1 for more information on Herbert Bedford.

[Bedford's] critical faculty is extraordinary, and, as regards composition, I have certainly learnt as much, if not more, from him than any other source'.[67] At the same time, as with White, she displays considerable self-deprecation: 'I have not at all a tidy brain, with all the ideas properly classified and pigeon-holed; nor have I the gift of putting into words much that probably slumbers within as mere instinct and sentiment.'[68] Lehmann's abilities as a composer, however, far outstripped her husband's, with a melody by Bedford performed at a New Symphony Orchestra concert in 1911 being described by one reviewer as 'unambitious'.[69]

While there is little evidence of collaborative composition among couples, other collaborations, such as that between Granville Bantock and his wife, Helena, who wrote lyrics for many of his vocal works, did occur.[70] Their marriage is described by their daughter, Myrrha, 'She [her mother] completed the 36 lyrics while they were still engaged inspired by their passionate and romantic love. This was, without any doubt, a meeting of two highly creative artists who were obviously intended for one another'.[71]

Although supportive marriages could lead to difficult decisions about career progression, an unsupportive partner or volatile relationship could stop a career altogether, as can be seen in the cases of Elsie Swinton, Ethel Barns and Morfydd Owen. It is also impossible to say how many other women stopped their compositional careers in very early stages through lack of encouragement or demands made by husbands/lovers or teachers: 'when the teacher is male, the relationship may lead to marriage and a silencing – at least temporarily – of her muse.'[72] Two examples of this are Harriet Cohen and Jane Joseph (1894–1929).[73] Cohen had an international career as a concert pianist, had studied composition at the RAM with Frederick Corder (1852–1932), producing a violin concerto and a nocturne for cor anglais and orchestra, but gave up composition after the composer Arnold Bax (1883–1953) became her lover, although she does not indicate that he discouraged her from continuing. Her pen name for composition, given to her by Corder and Bax, was 'Tania'.[74] Joseph took private composition lessons from Gustav Holst and also worked as one of his 'scribes', copying parts as well as teaching him Greek. In a letter to Joseph, Holst admits to feeling guilty about her work load which reduced her time for her own composition: 'I seem to divide

67 Lehmann, *The Life of Liza Lehmann*, pp. 66–7.

68 Ibid. pp. 173–4.

69 n.a., 'London Concerts' (reviews) *Musical Times*, 52/826 (Dec, 1911): p. 805.

70 See Appendix 1 for more information on Granville Bantock

71 Bantock, *Granville Bantock: A Personal Portrait*, p. 35.

72 Rhian Samuel, 'Women's Music', p. xvii.

73 See Appendix 1 for more information on Jane Joseph.

74 Cohen, *A Bundle of Time*, p. 30. Corder had wanted her pen name to be Natasha Rogorna after a Russian girl he had been 'fond' of but Bax suggested Tania. See Appendix 1 for more information on Frederick Corder.

my time with you between a) Objecting to your taking on things that prevent composition b) Making you do things that prevent composition.'[75]

Maude Valerie White eventually and perhaps unusually achieved independence to travel and live alone, having stayed with her trustee Mr Rose-Innes and his family after her mother's death, and then after his death with her sister in London. She remained unmarried, sensible of the benefits and freedoms, and the release from the pressure to marry when she had reached a certain age. 'For middle-age even now – is the most successful broom for sweeping tiresome complications out of a woman's life, and into how many women's lives has it not swept beautiful and faithful friendships, both with men and other women.'[76] There were, however, very few cases at this time of women who actually ceased composition upon getting married; in all of their writings, their determination to compose is evident.[77]

Motherhood also had an effect on the careers of women composers in this era, although the time actually spent with children by mothers varied considerably and was dependent on the class and generation of the woman composer. Of those women composers in this study who were married, most also had one or two children. At the same time, they did not tend to have large families. It cannot be argued that these mothers were any less productive as composers than other women but they were less likely to travel to the same extent as some unmarried women and they had fewer performances out of Britain. There were difficult choices, however, facing women composers who had children; for example Adela Maddison made the decision in the late 1890s to move to Paris to further her career, leaving her husband and children in London.[78]

In some cases, responsibilities of childcare had a greater effect on the work of unmarried women composers. This can be seen especially in the cases of Marion Scott and Katherine Eggar both of whom had to care for children after the death of siblings. As an unmarried woman, the responsibilities of caring for family members could be a heavier burden, than that faced by a married woman.

Another key decision in the lives of many women in this era was the possibility of joining a political or professional society. As the nineteenth century progressed, suffrage societies, in particular, became a significant force in the lives of many women. The first of these societies had been formed in the 1860s, and instigated the National Union of Women's Suffrage Societies (NUWSS), in 1897, by Millicent Fawcett.[79] The Union consisted mainly of women who 'were primarily concerned

---

[75] Imogen Holst, *Gustav Holst: A Biography* (London, New York, Toronto, 1969), p. 11. Similarly Imogen Holst herself was amanuensis for Benjamin Britten (1952–1964) and produced few compositions during this time.

[76] White, *My Indian Summer*, p. 53.

[77] In America Ruth Crawford Seeger was in a similar situation; see Judith Tick, *Ruth Crawford Seeger: A Composer's Search for American Music* (New York, 1997).

[78] Fuller, 'Women Composers', p. 308.

[79] The historical information on the NUWSS and WSPU presented here is mostly derived from Arthur Marwick, *Women at War*, pp. 22–6.

to secure votes for women on the same (undemocratic) terms as men'.[80] Emmeline and Christabel Pankhurst formed the Women's Social and Political Union (WSPU) in 1903 through frustration with the NUWSS and its seemingly passive methods. The violence with which the WSPU is associated did not reach its peak until the years preceding the First World War in 1914. The term 'suffragette' was first used in an article in the *Daily Mail* in 1906 and was then used by the public and members of the WSPU.[81] Despite Asquith's initial opposition to women's suffrage, there was considerable support for their cause from Liberal Members of Parliament and to a lesser extent within the Conservative ranks. The 'Cat and Mouse Act' introduced by Asquith's government in 1912 meant that suffragettes who had been released from prison due to ill health, particularly due to self-imposed starvation, could be re-arrested once their health had been restored. This appears to have done little to stem the increasingly militant activities of the WSPU. 'A small bomb damaged the coronation chair in Westminster Abbey, paintings (including the Velasquez 'Venus') were slashed, churches, railway stations and, in Scotland, three castles were damaged or destroyed by fire.'[82]

The WSPU did not maintain the support of all its members, however, and from 1910 different factions began to emerge. In 1910 a Mrs Despard formed the less extreme but still militant Women's Freedom League and this was followed by Sylvia and Adela Pankhurst's rejecting the WSPU to form The East London Women's Suffrage Federation. In 1914 some prominent members of the WSPU, including Gerald Gould, Laurence Housman, Louisa Garrett Anderson and Evelyn Sharp, formed the United Suffragists.[83]

Nevertheless, when the First World War broke out, the suffragettes who had initially opposed it rallied to the cause and used their organisational structure to co-ordinate their members' war effort.

> Many women of the middle and upper classes showed from the start great anxiety to contribute to the patriotic cause. Indeed one of the interesting psychological phenomena of the war is the way in which the suffragettes, who for ten years had been waging war on the Government and the community, now outshone everyone in their patriotic fervour and stirring appeals for national unity and endeavour.[84]

Yet, as Vera Brittain attests, young women who strove for roles closer to the front line of the war were often initially frustrated.[85] It can be argued though that women, such

80 Ibid., p. 22.

81 Lisa Tickner, *The Spectacle of Women: Imagery of the Suffrage Campaign 1907–1914* (London, 1987), p. 8.

82 Marwick, *Women at War*, p. 25.

83 Ibid., p. 26.

84 Marwick, *The Deluge*, p. 87.

85 Vera Brittain, *Testament of Youth* (London, 1978, first pub. 1933), pp. 140 and 142.

as the correspondent to *Ladies Realm* quoted previously, were increasingly finding positions outside the home in hospitals, the police force, administration, as drivers and in industry, although this was not always welcomed. David Cannadine claims:

> Not everyone approved of these 'grand ladies who are running hospitals in France.' Lord Crawford thought the Duchess of Westminster and the Duchess of Sutherland were particularly troublesome. They overspent, and expected the Red Cross to help them out. They shamelessly exploited their contacts in high places, and importuned busy generals and over-worked politicians.[86]

These criticisms also illustrate the tensions present in the shifts of power as women's position changed, as did notions of femininity.

Women musicians such as Ethel Smyth and May Mukle (1880–1963) were involved in the suffrage campaign.[87] In the case of Smyth, this included being arrested for breaking a Cabinet member's window and spending time in Holloway prison.[88] However, musicians also contributed to the cause through the composition and performance of suffrage anthems and other propaganda music and marching under the women musician's banner at rallies. Yet women composers in general tended not to enter the main political arena, choosing, rather, to focus on the status of women's music itself.

Travel habits such as those of Ethel Smyth, Maude Valerie White and Adela Maddison ceased with the start of the First World War in 1914. The war with Germany had a great effect on the lives of all women musicians and instigated changes that would have previously been inconceivable. Those women composers who had connections with or were living in Germany were among the first to be affected.[89] Performance opportunities ceased, performers of all nationalities who had resided in or travelled frequently to London returned to their countries of origin and London's orchestras and concert halls became reliant on British musicians. The numbers of male musicians eventually leaving London, to fight or undertake other war work, intensified this situation, creating a demand for female musicians.[90] This was particularly the case in the orchestral sector, but the numbers of smaller-scale concerts and opera performances decreased during the war years. A committee for music in war-time was formed by the heads of the conservatoires,

---

[86] David Cannadine, *The Decline and Fall of the British Aristocracy* (New Haven, London, 1990), p. 76.

[87] See Appendix 1 for more information on May Mukle.

[88] See Thomas Beecham, *A Mingled Chime: Leaves from an Autobiography* (London, 1943), pp. 117–18.

[89] Mabel Batten records Adela Maddison's escape from Germany through France in her diary entry for 12 August 1914. *Mabel Batten and Cara Lancaster Collections*, Lancaster Family Collection, London. See Chapter 4 for further details.

[90] Cyril Ehrlich, *The Music Profession in Britain Since the Eighteenth Century: A Social History* (Oxford, 1985), pp. 186–90.

Hubert Parry, Landon Ronald, Alexander Mackenzie and Granville Bantock, with Walter Wilson Cobbett as secretary, in order to negotiate artists and fees.[91]

Unless they were also performers, women composers did not necessarily benefit from these war-time changes, especially with the decline of recitals, for here the greatest numbers of works by women had been performed outside the private salon. Some women took time away from composition to be involved in war work; this included Ethel Smyth, who worked as a radiologist in France. Many more were involved in the war-relief effort in Britain, entertaining injured troops and organising charity concerts, such as the Oxford Ladies Musical Society concerts for soldiers.[92]

One of the most significant changes brought about by the war was the financial insecurity – previously unknown to upper-class women – that they now had to endure. Many female servants left domestic service to join women's military organisations such as the Women's Volunteer Reserve and the Women's Army Auxiliary Corps as they offered better pay and more challenging work.[93] The daughter of Granville Bantock describes her mother's reaction to this sudden lack of domestic help: '[T]o my mother, unused to fending for herself, it was a major catastrophe suddenly to be without servants in a large house, with a growing family and a shortage of money.'[94] This, in particular, meant that the time available for musical activities was reduced dramatically. And while it was also the end of so many women composers being able to rely on allowances from family money, more women undertook paid work. Maude Valerie White often had to economise to make her funds stretch, but was assured of a regular income from her publisher:

> My time in Venice was at an end. So was my money. It was time to go back to England. A financial earthquake (on a homeopathic scale) was imminent. I had a manuscript that would, I hoped, delay the catastrophe, and tide me over till the date of my next allowance, and on my return to London I disposed quite successfully of my one and only song I had composed during my five month absence. After all, in spite of Lord Byron's appalling suggestion that Barabbas was a publisher, I should indeed be an ungrateful wretch if I didn't admit that during the course of a good many years I, personally, have had every reason to be thankful of their existence, although there have been times when ... ! [95]

---

91 See Christopher Fifield, *Ibbs and Tillett: The Rise and Fall of a Musical Empire* (Aldershot, 2005), p. 95. Also see Appendix 1 for more information on Mackenzie, Parry and Ronald.

92 See Oxford Ladies Musical Society Archive, Bodleian Library, Oxford.

93 Janet S.K. Watson, *Fighting Different Wars: Experience, Memory and the First World War in Britain* (Cambridge, 2004), p. 19.

94 Myrrha Bantock, *Granville Bantock: A Personal Portrait* (London, 1972), p. 104.

95 White, *My Indian Summer*, p. 43.

Therefore despite differences in generation and class, women composers, like all British women, suffered increased difficulties in everyday life, yet found it easier to be professionals. Throughout the late nineteenth and early twentieth centuries, the barriers to education were becoming less significant and some women attained considerable success in their studies. Many of the pressures faced by women trying to make a living from composition were indeed the same as for men, but the standards women were expected to meet to maintain the favour of musical society were not. As will be examined in the specific cases of chamber music composers, Ethel Barns, Alice Verne Bredt, Susan Spain-Dunk, Ethel Smyth, Adela Madison and Morfydd Owen, these 'standards' affected not only the lives of women but also the genres and style in which they chose to write and their success as composers.

Chapter 2

Women and Chamber Music

> At its simplest form 'chamber music' will imply music of an intimate character played and heard for its own sake in private rooms rather than in great public halls and relying on a subtle use of medium for its effect.[1]

Many decades before Michael Tilmouth made the comments above, R.H. Walthew was cited in 1913 as viewing chamber music as 'music for friends'.[2] Since the mid-nineteenth century, however, the gap between music-making with 'amateur' players and the activities of virtuosic professional chamber players, especially playing string quartets, had been growing ever wider. By the beginning of the twentieth century, the most successful ensembles attracted large audiences in recital halls. Increasingly, works were being produced for ensembles of varying instruments. These ranged from Ethel Smyth's Songs for soprano, flute, strings, harp and percussion, 1908 – notably using the combination of voice and wind in chamber music before the French school and others – to Arthur Bliss's *Conversations* for flute and alto flute, oboe and English horn, and string trio written in 1920.[3] Tilmouth describes as this as a 'reaction against late Romantic gargantuanism',[4] while James McCalla feels a principal attraction of chamber music is its offer of freedom to experiment. He observes, for example, that with regard to the development of atonality, 'many composers took this step first in their chamber music'.[5]

A sense of experimentation, however, was only one of several reasons for writing chamber music around the time of the First World War, not the least of which were economic factors. As male composers were often scaling down the

---

1 Michael Tilmouth, 'Chamber Music' *TNG* (1980), p. 113 (This article does not appear in the Online version of Grove).

2 Walter Willson Cobbett, 'A Chamber Music Causerie', *Chamber Music: A Supplement to the Music Student*, 2 (August, 1913): p. 13. See Appendix 1 for more information on Richard Walthew.

3 Smyth uses wind and voice in her chamber music before Chabrier, Debussy, Ravel, Poulenc, Ives, Webern and Schoenberg; Stravinsky's *Pastorale*, 1907, for soprano and piano was only arranged for S, ob, eng hn, cl, bn in 1923. Stravinsky's first works for voice and instrumental ensemble were *Trois Poésies de la Lyrique Japonaise*, S, pf/ 2fl, 2cl, pf, str qt, 112-13 and *Pribaoutki*, male v, pf/ fl, ob, eng hn, cl, bn, vn, va, vc, db in 1914. See Appendix 1 for more information on Arthur Bliss.

4 Tilmouth, 'Chamber Music', p. 117.

5 James McCalla, *Twentieth Century Chamber Music* (London, 2003), p. x.

ensembles for which they wrote, female composers were scaling up, having previously, in general but not exclusively, written for solo piano and voice. What, therefore, was the relationship between domestic music making, the production of chamber music and women composers? This chapter will assess how women composers contributed to the explosion in instrumental chamber writing in this period and the circumstances in which they moved towards composing in forms that were perceived to be more 'intellectual'.

In early twentieth-century London, there was a renaissance of chamber music.[6] The halls holding the largest number of chamber music concerts were the Bechstein, Steinway and Æolian, but there were also frequent events at the Royal Albert Hall, and the Queen's Hall.[7] In these venues the predominant format of the concert was the single-artist recital; indeed their proliferation was criticised by the press on the grounds they were merely a promotional tool for the artists. The clashes in timetabling that resulted were a frustrating feature for some: 'At the same moment when A is giving a concert in the Steinway Hall, B is performing at Prince's Hall, C at St James's Hall while D, E and F may be similarly engaged at Messrs Collards, the Portman Rooms and the Marlborough Rooms.'[8]

Chamber music concerts were also held in private rooms and during 'At Homes', which could be large-scale, almost public occasions, or small intimate gatherings of acquaintances. The RCM Union used the concept of 'At Homes' as an opportunity for staff and students to play works by each other, as well as by more established composers. 'At Homes' often replicated a concert setting, their musical elements being taken seriously and 'professionally'. 'At large At Homes the hostess remains practically stationary near the drawing-room door, and guests entertain each other. During music they will be as silent as possible. When there is a lull in the entertainment they will proceed to the tea-room as they feel inclined.'[9]

The renaissance in the production and consumption of chamber music was mainly instigated by Walter Willson Cobbett, a businessman with a life-long passion

---

6 For this information the main sources are Walter Willson Cobbett (ed.), *Chamber Music: A Supplement to The Music Student.* June 1913–November 1916 and *Cobbett's Cyclopedic Survey of Chamber Music Vols I and II* (London, 1930); Thomas. F. Dunhill, *Chamber Music: A Treatise for Students* (London, 1913); Frank. V. Hawkins, *A Hundred Years of Chamber Music* (London, 1987) and Scholes, *The Mirror of Music.*

7 The Bechstein Hall 1901–1917 (reopened as The Wigmore Hall), Wigmore Street, seated 550; The Steinway Hall 1875–1924 (reopened as The Grotrian Hall), Lower Seymour Street, Portman Square seated 400–500; The Æolian Hall 1903–1943 (taken over by BBC), New Bond Street seated 400–500; The Royal Albert Hall 1871–present, Kensington, seats 8,000; The Queen's Hall 1893–1941 (bombed in Second World War), Langham Place Large Hall seated 3,000 and The Queen's Small Hall seated 500. See Lewis Foreman and Susan Foreman, *London A Musical Gazetteer* (New Haven and London, 2005), pp. 21–70.

8 Scholes, *The Mirror of Music*, p. 203.

9 n.a. *Etiquette for Ladies: A Guide to the Observances of Good Society* (London, 1923), p. 28.

Figure 2.1 Walter Willson Cobbett, Christmas card image photographed at 16 Avenue Road, London, December 1936

for chamber music. Having heard the Joachim string quartet play Beethoven at St James's Hall, he announced, 'It is not an exaggeration to say there opened up before me an enchanted world to which I longed to gain an entrance'.[10] After Cobbett retired from the City, he became chamber music's most influential patron, founding the Cobbett Phantasy competitions in 1905, editing the first journal dedicated solely to chamber music as a supplement to the *Music Student Magazine* from 1913–16 and, in the 1920s, establishing prizes for composition at the RCM and the RAM. In 1924 he also established a medal for services to chamber music whose recipients included Thomas F. Dunhill and Elizabeth Sprague Coolidge.[11]

At the outbreak of war, Cobbett added his voice to the call for foreign musicians to be treated with respect 'Let us hold in check the passions aroused by the brutality of German militarists, judge alien musicians in accordance with the services they have rendered us, and so achieve the greatest glory of all, a

---

[10] Cobbett is quoted as having said this in the BBC Radio 3 programme, *Music Weekly*, G. Sheffield and A. Lyle producers, 2/8/1987. Recording held at National Sound Archive.

[11] See Appendix 1 for more information on Thomas Dunhill.

victory over ourselves'.[12] Despite Cobbett himself feeling unable to play due to the psychological pressures of living through war, the columns on the possible demise of chamber music during the war in the journal *Chamber Music* only appear to have lasted until 1916. Indeed Cobbett seems to have been moved by an article in *The Referee* proclaiming his influence in the increase in chamber music during the war: '[I]t is a fact that since the outbreak of the War there has been a decided revival of chamber music and an increase in production of works suitable for such performances.'[13]

Cobbett had a specific influence on the chamber music written by women as, from his writings in *Chamber Music* and the *Cyclopedic Survey of Chamber Music*, he appears to have encouraged women to compose and perform such works. Indeed, in *Chamber Music*, Cobbett established a regular column for writers Katherine Eggar and Marion Scott to pronounce their views on women's music; here they also recounted their difficulties in obtaining performance materials. Cobbett comments:

> Those unacquainted with the subject may not be aware that woman is a factor of increasing importance in the world of chamber music, both on the creative and executive side. Indeed on the latter she bids fair to outnumber Man, a piece of good news for the feminists which none will grudge them.[14]

Thomas F. Dunhill was another champion of chamber music. A composer who attended the RCM with Marion Scott, he was an associate of the SWM.[15] His book, *Chamber Music: A Treatise for Students*, gives a positive view of the direction of chamber music at the beginning of the second decade of the century.[16] This extended passage enunciates his pleasure at a return to more intimate venues for chamber music in London:

> It may be true that we do not have to-day such a regular and comfortable succession of uniformly excellent performances, but it is also true that the chamber music which we do hear is generally listened to under far more favourable conditions, either in buildings more suitable in size than the old St James's Hall, or in the

12 Walter Willson Cobbett, 'Some War-time reflections', *Chamber Music*, 11 (November, 1914): p. 18.

13 Lancelot in *The Referee* cited in Walter Willson Cobbett, 'Obiter Dicta', *Chamber Music*, 20 (May, 1916): p. 57.

14 Walter Willson Cobbett, 'A Foreword', *Chamber Music*, 1 (June, 1913): p. 1.

15 See David Dunhill, *Thomas Dunhill: Maker of Music* (London, 1997) and Beryl Kington, 'Thomas F. Dunhill and Sibelius 7', *Journal of the British Music Society*, 18 (1996): pp. 54–65.

16 Dunhill, *Chamber Music*.

> private rooms of the wealthy and the cultured, where musical entertainments on the required artistic level are far more frequently given than formerly.[17]

A writer in *Chamber Music* – note that it was not Cobbett but R.H. Walthew – disagreed with Dunhill's optimistic attitude:

> Mr Dunhill does not believe in the decline of chamber music in England, and asserts that 'in the private rooms of the wealthy and cultured' there are far more frequent performances of music of the kind than formerly. It may be so! But are there as many amateur quartet parties as there were? How many members of big amateur orchestral societies have their weekly meetings of chamber music? Do not golf and motoring take up the time that used to be devoted to the practise of quartets and trios, in London at least?[18]

There were, however, enthusiastic amateurs who continued to host chamber music evenings, such as the Rensburg family, although the only female composer whose music was documented as having been played at these weekly social gatherings is Cécile Chaminade.[19]

Christina Bashford claims that audience behaviour at chamber music venues as well as concerts in general was changing, helping to raise chamber music to a more 'serious' art-form. This difference in attitude stemmed from the work of Thomas Alsager of the Beethoven Quartett [sic] Society and John Ella at the Musical Union who in the mid-nineteenth century had started to encourage less audience movement, less clapping and commenting between and during movements of pieces and supplied annotated programmes designed to be studied prior to the concert.[20] By the end of the nineteenth century an audience, even in the most intimate of settings, were less likely to disrupt performances, although the *Musical Times* reported: 'At last, in 1919 (March), we learn that reform is coming about. It is now happily possible, says the Editor, to hear oratorios performed without applause, though to secure this result it still seems necessary to print a request in the programme.'[21]

In Percy Scholes' (1877–1958) opinion, however, the concert-going public was too inhibited; he reports being:

---

17 Ibid., p. 8.

18 R.H. Walthew, 'A New Book on Chamber Music', *Chamber Music*, 2 (August, 1913): p. 25.

19 See Rensburg Collection, MS Mus 308, vols. 1 and 2, British Library, London. See Appendix 1 for more information on Cécile Chaminade.

20 See Christina Bashford, 'Learning to Listen: Audiences for Chamber Music in Early Victorian London', *Journal of Victorian Culture*, 4/1 (Spring 1999): pp. 25–51.

21 Scholes, *The Mirror of Music*, p. 219.

> repeatedly amazed to find how often the most able composers failed in their most hilarious scherzo to attain what was surely their aim – to provoke a smile. Either (a) London concert audiences in general entirely lack the sense of humour or (b) that sense is inhibited by some delusion that they are at High Mass or a Quakers' meeting.[22]

For British composers, the chamber-music renaissance was a means to greater definition of a national style. This was certainly a position Thomas Dunhill supported:

> It may be doubted if any country in Europe could furnish a more imposing array of earnest and ardent young musicians than is to be found in England at the present time, and it is extremely gratifying to note that the majority of these men [sic] are devoting a large part of their time to the composition of chamber music.[23]

Dunhill had observed that chamber music was now being played in venues such as the Æolian and Bechstein Halls, and also, as indicated above, in the 'rooms of wealthy'. All of these locations were frequented by women musicians, players and, to some extent, composers. So, while this new young generation of British composers included Frank Bridge, Arnold Bax, Arthur Bliss (1891–1975) and Cyril Scott (1879–1970), it also included women composers such as Ethel Barns, Edith Swepstone and Alice Verne-Bredt.[24] Not only were composers and writers Katherine Eggar and Marion Scott fighting for women's position in musical society, they were also fighting for that of chamber music. In an article on Cobbett, Marion Scott reveals her views: 'Latterly events have tended to stress the importance of publicity. It would be folly to underrate the value of big works written, prepared and performed in the public eye, but chamber music has lost none of its virtue as one of the true springs of music.'[25]

The advocates of chamber music argued their case partly on moral grounds, in that chamber music was a purifying force. Freed from the anxiety of the impending First World War and increasing political and societal problems, chamber music was music stripped to its essence: 'Indeed, it [chamber music] has contrived to keep itself singularly pure, and untainted with that turgid pessimism which has rendered unwholesome so much recent orchestral music, both British and foreign.'[26]

---

22 Ibid., p. 225.

23 Dunhill, *Chamber Music*, p. 9.

24 See Appendix 1 for more information on Scott and Swepstone.

25 Marion Margaret Scott, from article on Walter Willson Cobbett in Marion Scott's notebook dated 23 July, 1927, Marion Margaret Scott Archive, RCM, London.

26 Dunhill, *Chamber Music*, p. 9.

Richard Walthew justified advocating the continuation of chamber music during the First World War to readers of *Chamber Music*, which was a supplement to *The Music Student* in the war years:

> [T]here may seem to some people something incongruous, something selfish even, in the indulgence of a pleasure, however pure and rare, which does not bring us into any sort of relation with the movements and passions and heroisms of the world around us ... Although the subtler phases of our art must perforce retire into the background, for a time let us keep the flag of chamber music flying (if only in a remote corner of the field until happier times).[27]

The parallel fights for chamber music and women's rights – the latter via the SWM – lent succour to each other. Cobbett was a powerful ally, for not only did he advocate the composition of chamber music but actively supported lesser-known but 'worthy' composers in this genre. His remark, 'It should not be forgotten how much there is to admire in the work of second-class composers', has become famous.[28] This list of supposed second-rate composers included Edvard Grieg (1843–1907), Hubert Parry (1848–1918) and Heinrich von Herzogenberg (1843–1900).[29] Ironically, it included no women composers.

Cobbett was also concerned about the education of audiences, describing 1913 as 'a critical time when the practice of chamber music is threatened with temporary shipwreck by the inglorious facilities of mechanical music, and by the superior attractiveness to the listener, *not to the player*, of the modern orchestra'.[30]

Women were not only listeners, but also organisers and promoters of live chamber music, as exemplified by women's chamber music clubs. These combined professional concerts with opportunities for music making by the women members. The ratio of these two activities differed; an example cited by Eggar and Scott is the Oxford Ladies Musical Society (OLMS), which was founded in 1898 and in 1913 had 200 members: they held mainly professional concerts, but the concert room was open once a week for members to play together. On the other hand, Eggar and Scott claimed that the Dawlish Musical Club, which was founded in 1909 and had 40 members in 1913, was an important rural amenity providing professional coaching for performances by its members. Each club therefore served its own particular community's needs. Some clubs actively tried to influence their members' musical taste; for example Eggar and Scott pointed out that the Clifton Ladies' Musical Club had a policy of only playing works in

27 Richard R. Walthew in W.W. Cobbett, 'Some War-time Reflections', *Chamber Music*, 11 (November, 1914): p. 17.

28 Walter Willson Cobbett, 'Duo Repertory: Some Comments', *Chamber Music*, 1 (June, 1913): p. 8.

29 See Appendix 1 for more information on Heinrich and Lisl von Herzogenberg.

30 Ibid., p. 2.

their entirety and described it as 'creating a recognised demand for a better class of public concerts'.[31]

Although the OLMS may not be representative, it is interesting to analyse the circumstances under which the Society was formed and how its organisation was structured, particularly how this might have affected the performance of chamber works by women.[32] The OLMS was established in 1897 at a time when women were excluded from the Oxford University Musical Club, which programmed concerts of orchestral as well as chamber works. This exclusion was not mentioned in a speech at the inaugural meeting of the OLMS, when Mrs Burdon-Sanderson claimed, rather, that they were concerned simply with providing high quality chamber music for Oxford. However there is an obvious subtext to her speech, given that it was a *women's* organisation that was being founded.

While the members of the Society were exclusively female, they were allowed to bring a guest of either sex, but not resident in Oxford, to each concert. Thus, the audiences were undoubtedly predominantly female, although the exact extent is not documented. Perhaps, during the First World War, when Belgian refugees, wounded soldiers and disabled officer undergraduates attended, the proportion of men was a little higher.

The Society did not claim the promotion of works by women as one of their objectives; indeed, the nomenclature, 'Ladies', as opposed to the 'Women' of the SWM suggests a rather more *gentile* and less political atmosphere. At this time, the word 'lady' had not only connotations of 'good social position' but also acceptable behaviour. *Etiquette for Ladies* opined, 'True ladyhood is of the heart rather than the head, and one who would aspire to the title is only worthy if her entire life is the embodiment of the Golden Rule, than which there can be no higher standard of conduct'.[33]

For their concerts, the OLMS generally employed London musicians, many of whom played regularly in concert halls such as the Bechstein and the Æolian. In the period between 1910 and 1915, these included the instrumentalists, Marjorie Hayward, Jessie Grimson, May Mukle, Adrian Boult, Frank Bridge and Fanny Davies.[34] From surviving concert programmes, it can be deduced that, between 1900 and 1920, 15 works by Liza and Amelia Lehmann, Maude Valerie White, Amy Woodforde-Finden, Mary Scott, Dora Bright, Adela Maddison and Ethel Barns were performed – all works, apart from Mary Scott's violin solo, for voice and piano. The number of works by English male contemporary composers was somewhat larger, but these were mainly works for voice and piano, or piano solo

[31] Katherine Emily Eggar and Marion Margaret Scott, 'Women's Doings in Chamber Music: Chamber Music Clubs', *Chamber Music*, 1 (June, 1913): p. 10.

[32] The papers of the OLMS are found in the Bodleian Library, Oxford together with the Deneke Archive, which contains the papers of Margaret Deneke who was influential in the organisation and programming for the OLMS.

[33] *Etiquette for Ladies*, pp. 11–12.

[34] See Appendix 1 for more information on Davies and Hayward.

too. While many programmes are missing from the OLMS and Deneke archives, the international and historical spread of the 1910–1911 programme, together with its inclusion of contemporary English and international composers is quite admirable.[35]

One of the most influential women in OLMS was Margaret (Marga) Deneke (1882–1969), who was part of a wealthy London family who had resided in Denmark Hill before moving to Gunfield (House) in Oxford in 1914 to escape the Zeppelin raids. The chapel in the grounds of Gunfield, which had belonged to St Hugh's College, was converted into a music room holding an audience of 90, for private and more public performances of chamber music.[36] Marga Deneke describes the decor as being designed by Roger Fry's Omega studio, but that it did not fully materialise due to war-time pressures. 'The ceiling was to be bright green, a screen with a huge goose whose neck extended over several panels was to create a pool of comfort around the music room fire where we were to sit, when alone, on a carpet with bright blobs and an even brighter border.'[37] The décor no longer exists but it is clear that the music room was to reflect a twentieth-century design-aesthetic if not such a twentieth-century musical one.

The following composers had their music played at OLMS concerts between 1910 and 1911:

'A.L.'(*)	Geminiani	Simonetti Spohr
Arne	Gibbons	Paganini
Bach	Grieg	Pugani-Kreisler
Bantock*	Handel	Purcell
Bath*	Haydn	Schubert
Beethoven	Henschel*	Schumann
Bishop	Hollander	Schutz
Brahms	Joachim	Scott*
Carissimi	Jones	Sgambati
Chopin	Liszt	Spohr
Corelli	Lully	Strauss
Corkine	Mallinson*	Stucken
Dalcroze	Marenzio	Tartini
Debussy	Massenet	Tovey*
Dowland	Mozart	Vitali

[* = contemporary British composers (*) = Amelia Lehmann]

As can be seen from her influence on the committee of the OLMS, Marga Deneke was part of a group of philanthropic women (which included Katherine Eggar and Marion Scott in London) who exerted power over the programming of chamber music in this period. They were educated, wealthy, progressive women

---

35 Stucken: American; Dalcroze: Swiss; Simonetti: Brazilian.

36 For more information on Gunfield House, see www.victorianweb.org/art/architecture/homes/36.html. Gunfield became an annexe of St Edmund's Hall.

37 Deneke Papers, Box 10, Bodleian Library, uncatalogued.

with private incomes and seemingly unending energy for organising others. The power of these women over composers and performers of both sexes was not always appreciated. For example composer Dora Bright (1862–1951), also known as Mrs Knatchbull, was involved in programming concerts in London and Cambridge. She had studied at the RAM and was part of a group of young composers, including Edward German, known as 'The Party' and was the first woman to win the Charles Lucas medal for composition.[38] However, she was described in Edward Dent's biography as 'a wealthy woman whose well-intended patronage was not always well rewarded; Clive's [the singer Clive Carey] mother nicknamed her 'Mrs Snatch'em' and resented her possessiveness'.[39]

Marga Deneke is a pertinent example of a woman of the period who was politically aware and broadly supportive of women's rights – in her notebooks she notes all the parliamentary debates on voting rights for women – she was an established member of the feminist society run by students of Oxford University. Close family friends included the suffrage campaigner Millicent Fawcett, but Deneke did not actively promote women composers' works even though the OLMS audiences consisted mainly of women.

Whilst Deneke's was not an overtly anti-feminist approach, there were indeed vocal anti-feminists in this period. This attitude can be described as a separation of political thought from aesthetics. There are no references to women composers in Deneke's diaries and papers; it appears to have merely been an issue she considered unimportant.

How concerts are programmed is a complex issue. Indeed part of the lack of support for the work of women could be attributed to the desire of promoters to engage the best musicians from London in order to maintain a professional standing. The choice of repertoire was the joint responsibility of the organising committee and the musicians themselves; in some cases there is extended correspondence on programme content. When women composers and contemporary male composers were included, it was often due to their performer-spouses' including their works in their programmes, such as Charles Phillips including songs by Ethel Barns and Adine O'Neill (1875–1947) playing works by Norman O'Neill (1875–1934).[40]

On the other hand, women performers such as Marjorie Hayward, who led her own string quartet, do not appear to have actively promoted women's chamber music for the Oxford audiences either. Even Katherine Eggar, who performed at an OLMS concert in 1903 with Eveline and Stella Fife and Walter Lang, played a programme of works by Arensky, Schubert, Handel, Grieg, Purcell and Smetana.[41] Many of the contemporary English names listed previously, have disappeared

---

[38] See Appendix 1 for more information on Edward German.

[39] Hugh Carey, *Duet for Two Voices: An Informal Biography of Edward J. Dent compiled from his Letters to Clive Carey* (Cambridge, 1979), p. 33.

[40] See Appendix 1 for more information on Adine and Norman O'Neill.

[41] OLMS Archive, Bodleian Library, Mus top oxon e473.

from view by today; a group of women composers as illustrious as these men could easily have been included in this series.

A number of women composers, including, for instance, Susan Spain-Dunk, Rebecca Clarke and Marion Scott, would have played chamber music professionally. Marga Deneke, for example, was often required to provide piano accompaniment for visiting musicians such as the violinists Joseph Joachim and John Kruse. Her mother actively discouraged her from pursuing writing prose instead of performing music, as it was far more useful to the family for Marga to play the piano.[42]

The all-female quartet was at its height in the 1910s; and in London these included the Grimson, Langley-Mukle, Solly, and Lucas string quartets and the Henkel piano quartet. Scott and Eggar felt that, 'Taken all in all there are few departments of music where a woman's special artistic qualities can be put to better use than quartet playing'.[43] Within the SWM there were several amateur and professional string quartets and a reserve of players to form chamber ensembles of different instrumental combinations. It was not too difficult, therefore, for composers to find opportunities to have their compositions played, especially in comparison with the formidable task of finding a willing and available orchestra to try out larger works.

Another practical reason for women to write chamber music was that, while it represented a movement away from the predominant media of solo piano and vocal music, it did not require orchestration skills on a vast scale. Orchestration skills learnt during a woman composer's education, however, would enhance a composer's understanding of instrumental textures involved in writing chamber works. The suitability of chamber music for women composers not only stems from its historical domestic setting but also from chamber music's comparatively modest dimensions, compared with the romantic orchestra. While male composers covered the whole gamut, women were more likely to confine themselves to smaller forces.

Of the professional chamber-music concert series, the South Place Concerts helped women's position in the chamber music world. The concert series was founded in 1887 at South Place Chapel in Finsbury and continuing in a different form, the Conway concerts, at the Conway Hall, is the longest running series of weekly chamber music concerts in London. It was part of a movement in the late nineteenth century to organise 'concerts for the people', which included the People's Concert Society – out of which the South Place Concerts were formed – as well as the Kyrle Society. Scholes describes the situation: 'There was a great desire to give the people their share of good things of life and also, as in the Manzier, Hullah and Curwen movements, to make their own good things.'[44]

42 Deneke Archive, box 10.

43 Eggar and Scott, 'Women's Doings in Chamber Music: Women in the String Quartet', *Chamber Music*, 3 (October, 1913): p. 12.

44 Scholes, *The Mirror of Music*, p. 202.

Many of the same performers appeared at the South Place Concerts as at the Bechstein Hall; however, at the former venue there was only one concert per week, which before the Second World War would include an ensemble, solo piano and piano plus voice. There were no solo song recitals, which made up the bulk of concerts in which women were involved at the Bechstein Hall. Alfred J. Clements was the first Hon. Secretary of the South Place Concerts, serving until his death in 1938. He received the Cobbett medal for services to chamber music and his organisational skills and tastes are described by Frank V. Hawkins:

> Mr Clements displayed a genius for arranging programmes and getting the best possible artists to perform them. More remarkable was the brilliant foresight which enabled him to visualise an audience which would come Sunday after Sunday and listen to programmes which rarely if ever made any concession to popular taste, but contained only the very finest inspirations of chamber music composers.[45]

Between 1887 and 1987, 1,121 chamber works were played and, out of these, 13 works were incontrovertibly by women (see table 2.1).[46] At first glance this statistic seems a depressingly small percentage but, surprisingly, women composers active between 1887 and 1920 fare considerably better than those active after 1920. This of course may reflect more on the status of the concert series than on the women composers themselves, but of th e 13 works by women only three were by women active after 1920: Elizabeth Maconchy, Imogen Holst (1907–1984) and Freda Swain. Indeed, for all of the women composers included, their works were generally only played once, the exception being Edith Swepstone's Piano Quintet in E minor, which was played four times. Swepstone appears to have had significant influence at the South Place Concerts as her pieces account for over half of those by women.

Frank Bridge, Arnold Bax, Norman O'Neill and Herbert Howells (1892–1983) are the male composers on the list who are the closest to the women in age, training and experience.[47] In general, a greater number of pieces by males than by females were played. Regarding the number of performances of individual pieces, however, these male composers fare little better than the women: though one piece by Bax was played nine times, most of his pieces were only played once.

However, few composers have established a reputation and ultimately a place in the canon through writing only chamber music. Marcia Citron, claiming that not

---

45 Hawkins, *A Hundred Years of Chamber Music*, p. 10. Hawkins was involved with the organising committee of the South Place Concert series (as was his father) so this description may possibly be in some aspects inflated.

46 Other names which might belong to women are: Boyce (likely to be Ethel Boyce), Holland (possibly Ruby Holland or Theodore Holland) and Zimmerman (likely to be Agnes Zimmerman). These have not been included in the statistical information.

47 See Appendix 1 for more information on Swepstone and Howells.

Table 2.1 Works Composed by Women at South Place Concerts 1887–1987

Composer	**Work**	**Performances**	**Overall works played**
Susan Spain-Dunk	Sextet E minor Op.55	1	1
Edith Swepstone	Piano Quintet E minor	4	7
	Quintet D Hn and Str Qt	1	
	Quintet E♭ Pf and Wind	1	
	String Quartet *Lyrical Cycle*	1	
	Piano Trio D minor	1	
	Piano Trio G minor	1	
	Piano Trio A minor	1	
Imogen Holst	Phantasy String Quartet	1	1
Elizabeth Machonchy	String Quartet no. 3 Op. 15	1	1
Ethel Smyth	String Quartet E minor	1	1
Cécile Chaminade	Piano Trio A minor	1	1
Freda Swain	Piece for violin and harp	1	1

all genres are equal, observes that ranking is affected by the status of performers of the piece and its audience, as well as its perceived complexity. Women composers have historically been associated with simple rather than complex forms, and therefore have suffered from a consequent diminution of status. In any case, Citron questions the validity of such ranking of genres:

> The distinction between complex and simple style has served as a fundamental criterion in the relative valuation of genres and sub-genres. The ranking rests on the assumption that complexity is desirable: it shows skill and competence, qualities deemed necessary for good composition. Skill is a relative term, and the demonstration of skill to 'whose satisfaction' is an open question.[48]

Questions concerning taste involve not only contemporary differences, but also historical ones. With regard to nineteenth-century women, Citron argues:

> Many female composers and listeners seemed to prefer musical simplicity, at least as gauged by the many tuneful songs and piano works composed by women. Such works would be considered lower genres, particularly if performed in private settings. Of course they might be performed just because of the simpler style, as well as for reasons of custom and access. The works might be assigned

48 Citron, *Gender and the Musical Canon*, p. 131.

> dismissive judgements, for example that they do "not rise above charming salon music", which appears in the entry on Cécile Chaminade in the *New Grove*.[49]

There is, however, a danger with this kind of binary approach, which in itself is simplistic. In addition, for composition, 'simple' does not necessarily equate with 'less skilful'. Yet it should be acknowledged that judgements linking quality to complexity or simplicity vary with historical period. Counterpoint – its zenith being the fugue – was the peak of intellectual music in the nineteenth century – the student who was able to demonstrate skill in its techniques thus showed learning.

> Fugal theory came to focus increasingly on one of two strains: either fierce, partisan debate about what constituted a 'proper' fugue, principally for the purpose of evaluating music of the past, or the establishment of a rigid model to be followed to the letter by any student wishing to master the ideal fugue.[50]

As discussed previously, the emphasis on complex compositional techniques in the assessment of quality in music led to an easy dismissal of women's work in the late nineteenth and early twentieth centuries.[51] While, in the early twentieth century, there was a resurgence of more simple kinds of music, with the promotion of the English phantasy and foundation of the folk song movement, intellectual forms such as 'fugue' and sonata form held sway in a composer's curriculum.[52] Indeed, in the 1920s there was a backlash against the perceived threat of simple music to the structure of the canon. 'Simple music, as seen in madrigals, church services, and music suitable for small vocal ensemble, is as it were, the "silver" of musical currency, but it cannot claim to greater value than the "gold" of the same currency on the score of a greater power of divisibility.'[53]

Despite their difficulties in securing performances, women composers did have works presented at all the various venues discussed in this chapter. It seems that they were optimistic: the era was perceived as a time of change, and their success had not yet peaked. Katherine Eggar and Marion Scott, writing in *Chamber Music*, describe it thus:

> We regard the present as a time in which the new idea is maturing, and the efforts at expression which we see seem to us the essays of a strength which has not yet 'found itself'. The old forms are being stretched, bent, twisted, burst; when they

---

49 Ibid., p. 132.

50 Paul M. Walker, 'Fugue: The Romantic Era', *Grove Music Online, Oxford Music Online* <www.oxfordmusiconline.com> [accessed 14 October 2009].

51 Samuel, 'Women's Music', pp. xiii–xiv.

52 This issue is discussed in greater depth in Chapter 4.

53 Robert Hull, 'On Simplicity in Music', *MT*, 67/1005 (November, 1926): p. 996.

> can no longer do duty, something, to which just now our eyes are holden, will have taken shape.[54]

That these changes should result from the *modification* of tradition rather than from its radical annihilation – as was soon to happen on the continent, at least superficially, with regard to tonality and the Second Viennese School – is both a reflection of British attitudes and, more importantly, female ones: the women composers to whom doors were opening would surely wish to enter areas previously denied them.

It is perhaps ironic that the discussion of the concept of the 'author', beginning in the late 1960s with Roland Barthes and Michel Foucault, which has connotations for the musical canon, has been felt by some feminist critics to have actually prevented women from gaining the kudos and power allocated to male authors in the past.[55] Rita Felski addresses this issue of 'sabotage' but argues:

> Yet most of those who proclaimed the death of the author were, I suspect, indifferent rather than openly hostile to feminist criticism. Obsessed with their own oedipal relationship to male myths of authorship, with debunking Shakespeare or bringing down Racine, they did not pause to think that not all authors carried the same metaphysical weight.[56]

But a fight for space was now taking place amongst various groups of composers including women. Chamber music provided a respectable backdrop for this 'battleground' and aided the advancement of women's work. With a few notable exceptions, women had not previously composed in the more 'serious' forms of chamber music. Eggar and Scott had confidence that the enthusiasm for chamber music would be beneficial to women: 'Yes there is every reason to be hopeful – women are making efforts – almost super-human efforts; and some of us have already made efforts in the direction of chamber music.'[57]

---

[54] Eggar and Scott, 'Women's Doings in Chamber Music: Women as Composers of Chamber Music', *Chamber Music*, 8 (May, 1914): p. 75.

[55] See Roland Barthes, 'The Death of An Author', in *Image-Music-Text: Essays Selected and Translated by Stephen Heath* (London, 1977), pp. 142–8 and Michel Foucault, 'What is an Author?', in *The Foucault Reader: An Introduction to Foucault's Thought*, ed. Paul Rabinow (London, 1984), pp. 101–20.

[56] Rita Felski, *Literature After Feminism* (Chicago, 2003), pp. 58–9.

[57] Eggar and Scott, 'Women's Doings in Chamber Music: Women as Composers of Chamber Music', p. 60.

Chapter 3
The Society of Women Musicians

> It is doubtful if in any part of the world there exists a body of ladies which accomplishes more in the promotion of the interests of good music with *so little assumption of importance* than the Society of Women Musicians.[1]

The Society of Women Musicians held its inaugural meeting at the headquarters of the Women's Institute at 92, Victoria Street, London, on 15 July 1911, followed by its first full meeting in on 11 November 1911.[2] It was organised by the three women who dominated its early years, Gertrude Eaton (1861–?), Katherine Emily Eggar (1874–1961) and Marion Margaret Scott (1877–1953). During the rest of its 60-year existence, it attracted hundreds of musical women members and some males. This chapter will consider its first nine years, when members initiated debates on women's role in music; it will enquire who its members were at this time; how much influence it wielded on musical society, what its political position was and how this affected the image of women composers in general, as well as their chamber music output. Were SWM composers typical of contemporary women composers? Why might a women composer have chosen not to become a member of the SWM? How did the SWM reflect the development of chamber music by women?

The objectives of the SWM were stated in the constitution of 1911, to be:

- To supply a centre where women musicians can meet to discuss and criticise musical matters.
- To afford members the benefits of co-operation and also when desired of advice with regard to the business side of their professional work.
- To bring composers and executants into touch with each other and to afford practical opportunities to composers for trying over compositions.
- To promote such other subjects as may be deemed desirable by the council for the advancement and extension of the Society's interests generally.[3]

---

1 W.W. Cobbett, 'Society of Women Musicians', *Cobbett's Cyclopedic Survey of Chamber Music*, vol. 2, p. 435.

2 There has not been a full-length study on the SWM but previous studies which have mentioned SWM activities include Paula Gillett, *Musical Women in England*, pp. 219–22, Fuller, 'Women Composers', pp. 79–81 and Pamela Blevins, *Ivor Gurney and Marion Scott: Song of Pain and Beauty* (Woodbridge, 2008), pp. 12–14 and 102–104.

3 SWM Constitution and Rules, 1911.

The language used in the constitution illuminates the social objectives of the SWM council. They clearly felt there was no suitable forum for academic and critical discussion of the professional and amateur woman musician. They were also keen to promote a sense of community between women musicians. Whether or not this was a popular goal will be discussed later. Women composers were given a special focus; the constitution refers specifically to services for them. The last objective quoted above, however, indicates the SWM was (understandably) more concerned with its own survival and interests than with that of individual members or specific groups. It should be noted that the objectives are set out in neutral language, for example there is no overt statement of aims to increase the status of women musicians and promote compositions by women, even though, in later speeches by and activities of its members, it is clearly enunciated.[4]

In the period between 1911 and 1920, the organisation included approximately 423 female members and 49 male associates.[5] There were amateurs as well as professional performers and composers; many had studied together, were part of the same social circle, and played together in various ensembles. Considerable numbers of women from the same families were members together; indeed during the time in question, there were up to 26 groups of sisters and up to 15 groups of mothers and daughters.[6] A typical member of the SWM was moderately well off, had studied at the RCM or RAM, was based in London and performed at a mixture of amateur and professional levels but with limited success. This is not to say there were not notable exceptions to this profile: while no working women seem to have joined, women from aristocratic backgrounds included Lady Mary Trefusis and Madame Marie Mely (the Comtesse Vanden Heuvel); there were also extremely successful professional musicians such as the cellist May Mukle and the violist Rebecca Clarke.[7]

The three founders of the SWM were women of music-college background who were well connected and persuasive in attracting others to their cause. Gertrude Eaton was a graduate of the RCM and was for a time Hon. Secretary and Treasurer of the RCM Union. She was involved with the Women's Institute and the suffrage movement, and later was vocal on prison reform, negotiating with the Women's Institute to allow the SWM access to meeting rooms and storage space.[8] Katherine

---

4 This will be discussed later with reference to the SWM's political position. See Paula Gillett, *Musical Women in England*, pp. 219–22.

5 The number for members is approximate because some women used several names i.e. different married names and professional names.

6 These statistics are taken from membership lists where surnames are the same.

7 See Appendix 1 for more information on Mely and Trefusis. A full list of SWM members from 1911–1920 is given in Appendix 2.

8 For further information on the connections between the SWM and the WI see Lorna Gibson, *Beyond Jerusalem: Music in the Women's Institute 1919–1969* (Aldershot, 2008), pp. 38–41 and pp. 189–191. Eaton's relationship with the WI cooled following the decision for the SWM to move to more suitable headquarters in 1920, see SWM Archive, letters between Gertrude Eaton and Mrs Roskill.

Eggar studied composition with Frederick Corder at the Royal Academy.[9] She was also a pianist, having studied in Berlin and Brussels and London. She exerted considerable influence in the early years of the SWM, giving an inflammatory speech at the inaugural meeting, sitting on the council of the SWM throughout this period and becoming president of the SWM, 1914–1915.[10] Her speech on becoming president included her opinion on the position of women musicians during the First World War and the position of women in society generally.

Katherine Eggar's close friend, Marion Scott, was a music critic writing for the *Musical Times* and the *Christian Science Monitor* among other publications, a violinist leading her own quartet and a composer. She followed Eggar as president in 1915–16. She appears to have been a less politically controversial figure than Eggar, although the organisation behind the memorial service for Scott by Eggar in 1954 shows the strength of the relationship, although there is no evidence that this was other than platonic. Scott is at present mostly remembered for her support of Ivor Gurney and the promotion of his works.[11] Her entry in *TNG (rev.)* briefly mentions her compositions and concentrates on her reputation as a writer. Even here, however, she is complimented (in gentlemanly fashion!) for her feminine style, her writings described as being 'remarkable for their grace'.[12]

Neither Eggar nor Scott has gained emancipation to the status of a 'serious' composer, even in comparison with other woman composers of the period; academic writing almost without exception refers to their links with the SWM. They were tireless and formidable activists, and the time and energy they lavished on the SWM was undoubtedly partly due to the fact that they both remained unmarried and had considerable private incomes. Indeed at the time of her death Scott's estate was worth £30,401.2.11 although, surprisingly, the amount bequeathed to the SWM in her will was a modest £100, an amount which was repeated in Eggar's will eight years later.

The three founders were active organisers during their education at the RCM and the RAM; both Eaton and Scott held committee positions in the Royal College Union after graduation. The influence of relationships established through the music colleges on the SWM can be seen in the committee of the Royal College Union in 1915; those in the most senior positions were Miss Beatrix Darnell (Hon.

---

9 Sophie Fuller, 'Eggar, Katherine Emily', *Grove Music Online, Oxford Music Online* <www.oxfordmusiconline.com> [accessed 14 October 2009]. Extensive information on Katherine Eggar's role in the SWM is contained in the SWM Archive. The archive of the SWM is held at the RCM, London but is uncatalogued. As part of my research a catalogue was produced of all items.

10 Extracts from Katherine Eggar's speech are given in Appendix 3.

11 See Appendix 1 for more information on Ivor Gurney.

12 Eric Blom and Peter Platt, 'Marion Scott' in *TNG* (rev), 2001 and Eric Blom and Peter Platt, 'Scott, Marion M.' *Grove Music Online, Oxford Music Online* <www.oxfordmusiconline.com> [accessed 14 October 2009]. In the online version the comments quoted above have been removed.

Treasurer), Mr Harold Darke (Ass. Hon Treasurer), Miss Marion Scott (Hon. Secretary), Miss Mabel Saumarez Smith (Ass. Hon Secretary), and Mrs Connah Boyd and Dr F.G. Shinn (Hon. Auditors).[13] Of these Darnell, Darke, Scott and Saumarez Smith were all members of the SWM. The social events of the societies of Royal College and Royal Academy graduates, such as the Royal College Union's 'At Homes', would have provided ideal recruitment opportunities for the SWM. Although there were many SWM members who had trained at the RAM or who held teaching positions, there were very few members between 1911 and 1920 who were students. Unlike the RCM there appears not to have been such a close relationship between the SWM and the RAM as an institution.

The SWM professional performer members included the vocalists, Evangeline Florence, Agnes Larkcom, Marie Brema, Elsie Hall, Jeanne Jouve and Gladys Moger, pianists, Alma Haas, Lily Henkel, Fanny Davies and Adelina de Lara, and string players, May Mukle, Rhoda Backhouse, Cecilia Gates and Rebecca Clarke.[14] Unsurprisingly, many married members had husbands employed in the music industry, such as the composer Ethel Barns (the singer Charles Phillips) and the singer Gladys Moger (the musical agent Philip Ashbrooke). Approximately three-quarters of the members of the SWM, however, were unmarried.[15]

Many SWM members who did not have training in composition and could not be defined as professional composers used their membership to start or develop their compositional skills. This can be seen from the sheer numbers of women who had their works played at SWM concerts. Other members were acknowledged composers and had achieved considerable commercial and critical success prior to joining. This group included the first president, Liza Lehmann, whose mother Amelia published compositions under the initials A.L.; Liza was a recital singer until her marriage to Herbert Bedford in 1894. She had studied composition with the Dutch composer Niels Raunkilde (1823–1890), and by the time of her presidency of the SWM she had produced a considerable number of vocal works and had just completed a tour of America featuring her compositions. In 1911 she was increasing the amount of teaching she undertook; subsequently she obtained a post at the GSM and produced a thesis on singing tuition.[16]

One established composer who was involved with the SWM on a regular basis was Ethel Smyth, probably the best-known British woman composer of the

---

13 See *RCM Magazine*, 11/ 3 (Easter, 1914). See Appendix 1 for more information on Darke and Saumarez Smith.

14 See Appendix 1 for more information on Larkcom, Brema, Hall, Moger, Haas, Henkel. Davies, de Lara, Mukle, Backhouse, Gates and Clarke.

15 Statistics from the SWM member list; this calculation is approximate as 'Miss' is assumed to be unmarried, 'Mrs' and 'Madame' assumed to be married. However, married women performers sometimes chose to retain their maiden names professionally. Foreign members were often called Madame whether they were married or not.

16 See Stephen Banfield, 'Lehmann, Liza', *Grove Music Online, Oxford Music Online* <www.oxfordmusiconline.com> [accessed 14 October 2009].

Figure 3.1 Ethel Barns

twentieth-century. Smyth had an erratic relationship with the SWM; there is no evidence that she attended the composer-group meetings but she did use the SWM concerts as a platform for her works and gave occasional lectures to members.[17]

Ethel Barns was also a well-established composer based in London, being known primarily for her chamber works. She was a violinist and pianist as well as composer, studying composition at the RAM with Ebenezer Prout.[18] Together with her husband, Charles Phillips, she instigated the Barns-Phillips concert series at

---

[17] See Sophie Fuller, 'Smyth, Dame Ethel (Mary)', *Grove Music Online, Oxford Music Online* <www.oxfordmusiconline.com> [accessed 14 October 2009]. For more detailed information on Smyth see Chapter 4. Smyth was grateful for the SWM's supportive congratulations on *The Wreckers* in 1939.

[18] See Appendix 1 for more information on Ebenezer Prout.

the Bechstein Hall.[19] Barns also used the SWM concerts as a platform for her new works, but was only a member until 1914.[20] She was part of a younger generation of woman composers, which also included Rebecca Clarke, which Stephen Banfield describes as 'the generation between the late Victorians (Smyth, Lehmann, White) and the new independents (Maconchy, Lutyens)'.[21]

Rebecca Clarke was a professional viola player, a member of the Queen's Hall Orchestra under Henry Wood and numerous string quartets. She studied composition at the Royal College of Music with Charles Villiers Stanford (1852–1924), as did her contemporaries, Frank Bridge (1879–1941) and Eugene Goossens (1867–1958).[22] Like Barns, Clarke wrote chamber music. Her best-known work the Viola Sonata, composed 1918–19, is now so ubiquitous that it can be considered to have entered the canonical viola repertory.[23]

Another sub-category of SWM composer-members is women who are remembered as professional performers – some had global reputations – but who also composed. These included the pianists Kathleen Bruckshaw, Ruby Holland and Elsie Horne, Elsie's sister, the singer Marie Horne, and the most well known of these, May Mukle.[24] Mukle (1880–1963) was an internationally renowned cellist who was a close friend of Rebecca Clarke, playing in the English Ensemble piano quartet with Clarke, Kathleen Long and Marjorie Hayward.[25]

Other SWM members who were primarily known as educationalists and writers on music also had works played at the Society's concerts. Among this group were the teacher Emily Daymond and writer Kathleen Schlesinger.[26] Lucie Johnstone was a singer and teacher who published compositions under the name of Lewis Carey and was involved in the running of the SWM including the careers advisory committee.[27]

This small sample of SWM membership clearly identifies the music-college connection. Indeed the SWM was the ideal venue at which female graduates of these institutions could socialise, discuss musical ideas and further their careers. It could be argued the SWM functioned in some ways on the same level as gentlemen's clubs of this period, providing a safe place to make contacts.

---

[19] The Bechstein Hall was renamed the Wigmore Hall in 1917.

[20] See Sophie Fuller, 'Barns, Ethel', *Grove Music Online, Oxford Music Online* <www.oxfordmusiconline.com> [accessed 14 October 2009]. For more information on Barns and a list of writings on Barns see Chapter 5.

[21] Banfield, 'Rebecca Clarke', p. 119.

[22] See Appendix 1 for more information on Eugene Goossens.

[23] Liane Curtis, 'Clarke [Friskin], Rebecca (Thacher) [Helferich]', *Grove Music Online, Oxford Music Online* <www.oxfordmusiconline.com> [accessed 14 October 2009].

[24] See Appendix 1 for more information on Bruckshaw, Elsie and Marie Horne.

[25] See Appendix 1 for more information on Kathleen Long.

[26] See Appendix 1 for more information on Daymond and Schlesinger.

[27] See Appendix 1 for more information on Lucie Johnstone

The most prominent foreign woman composer to be associated with the SWM was the French composer, Cécile Chaminade (1857–1944). A resolution to admit foreign members was not brought forward for discussion until 1920 but Chaminade agreed to take on the presidency in 1913–1914.[28] While she played no active role in the running of the SWM, a concert of her works was organised at the Æolian Hall when she visited London on June 30 1914. She played at the concert with SWM members Alma Haas, Beatrice Langley, May Mukle and Ernest Groom. Other members with works in this prestigious event included Lewis Carey (Lucie Johnstone), Isobel Hearne, Bluebell Klean, Mabel Saumarez-Smith, Marion Scott and Katherine Eggar.[29]

In the period between the formation of the SWM in 1911 and 1920, there were 49 male associates. They ranged from those who were related to female members and were also musicians in some capacity, to those involved in teaching, such as Albert Visetti.[30] Young male composers, such as Arthur Bliss (1891–1975) and Ivor Gurney (1890–1937) also benefited from SWM activities. The male associate with probably the most influence within the SWM, however, was Walter Willson Cobbett.[31]

As discussed in Chapter 2, Cobbett, in addition to other activities such as editing the *Cyclopaedic Survey*, first published in 1929, held competitions for the composition of chamber music, starting as early as 1905; SWM members were closely associated with these, submitting compositions and playing the works selected for prizes. It was at Cobbett's insistence that the chamber music competition revived the form of the English Phantasy. As his own encyclopaedia claims: 'He set British composers to work, with modern methods in a form, which was their own particular inheritance. There were no prescribed structural limitations, but the works were required to be tersely designed in one continuous movement.'[32]

Indeed SWM member Susan Spain-Dunk's piano trio and violin sonata both won Cobbett prizes.[33] While Cobbett's financial assistance certainly encouraged composers of both sexes to write chamber music, the SWM gave women added impetus. The result was that larger numbers of women, who had previously only written piano pieces or songs or had never composed at all, were motivated to compose in this medium. Yet some still regarded larger chamber ensembles as inappropriate for women; as late as the 1950s, an unidentified correspondent

---

[28] SWM members living abroad for not less than one year were allowed a discounted rate; foreign musicians visiting London for up to 6 months were allowed temporary membership.

[29] See Appendix 1 for more information on Klean and Langley.

[30] See Appendix 1 for more information on Albert Visetti.

[31] For a full list of male associates see Appendix 4.

[32] Thomas F. Dunhill, 'British Chamber Music' *Cobbett's Cyclopedic Survey*, 1: pp. 197–98.

[33] See Chapter 5 for a detailed discussion of the Phantasy competitions.

wrote to Katherine Eggar, imminently a panel-member for a SWM composition competition, declaring that the Trio was a particularly suitable form for women to employ.

Cobbett also established the Cobbett Free Library, which aimed to contain 'every important chamber work' and was housed and administered by the SWM. This was an important resource for the general public but especially SWM members, amateur and professional, who played in chamber ensembles. It was not, however, always well used, as Librarian Hilda Moon had to remind members in 1913 of its existence! Cobbett worked closely with Katherine Eggar, Marion Scott, and Susan Spain-Dunk – who played viola in his private string quartet – indeed they contributed articles for *Cobbett's Cyclopedic Survey of Chamber Music*, Scott writing articles on Thomas Dunhill and Herbert Howells and Eggar on Cécile Chaminade. Other contributors to this volume who were also associated with the SWM included Herbert Bedford, Rebecca Clarke, Fanny Davies, Thomas F. Dunhill, Stella B. Fife, Amina Goodwin and Percy A. Scholes.

Cobbett's competitions provided a platform for new works, although there were not vast numbers of women amongst the top prize-winners. It was rather through his support of the SWM that he advocated the work of women composers. But his *Cyclopedic Survey of Chamber Music* had 63 individual entries on women composers of chamber music, including SWM members, Barns, Chaminade, Eggar, Smyth and Spain-Dunk, while the entry, 'Women composers' mentioned SWM members, Dorothy Kalitha Fox, Dorothy Goodwin-Foster, Agnes H. Lambert, Fiona McCleary, M.E. Marshall and Monica E.M. Smith.[34] Significantly, Cobbett himself felt that women should not try to write like men: '[T]he composer destined to achieve greatness in the future is more likely to be simply – herself; not woman pranked in male garb.'[35]

There had been a precedent for the SWM in the form of the Royal Society of Female Musicians, set up in 1839, but by 1886 this organisation had amalgamated with the Royal Society of Musicians.[36] The Society of Female Artists was founded in 1855 and the Theatrical Ladies' Guild in 1891.[37] Women musicians involved in the suffrage movement formed a sub-group of the Actresses' Franchise League and marched under their banner in the Women's Coronation Procession in 1911.[38]

---

34 See M. Drake Brockman, 'Women Composers' *Cobbett's Cyclopedic Survey*, 2: pp. 591–3. Fox, Goodwin-Foster, Mcleary and Smith were not SWM members pre-1920. M.E. Marshall is very likely to have been SWM member, 'Mrs Marshall' but this is not conclusive. Liza Lehmann also has her own entry but is omitted from the entry on women composers. See Appendix 1 for more information on Fox, Lambert, Marshall and Smith.

35 Ibid., p. 593.

36 Fuller, 'Women Composers', p. 79.

37 Barbara Penketh Simpson, 'History' *Society of Women Artists* <www.society-women artists.org.uk /history.html> [accessed 20 May 2009] and Fuller, 'Women Composers', p. 38.

38 Fuller, 'Women Composers', p. 38.

On the international scene, the SWM was the first of its kind, with the American Society of Women Composers being instituted 13 years later in 1924. Many SWM members had international connections, with performers such as May Mukle and Rebecca Clarke touring America and Marion Scott writing regular articles for the American publication, *The Christian Science Monitor.* SWM members appear not to have been directly involved, however, with their American counterparts.

Perhaps the activity of most significance to SWM members was its organisation of events. In the first year these included lectures by members and guest speakers on an eclectic range of topics such as piano technique, French lyric diction, Indian music, Polish folk songs, the music copyright bill and brass instruments. These would conclude with chaired discussions between the members present.[39]

One of the most pertinent activities for composers was the establishment of a two-day composers' conference in 1912, which became an annual event. The first included papers by two prominent speakers, Ralph Vaughan Williams on 'What should be the aims of our young composers?' and Dr R. R. Terry on Gregorian rhythm.[40]

The composer-members could also attend fortnightly composer meetings run by Katherine Eggar. According to the *Music Student* in 1918, the composer group:

> demonstrated that women musicians were doing something higher than writing mere 'Shop Ballads'. String Phantasies, piano solos and nine settings of Blake's *The Sunflower*, composed by members of this little group of enthusiasts, were put before an audience. The nine vocal items formed a sort of flower show, and the audience, by vote, awarded its approbation to the best developed and most beautiful specimen in the exhibition.[41]

The tone of the above extract reveals the attitude of the author to the composers of the SWM. The author, given as 'P.A.S.', is most likely to have been Percy Scholes, editor of the *Music Student.* The reference to 'women musicians' rather than 'women composers' and the term 'little group of enthusiasts' bestows a definite amateur status on the composers of the works. It is perhaps unsurprising that, given all the settings of 'The Sunflower', Scholes evoked a flower show – and its feminine connotations – and linked this to amateurism; nonetheless the tone of this part of the article is surprisingly condescending and dismissive in an edition of the *Music Student* devoted to the SWM.

Some non-composer SWM members showed considerable support of women composers in general and made efforts to promote their work. The SWM

---

39 SWM Archive, RCM, London Notice of 4th Annual Composer Conference 1915, box 178 and Events Fixtures Pamphlets and Report on Composer Conference in *Musical News*, p. 16.

40 SWM Archive, Notice of 1st Composers Conference, 1911, box 176.

41 P.A.S. (Percy Scholes), 'The Society of Women Musicians: A Model for Men', *Music Student*, May 1918: p. 335. See Appendix 1 for more information on Percy Scholes.

encouraged a supportive atmosphere: 'As one of the chief aims in founding the SWM was to encourage serious composition among women, the Council very earnestly beg the Society to give their fellow-members the friendly support of their attendance on this occasion.'[42]

This can also be seen in correspondence in 1908 between SWM member Cecilia Hill who was Organising Secretary for the Herts and North Middlesex Competitive Music Festival and SWM composer M.E. Marshall. Having won second prize in 1907, Mrs Marshall won first prize in the 1908 competition for her violin compositions: 'Just a line in delighted haste to say you have *first* prize for composition; and the violin pieces are to be performed on Thursday's concert … There were six candidates. The other 5 were all *men* poor things! Hurrah!'[43]

Although the SWM accepted male associates who were able to participate in SWM activities, it was not unusual for male musicians to strike condescending attitudes towards the SWM. Even when well-respected musicians spoke at SWM functions and conferences they could sometimes be perceived as underestimating the intellect of their audience. Arthur Bliss succumbed to this in a paper he gave to the SWM in 1921, where he referred to the inability of 'fine ladies' to understand modern music – in this case Stravinsky's *Rite of Spring* – due to their lack of two essential characteristics, being neither male nor a child:

> Listen to it, if you can, unprejudiced. 'I appeal', I am sure he [Stravinsky] would say 'not to the professional, steeped in music, but to the man who can come and listen with his imagination aware, and his other faculties in subjection. It is the child to whom the work makes the strongest appeal, who is attracted at once by the simplicity of its message, and convincing sincerity with which the message is conveyed. I am afraid the fine ladies whom I see applauding it so vigorously have neither the one nor the other characteristic, but only find in it a sensation all the more delicious for being totally incomprehensible.[44]

What occurred in Eggar's composer meetings is unclear, although the annual reports of the SWM indicate they were for criticism rather than technical instruction. Indeed Eggar's influence and ideology may have been a reason why some of the women composers still familiar to us, such as Ethel Smyth and Ethel Barns, remained members of the society only briefly. This will be discussed in more detail later.

The SWM provided a platform for established women composers, as well as novices, to present their work. This opportunity appears to have been exploited to the full even by professionals who played no role in Eggar's composer meetings.

---

42 SWM Archive, RCM, London, Notice of Autumn Events, box 176.

43 Correspondence between Cecilia Hill and Mrs Marshall, 20 February 1908, see McCann Collection (Apollo Online), RAM, London.

44 Arthur Bliss, *As I Remember* (London: Faber and Faber, 1970), p. 252. Transcript of 'What Modern Music is Aiming At' a paper given to the SWM, 2 July 1921.

The list of women composers in Table 3.1 includes well-established women composers: Barns, Lehmann, Smyth, del Riego and White. Many on the programme were involved in performing their own works as well as those of others. These concerts in combination with rehearsals, composers' meetings and general society functions meant that professional and amateur women composers were able to converse with performers, so that the in-house orchestra, choir and instrumentalists could experiment with new works. The in-house ensembles were active and appear to be continually shifting to meet the demands of the instrumentation for the works scheduled. The musicians also worked with outside ensembles, for instance the SWM orchestra collaborated with the Choir of Westminster Cathedral in June 1913 to perform lesser-known works of Bach, under R.R. Terry.[45]

The first public concert of the SWM, Queen's Small Hall, 25 January 1912 featured the following composers:

Ethel Barns
Kathleen Bruckshaw
Emily Belcher
Louise Burns
Cécile Chaminade
Frances Davidson
Katherine Eggar
Ella Faber
Minna Gratton
Adela Hamaton
Elsie Horne
Marie Horne
Lucie Johnstone
Agnes Lambert
Adelina de Lara
Liza Lehmann
Marie Mely
May Mukle
Muriel Overton
Caroline Percival
Dorothy Pyke
Teresa del Riego
Mabel Saumarez-Smith
Marion Scott
Ethel Smyth
Julia Cook Watson
Maude Valerie White

After the opening concert, which was devoted to members' works, most SWM concerts, such as the one programmed on 24 February 1913, did not feature work solely by SWM members. As well as songs by Agnes Lambert and a Phantasy Trio by Alice Verne-Bredt, there were works by Coleridge-Taylor, Stanford, Glazounov, German, Palestrina, di Lasso and Brahms.[46] This was also the case for the first concert of 1915, held at SWM headquarters and organised by the pianist Elsie Horne, with works by herself, Rachmaninov and Delibes.[47] In later years, the SWM returned to only SWM composer-concerts in an effort to promote a younger generation of composers. On 18 December 1920, there was a performance of works by younger members including Elsie Hamilton, Ruby Holland, Jane Joseph,

---

45 n.a. 'Occasional Notes' *MT*, 54/ 845 (July, 1913): p. 444.

46 This concert did not receive a favourable review from Evelyn Kaesman in *The Musical Courier* (Feb, 1913) who felt the compositions were not original.

47 Anon, 'London Concerts' *MT*, 56/864 (February, 1915): p. 108.

M.E. Marshall, Kathleen Richards – later the wife of composer Benjamin Dale and contributor to Ethel Smyth's biography by Christopher St John – and Joan Spink.[48]

Some SWM concerts, for example the Chaminade concert, were well attended; the Liza Lehmann memorial concert in 1918 had to be repeated because of the demand for tickets. Such popularity with audiences was not always evident, however, and in October 1913 the players and composers involved in a SWM concert complained they had played to themselves. It appears that, even within the community of women musicians, a famous name was needed in order to draw large audiences. Indeed it could be argued that while the SWM had worked to dismantle the male canon, it was replacing this with an elite selection of idolised women composers such as Chaminade and Lehmann. Programmes by well-known women composers did not often also include works by lesser-known women.

The SWM were keen to promote a sense of professionalism in order to be taken seriously by London's musical society. They divided themselves into professionals and amateurs, although it is not clear how they made this distinction and indeed implemented it. It should be remembered that many women composers moved between these categories throughout their lives, depending on their circumstances, and that amateurs at this time were not necessarily badly trained. Amateurs and professionals were only segregated in that professionals paid a lower subscription fee than amateurs.

In this time-period the society also set up an advisory committee to give career advice for women wanting professional careers as performers or composers. The members on the advisory panel for composers were Katherine Eggar, Thomas F. Dunhill – a well established composer – and Adela Hamaton, who had compositions played while at the Royal Academy but did not subsequently establish a considerable reputation in the professional world.[49]

Politically the SWM was not directly connected to the suffrage movement, although several of its members were involved in it at some level, but the relationship between the suffrage movement and the SWM was complex. On a practical, if not ideological, level, there were many similarities between them: the regular meetings, the campaigns for new members, the distribution of propaganda, posters and advertising. Each of the two women's societies would have provided ideal opportunities to recruit for the other. Suffragette members in the SWM would have been well-versed in promoting a cause with continual enthusiasm and energy; this was put to good use in the tussle between various SWM members and the Associated Board of the Royal Schools of Music over women examiners, which lasted, 1937–1956. A perceived link to the suffrage movement, however, could have discouraged some women musicians from joining the SWM. Indeed for some the notion that the SWM had a political agenda, whatever that may have been, was a reason not to join. Katherine Eggar was sensitive to this:

---

48 See Appendix 1 for more information on Benjamin Dale.

49 See Appendix 1 for more information on Adela Hamaton.

> Perhaps in the minds of some there is a lurking fear that we are a suffragist society in disguise; our only connection with the Suffragist movement is a similarity of ideals. In both political and musical life there is a great deal of wire pulling and party policy; one does not need to know much about musical dealings in general, to know this.[50]

The press, initially supportive of the SWM's objectives, was increasingly critical of perceived suffragist tendencies within the organisation. The members themselves appeared to realise the risks involved in taking too much of a suffragist line, for example, Gertrude Eaton declined to take a lead in their campaign for women to receive doctorates in music as she felt she was too closely allied to the suffrage cause. Women artists in general were much more closely linked with the suffrage movement than women musicians, mainly through the Suffrage Atelier, which produced visual propaganda.[51]

Eggar's speech at the inaugural meeting in 1911, however, projects a feminist tone in discussing women's suffrage. '[W]e want women to join us who will take an active share in vitalising the artistic conception.'[52] The SWM encouraged women to take an increasingly active role in shaping their position within musical society and thus a more confident notion of identity as a woman composer. Contrasting with advice given in the RAM student magazine, *The Overture*, in the 1890s, women in the early twentieth century were much less likely to publish under pseudonyms or initials.

> [T]he woman composer has a great deal of prejudice to overcome, and her best plan is to give the public only her surname and the initial letter of her Christian name. Then she will stand some chance of getting a certain amount of unbiased criticism – till she is found out.[53]

Were the SWM's composer-members typical of women composers generally? Here, its public image is significant: the SWM in the war years spanned three generations, yet the youngest of these was the least represented. Its members were eager consumers, ensuring sales of sheet music, as can be seen in the hugely successful Chaminade concert at the Æolian Hall during her presidency in 1914. The benefits of membership for the professionally more-established included, as mentioned earlier, a platform for new works. The first two movements of Ethel

---

50 Katherine Eggar, *Address at Inaugural Meeting*, SWM Archive, RCM, London, see Appendix 3.

51 Tickner, *The Spectacle of Women*, pp. 20–22. The Suffrage Artelier was founded in 1909 by Clemence and Lawrence Housman as a society, which promoted women's suffrage through crafts and visual arts. Artists submitted work that was sold through the Artelier. See http://vads.ahds.ac.uk/collections/FSB.html.

52 Eggar, *Address at Inaugural Meeting*, SWM Archive, RCM, London, see Appendix 3.

53 n.a. 'Correspondence to the Editor', *The Overture*, 4/1 (March, 1893): p. 16.

Smyth's String Quartet in E minor, played here, were praised in the *Musical Times*: 'They were remarkable for an originality which had no recourse to the eccentric.'[54] Some women had only fleeting association with the Society; for example, as mentioned earlier, Maude Valerie White was a member throughout this period but lived abroad, and Ethel Smyth was only a member for three years during this period, although she returned in later years.

The First World War certainly had an impact on membership, as many women were involved in the war effort, but it does not explain all of the lapses in membership that occurred at that time. It is possible that those who had established careers were anxious about being too closely linked to the Society, resulting in a loss of identity and a loss of acceptance in the mainstream, while also being concerned about the expectations placed upon them by the SWM.

One possible source of discontent, especially for the more established composers, could have been the extent of the power exerted by certain women within the SWM. Katherine Eggar, for instance, was influential not only in the administration but also in the formation of the Society's ideology. Indeed her presidential speech in 1915 clearly reveals her views on the position of women and their proposed path. It can almost be read as a war-cry, similar to many suffrage speeches but with a musical message. Eggar was eager for change within musical society and for women to pursue intellectual interests:

> Think of all the stuffiness and all the cobwebs which have been swept away by the breezes, and, it must be owned, destructive gales, of modern thought and feeling. Can you not see what this has meant for women themselves, to have got used to travelling, to having clubs, to looking after themselves, to having big and serious interests of their own, to being a vital part of a world larger than their own sitting rooms? Can you not see what it has meant for the world, for men in all classes of society to become accustomed to women doctors, women guardians, women clerks, women gardeners, women speakers, women farmers, women professors?[55]

In the same speech, Eggar also discusses the popular idea – in her opinion unjustified – that if women had had the vote, war would have come sooner; this was of course something well beyond the remit of a musical society: 'I really can hardly believe that if women, trained for years to that work, had been in the cabinet, they would have made more of a hash in questions affecting the empire than men.'[56]

---

[54] n.a. 'Chamber Music' *MT*, 53/829 (March, 1912): p. 181. Smyth did not complete the final two movements of the String Quartet until 1912 and her return to writing this work may have led to the performance of the first two movements.

[55] SWM Archive, RCM, London, Presidential speech of Katherine Eggar, p. 3.

[56] Ibid., p. 4.

More pertinent for the composer members, however, was that she also had strong opinions on the type of work women should produce:

> I beg you, I beseech you, if you *must* write songs, if you must link music with words, to maintain a high literary standard, a high standard of sentiment at least. Have fine taste in poetry, and remember that your music has got to express something more still . . . Music only begins to be relevant when there is something to be said which words cannot compass alone, some idea which eludes definition. Apart from that, music is merely a frivolous ornament.[57]

Eggar was herself a keen exponent of chamber music but these can be considered strong words given that two of the country's foremost ballad writers, Liza Lehmann and Maude Valerie White, were members of the SWM. However, Eggar felt that 'the Society might be the means of stimulating the imagination of women to loftier flights in that atmosphere than they had at present attempted'.[58] Indeed Eggar and Scott considered there was no longer any reason why women should not write in this genre and to some extent blamed the women composers themselves for not rising to the challenge: 'There have been insuperable barriers which have prevented women from being composers; but many of those barriers have now been removed, and the time has come for us to feel ashamed if we are any longer "Nefarantoj" – *habitual not – doing ones.*'[59]

The difficulties encountered by Eggar and Scott in finding chamber music by women on which to comment highlights the reluctance of publishers to publish chamber music by women and indeed chamber music at all. This is a response from one such publisher, as quoted by Eggar and Scott, which omits both the male composer's and the publisher's name, presumably for fear of jeopardising their own publishing careers. 'The only thing we handle in the way of chamber music is ...'s pianoforte quintet. That, we take it, will not interest you, as the composer has the misfortune to belong to the sterner sex.'[60]

However, over the course of writing two more articles on the subject, Eggar and Scott managed to trace a bulk of music, which had remained in manuscript, published privately or published for a short time. These included works by Ethel Smyth, Oliveria Prescott, Fanny Hayes, Josephine Troup, Dora Bright, Cécile Hartog, Adela Hamaton, Marion Arkwright, Margaret Meredith, Bluebell Klean, Ethel Barns, Alice Verne-Bredt, Ethel Bilsand and Susan Spain-Dunk.[61] Considering that many of the women composers discussed in print by Scott and Eggar were well known to the authors – some were members of the SWM and

---

57 Ibid., p. 8.

58 n.a. 'The Society of Women Musicians', *MT*, 52/822 (August, 1911): p. 536.

59 Eggar and Scott, 'Women's Doings in Chamber Music: Women as Composers of Chamber Music', *Chamber Music*, 7 (March 1914): p. 60.

60 Ibid.

61 See Appendix 1 for more information on Bilsand and Hartog.

personal friends – the candour of the assessments is surprising. At the same time, there seems a correlation between length of comment and familiarity of the authors with the composer. Susan Spain-Dunk, for example, is described as 'a composer of real promise, and one who ought to count for something in the progress of women chamber music writers'.[62]

Bluebell Klean, one of the younger SWM composers, is described as being 'of more than usual merit'.[63] Adela Hamaton, on the SWM advisory committee for young composers, is criticised for composing as a pianist: 'the effect is rather too much that of a piano solo accompanied by strings.'[64] Cécile Hartog, another regular SWM member, has a mixed review: 'A conscientious student's tendency to overdo a "figure" and to work the subject rather threadbare does not prevent a genuine musical sincerity from pervading the whole work.'[65]

Despite the possible negative aspects of Eggar's position in the SWM, there were women who thrived under her mentoring, some of whom would not have attempted composing had it not been for their membership of the Society's composer group, whose meetings often took place in Eggar's home. At the SWM annual birthday party in 1916, the gratitude of the composer group was recorded:

> Miss Katherine Eggar was presented with a handbag by the members of her 'Group of Composers' as a small token of their thanks for the inspiration she had given them during the year in directing the meetings of the group at her own home and at Æolian Hall. Miss Lucie Johnstone (hon. Secretary) expressed the thanks of the membership and Miss Kathleen Bruckshaw presented the bag to Miss Eggar.[66]

The image of the SWM as an amateur society may have also discouraged professional women composers from joining or participating in events. It is true that the majority of members were amateurs, and a number of events were strictly geared towards them – cream teas, etc. – but other events, such as concerts at prestigious venues, had a definite professional flavour. The amateur events included two social occasions organised by Gertrude Eaton in 1914 at the Halcyon Club, the first hosted by Eaton, Lucie Johnstone and Mrs Frank Dawes, and the second by Alma Haas, Adela Hamaton and Lily Henkel.[67] Despite the possibility of alienating professional women, these events were probably essential in maintaining enough members to safeguard the future of the SWM.

---

62 Eggar and Scott, 'Women's Doings in Chamber Music: Women as Composers of Chamber Music Third Paper' *Chamber Music*, 8 (July, 1914): p. 98.

63 Ibid. p. 97.

64 Eggar and Scott, 'Women's Doings in Chamber Music: Women as Composers of Chamber Music Second Paper', *Chamber Music*, 8 (May, 1914): p. 76.

65 Ibid.

66 n.a. 'Society of Women Musicians' *MT*, 57/883 (September, 1916): p. 419.

67 SWM Archive, RCM, London, 3rd Annual Report 1914, box 178.

The number of well-known names connected with the SWM in various capacities shows that the organisation, on the surface at least, occupied a respected place in musical society. It is perhaps ironic that those closely involved with the committee of the SWM, such as Scott and Eggar, were responsible both for the SWM's success and its limitations.

Chapter 4

The Other Side of London's Musical Society: Adela Maddison, Ethel Smyth and Morfydd Owen

I've tried in my noddle to carry
The laws of Macfarren and Prout
But henceforth I cotton to Parry:
He says the Sonata's played out.
The Rondo would puzzle old Harry
The first movement – what's it about?
I bless my deliverer, Parry,
He says the Sonata's played out.
No more second subjects to marry
To first subjects. 'working' I scout;
I'll write as I please, Doctor Parry,
For now the Sonata's played out.[1]

This chapter will ask to what extent did chamber music of women composers of the early twentieth century conform to male ideals? An examination of the outlook of women composers of this period, in particular, their desire to distinguish their compositional activities from those of their male colleagues, can begin to answer this question.

While the SWM provided a platform for many women composers, others either chose not to become members of the organisation or else, having been members for a period of time, distanced themselves from it, inhabiting a different and in some cases more international musical milieu. Adela Maddison and Morfydd Owen, who were never members of the SWM, and Ethel Smyth, who was a fitful member, will be the focus of this chapter. Why did they not involve themselves very much with the Society? Did their creative output differ from what the SWM was advocating for women composers? And is this distance from (and perhaps lack of interest in) female communities reflected in any way in their music? Do the quintet, quartet and trio of Maddison, Smyth and Owen conform to traditional male ideals more than those of SWM members?

---

1 n.a., 'Songs of the Century: no. 1, The Youthful Composer's Pæan of Joy', *The Overture*, 4/1 (March, 1893): p. 7.

Perhaps the most obvious aspect of the nineteenth century's (male) heritage in chamber music at this time is sonata form. The gendered implications of this form, discussed in much feminist musicology in the late twentieth century, seem, at least on the surface, to have been ignored at the beginning of the same century. Yet, what exactly did British theorists write about it and what did they advocate to their students?

James Webster, in his entry on Sonata Form in the *New Grove Dictionary of Music and Musicians*, describes what he considers to be its five main aspects in the Romantic era.[2] These include an emphasis on 'striking and original' themes; the lack of exact repetition especially of the main theme, the increased importance of the coda regarding the climax of the piece rather than the recapitulation and expanded tonal relations, that is, 'acceptance of major and minor as equally valid representations of the tonic'.[3]

The fifth of Webster's 'aspects', however, is the significance of the second theme, which, he claims, had increased in importance in the Romantic era: '[S]onata form was based on the duality of two contrasting themes – often characterised as "masculine" and "feminine" – rather than on the tonal duality of the exposition.'[4] As Susan McClary has observed, this masculine/feminine dichotomy was originally outlined by A.B. Marx in *Die Lehre von der Musikalischen Komposition Practisch – Theoretisch*.[5] Scott Burnham quotes the relevant passage:

> The *Haupsatz* [main theme] is the first to be determined, thus partaking of an initial freshness and energy, and as such is the more energetic, pithy, and unconditional formation, that which leads and determines. The *Seitensatz* [subsidiary theme], on the other hand, is created after the first energetic confirmation and, by contrast, is that which serves. It is conditioned and determined by the preceding theme, and as such its essence is necessarily milder, its formation is one of pliancy rather than pitch – a feminine counterpart, as it were, to its masculine precedent.[6]

At the same time, Burnham argues – in answer to the condemnation of critics such as McClary – that Marx did not view the themes in a way that had negative connotations for the term, 'feminine':

---

2 James Webster, 'Sonata Form', *Grove Music Online,* Oxford Music Online <www.oxfordmusiconline.com> [accessed 14 October 2009].

3 Ibid.

4 Ibid.

5 McClary, *Feminine Endings*, pp. 13–15. A.B. Marx, *Die Lehre von der Musikalschen Komposition, Praktisch – Theoretisch,* 2nd edn (4 vols, Leipzig, 1841–1851), III (1848) as discussed in Scott Burnham, 'A. B. Marx and the Gendering of Sonata Form', *Music Theory in the Age of Romanticism*, ed. Ian Bent (Cambridge, 1996), pp. 163–86.

6 Marx, *Die Lehre*, pp. 272–3 quoted in Burnham, 'A. B. Marx and the Gendering of Sonata Form', p. 163.

> What Marx needed was a way of expressing the interdependence of two themes (or group of themes) which together form a balanced whole. His dynamic conception of formal process constrains him to regard the initial thematic utterance as primary and determining. And the *Seintensatz* is clearly the unmarked component of the pair, that which must be so many things for, and with, the *Haupsatz.* Marx's metaphor of gendered themes is a poetic attempt to address this complexity.[7]

Yet, late twentieth-century feminist musicologists in general have seen Marx's interpretation of the relationship of the two themes as a metaphor for the relationship between males and females in his contemporary society: at its extreme, one, powerful and active, the other, gentle and compliant.[8] Liane Curtis admits that feminist musicologists have used this nineteenth century model and this latter interpretation – also explored by Hugo Riemann and Vincent D'Indy – as a basis for the development of feminist analyses of instrumental music.[9] With regard to the composer Rebecca Clarke, however, she argues that, although Clarke would have been familiar with German music theorists and her viola sonata can be analysed as a subversion of gendered codes, she (Curtis) is unwilling to privilege the theorists' view 'over how the work may have been understood by the composer and by performers, audiences and critics of the time'.[10]

Curtis goes on to point out, while Marx and others have interpreted first and second themes as 'masculine' and 'feminine', there is no evidence that British educators or composers, including women composers, considered them in this gendered way: the metaphor may indeed have remained at a more innocent level of a 'strong' first theme and a 'more lyrical' second theme. Of course it is impossible to read the subconscious attitudes of composers to such subtle trends; but the writings of British theorists and pedagogues of this time can indeed offer some insight.

Three important British treatises of this era, which discuss sonata form, are *Applied Forms: A Sequel to 'Musical Form'* by Ebenezer Prout (1895), *Musical Composition: A Short Treatise for Students* by Charles V. Stanford (1911, 1930) and *Form in Music with Special Reference to the Designs of Instrumental Music* by Stewart Macpherson (1908).[11] They are all based on their authors' teachings at the RCM and the RAM and would have influenced not only students in their respective institutions but composers who had studied in Europe and those who had no formal training. While all three pedagogues used early nineteenth-century sonata form as

7 Burnham, 'A. B. Marx and the Gendering of Sonata Form', p. 183.

8 McClary, *Feminine Endings*, pp. 11–16.

9 Liane Curtis, 'Rebecca Clarke and Sonata Form: Questions of Gender and Genre', *Musical Quarterly*, 81/3 (Fall 1997): pp. 393–429. Those who have used this model include Marcia Citron in her analysis of Chaminade and Susan McClary on sonata form.

10 Curtis, 'Rebecca Clarke and Sonata Form', p. 401.

11 See Appendix 1 for more information on Stewart Macpherson.

a model for their teaching, in their published treatises they acknowledged some of the variants which Romantic and early twentieth-century composers had applied to the form. The treatises highlight not only how sonata form was taught, but also the ways in which composers considered its different aspects.

Stanford draws the attention of his students to the details of sonata form: the main theme is of vital importance as it is the basis of variation and it 'should contain sufficient material to vary'; other demands he makes on the main theme are, 'secondly, that it should have at least one striking feature; thirdly that it should be simple'.[12] The first and second subjects should contrast 'but not lose character'. Prout goes further, deeming 'unity' rather than logic as the special characteristic of sonata form, using Beethoven and later Romantic composers as examples. As with Stanford, he suggests there must be contrast between the first and second subjects. Significantly, however, he also stresses the link between them: 'In modern compositions the second subject is mostly constructed of entirely different thematic material from the first; at the same time, the contrast must not be too violent; the second subject ought rather to be like *a continuation of the trace of thought of the first.*'[13]

Macpherson also emphasises flow within sonata form. He recommends that, while the first subject should be 'strongly-marked' and of 'definite character' – so as to be remembered by the listener and have scope for development – it should flow into the second:

> [I]t should be remembered that often this gradual obliteration of the key and feeling of the first theme, so as to lead without a palpable break into the second subject, evinces a higher level of constructive skill, and is the outcome of that desire for greater continuity which has characterised the writings of the more modern masters, from the time of Beethoven onwards.[14]

As with Prout, Macpherson instructs that the first and second subjects should not be too contrasting: 'a most necessary matter in a movement whose aim is to preserve continuity and a certain degree of unity of style throughout.'[15] With regard to first and second themes, therefore, these authors stress both contrast and unity. But in none of the above treatises is there any reference to the notion of 'masculine' and 'feminine' themes, or even descriptions of them that might be interpreted as such.

A number of SWM members, as well as other women composers, were likely to have studied from the theses of Prout, Stanford, Parry and Macpherson as part of a music college education. What of the British contemporary music they listened

---

[12] Charles Villiers Stanford, *Musical Composition: A Short Treatise for Students* (London, 1911, 1930), p. 53.

[13] Ebenezer Prout, *Applied Forms: A Sequel to 'Musical Form'* (London, 1895), p. 145.

[14] Stewart Macpherson, *Form in Music with Special Reference to the Designs of Instrumental Music* (London, 1908), p. 128.

[15] Ibid., p. 129.

to? The composer who was perhaps the most concerned with recurrence of material from previous movements within sonatas was Cyril Scott (1879–1970). He was born in the generation between Maddison and Owen and, like Smyth, studied in Germany. In an article in the *Monthly Musical Record* in 1917, like his predecessors Stanford, Prout and Macpherson, Scott states sonata form should be logical and possess unity, and should also have flow.[16] He feels sonata form is still developing because it still lacks logic and unity and a connection between movements. The solution for this, he claims, is the recurrence of themes from previous movements: 'the free-fantasie section of the finale should be treated as an arena for all previous themes to re-enter, and so disport themselves once more before their final exit.'[17] This is within the context of Romantic music, which, as opposed to Classicism and 'Futurism', is the 'most rational and productive of great art', and sonata form should develop within its parameters.[18] Indeed, Scott specifies that his Sonata no. 1, composed in 1908, should be played continuously despite its division into sections. The sonata contains little exact repetition; as Lisa Hardy writes, 'Thematic transformation is an important part of Scott's style'.[19] The frequent changes of bar, time signatures and harmony are reminiscent of the phantasie style.[20]

Other British sonatas written in the late nineteenth century, such as the Piano Sonata by Edward German (1862–1936) in 1884 and the Sonata in F minor by William Yeates Hurlstone (1876–1906) in 1894, also show awareness of techniques used by Beethoven and Liszt and, as Scott later advocates, the 'main themes from the first and second movements recur in the final movement and the same motif opens the first and third movements'.[21]

European composers' treatment of sonata form in the early twentieth century was often conventional, differing little from nineteenth-century practices. However, both Skryabin (1871–1915) and Debussy (1862–1918) notably created increasingly complex sonata forms; Skryabin's 9th Sonata (1913) places an emphasis on the second subject: it 'has a distinct second subject ('*avec un langueur naissante*'), frail and simple, but has no recapitulation, at least not until the last line'.[22] In the 6th (1911) and 7th (1911) Sonatas there are climaxes before the recapitulation and codas are significant to the overall structure, as they 'reach into unsuspected thematic and textural territory'.[23]

---

16 Cyril Scott, 'Suggestions for a more Logical Sonata Form', *Monthly Musical Record*, xlvi (1 May, 1917): pp. 104–5.

17 Ibid., p. 104.

18 Cyril Scott, *The Philosophy of Modernism in its Connection to Music* (London, 1917), p. 8.

19 Lisa Hardy, *The British Piano Sonata, 1875–1945* (Woodbridge, 2001), p. 54.

20 See Chapter 5.

21 Hardy, *The British Piano Sonata*, pp. 39–40. See Appendix 1 for more information on William Hurlstone.

22 Hugh Macdonald, *Skryabin* (New York, Melbourne, 1978), p. 63.

23 Ibid., p. 62.

What then was the response of women composers to such developments and how did they take them forward?[24] Did SWM members, some intent on creating a female tradition, respond differently from those who rejected the organisation with its implied feminist ideals? Of course, this question cannot be answered definitively without a detailed investigation of the output of every British female composer of the time, an exercise well beyond the scope of the present study; in the meantime, however, some initial light may be cast on the subject by carefully scrutinising works by several non-members, as well as members, of the SWM.

Adela Maddison

Maddison (1866–1929) had grown up in London but spent most of her professional compositional career in Paris and Berlin before returning to London during the First World War.[25] She was from a respectable Irish family and married Fred Maddison at the age of 18. She was a prolific composer in her teenage years; her husband owned part of the music publishers, Meltzer, who were the first to publish her compositions. During her marriage she lived near Hyde Park and put on musical evenings in her salon; it was here the Maddisons met Gabriel Fauré (1845–1924), who encouraged Adela's compositional development to the extent that she left her husband and children to move to Paris at some point in the late 1890s. There is some speculation amongst scholars as to whether she had a sexual relationship with Fauré but, as Sophie Fuller points out, relations with Fred Maddison were not severed completely as Adela Maddison cared for her ailing husband before his death in 1906.[26]

Whatever the reasons for the move to Paris, Maddison's career peaked on her move from Paris to a new base in Berlin sometime between 1904 and 1906. The diary of her friend Mabel Batten (1856–1916) records her visiting London in 1911 and 1913.[27] Indeed Maddison was in London in June, 1911, a month before

---

[24] For a catalogue of instrumental chamber music composed by women in this period see Appendix 5.

[25] The main sources for discussion of Adela Maddison are Fuller, 'Women Composers', pp. 299–325; Fuller, 'Devoted Attention'; Jean Nectoux, *Gabriel Fauré A Musical Life*, trans. Roger Nichols (Cambridge, 1991), pp. 281–3 and Robert Orledge, *Gabriel Faure* (London, 1979), pp. 16–17, 39 and 95.

[26] See Fuller, 'Devoted Attention'. Although biographies of Fauré refer to Maddison as his mistress, Sophie Fuller's more recent research, which claims a wholly lesbian identity for Maddison, suggests the move to Paris was primarily for artistic reasons rather than solely to maintain a relationship with Fauré. According to Sewell Geneology <www.sewellgeneology.com/p407.htm> [accessed 22 April 2009] Frederick Brunning Maddison (1850–1906) married Mary Adela Tindal on 14 April 1883 at Christ Church, Lancaster Gate, London and their children Diana and Noel, were born in 1886 and 1888 respectively.

[27] Mabel Batten's Diary, Mabel Batten and Cara Lancaster Archive, Lancaster Family Collection, London.

the inaugural meeting of the SWM, and chose not to engage with the Society following her permanent return to London after the outbreak of war in 1914. It is possible that she was unaware of the Society's activities in this period, lacking the music college connections through which many SWM members were recruited. Ethel Smyth, who might have been in a position to advise her, had ceased her own membership, and it is unlikely Maddison would have had close connections with other British women composers. She did, however, attempt to regain her reputation in London by having 12 of her songs included in a concert at the Æolian Hall on 30 April 1915.[28] The press review in the *Musical Times* suggests Maddison perhaps had an organisational role:

> At Adela Maddison's concert on April 30 no fewer than 12 songs by the composer were sung. If somewhat unequal in merit, the best showed her to be a composer with ideas and some facility in handling modern harmonic resources. We were most pleased with 'The Poor Man's Love Song', and a declamatory setting of Longfellow's 'Sail On, O Ship of State'.[29]

The amateur nature of the SWM may not have appealed to an established composer like Maddison, whose opera *Der Talisman* was performed eight times at Leipzig. Although orchestral works by British women had been heard in London, Maddison and Smyth, for instance, appear to have been considerably more successful at mounting large-scale opera in Germany.[30] Another example, Dora Bright (1862–1951), had also nurtured her career in Germany with the performance of her piano concerto in Dresden, Cologne and Leipzig in 1889 before presenting it at the Crystal Palace in 1891.[31]

Maddison was, however, involved with groups of creative women in Paris and Berlin and had a powerful ally in the Princesse de Polignac who promoted her works. According to Fuller, after ceasing contact with Fauré, Maddison was in a relationship with Martha Mundt, secretary to the Princesse, which meant that the couple moved in upper-class and aristocratic lesbian artistic circles.[32] This

---

[28] Sophie Fuller, 'Women Composers', p. 315. The other works in the concert were piano music by Ravel and violin sonatas by Franck and Delius.

[29] n.a. 'London Concerts', *MT*, 56/868 (June 1915): p. 364.

[30] A number of British women had orchestral works performed in this period including Ethel Barns (*Concertstück* at the Promenade Concerts in 1910), Edith Swepstone (whose orchestral works were performed regularly by the Bournemouth Municipal Orchestra under Dan Godfrey) and Dorothy Howell (*Lamia* at the Promenade concerts in 1919). Liza Lehmann was one of the few women composers to have her light operas performed in England. These included *Sergeant Brue* in 1904, *The Vicar of Wakefield* in 1906 and *Everyman* in 1915.

[31] Nigel Burton, 'Dora Bright' *NGDWC*, (eds) J.A. Sadie and R. Samuel (London, 1994), p. 85, revised and abbreviated as Sophie Fuller, 'Bright, Dora'. *Grove Music Online*, Oxford Music Online. <www.oxfordmusiconline.com> [accessed 18 April 2009].

[32] Fuller, 'Devoted Attention', p. 87.

group included Ethel Smyth, the singer Mabel Batten and the writer Radclyffe Hall. The Princesse de Polignac, who was the extremely wealthy American heiress of the Singer sewing machine empire, had two unconsummated marriages with French aristocrats.[33] She did not directly commission Maddison, but, according to biographer Sylvia Kahan, was responsible for securing the Leipzig opera house for the performances of Maddison's opera, *Der Talisman*, and unsuccessfully campaigned for Maddison to be awarded the French honour of the *Palmes Académiques* in recognition of her compositional output.[34]

Although Kahan argues that the Princesse de Polignac did not show bias towards lesbian and gay composers, it seems that Maddison's relationships with other women (sexual or otherwise) did not disadvantage her. Fuller argues for an empowering lesbian identity:

> As Fred's wife or Fauré's lover, she was regarded, both by contemporaries and later scholars, as little more than a decorative appendage or a lovesick nuisance. But as Mundt's lover and friend of women such as Batten and Polignac, she took her place in the circle of independent, creative women, defined by and valued for her art.[35]

It is difficult, however, to conclude that Maddison was defined solely by her art within this group and that the group dynamic was always positive. Maddison's increasingly pleading letters to Batten during the early years of the First World War suggest previous support was no longer forthcoming.

Due to her German nationality, Martha Mundt lost employment in the Princesse's retinue in the build-up to the First World War. As a result, Maddison herself lost favour with the Princesse. Maddison and Mundt returned to London after the outbreak of war having to rely on the support of the singer Elsie Swinton and Mabel Batten, who were from wealthy backgrounds. Maddison writes in a letter to Batten: 'I know you yourself are worried, poor dear Mabel. I feel a brute writing all this. *I don't want money* and hate anyone thinking I am begging at this terrible moment but if the roof can be provided somehow – I can for a time manage our food etc'.[36] According to Fuller, Mundt was thereafter forced to return to Berlin and her separation from Maddison lasted until they were reunited in Switzerland in 1921.[37]

While the SWM in London also offered an echo of this kind of environment for women composers, it lacked the extreme wealth and opulence and the intimacy of sexual relationships that the Princesse de Polignac's circle provided. A society

33 Kahan, *Music's Modern Muse*, p. 31.

34 Ibid., p. 163.

35 Fuller, 'Devoted Attention', p. 87.

36 Letter from Adela Maddison to Mabel Batten (later sent on to Cara Harris nee. Batten), 1914, Mabel Batten and Cara Lancaster Archive, Lancaster Family Collection, London.

37 Fuller, 'Devoted Attention', p. 87.

such as the SWM was unable to provide the same level of financial support as individual patronage and it is notable that while, during the war, Marion Scott spent most of her resources on helping individual composers such as Ivor Gurney and Herbert Howells, she did not offer this assistance to Maddison or any other woman composer.[38] The cases of the Princesse de Polignac and Marion Scott perhaps highlight the sexual/intimate undercurrents of individual patronage mostly absent from the SWM. Although the organisation contained lesbian and bisexual members, such as the cellist, May Mukle, a lesbian aesthetic was not part of the group's *raison d'être*. The ideals and perceived frivolity of those surrounding the Princesse de Polignac's entourage were not always shared by those, such as Katherine Eggar and Marion Scott, involved in the women's and temperance movements.[39]

As discussed previously, war-time economies were not conducive to the performance of large-scale pieces. In addition, by 1916, the promotion – by Cobbett, Dunhill, Eggar et al. – of chamber music as *the* medium for women composers had spread through the Cobbett competitions and coloured speeches to the SWM and articles in the press. Maddison's return to London marked her return to composing chamber music, if only one ensemble work (a piano quintet) and various pieces for solo piano or piano and violin. This probably pragmatic choice conformed to the SWM's convictions about the medium. The Piano Quintet was composed in 1916 in London and first performed as part of a concert of Maddison's works on 21 June 1920 at the Bechstein Hall, although it was not published until 1925.[40] Ironically, if Maddison had been involved with the SWM, there might have been other performance opportunities and assistance with earlier publication.

In her quintet, Maddison exploits sonata form but not entirely faithfully (see table 4.1). The first movement exhibits a binary form, the second – with an introductory section, X – a variant of ternary form, the third, a simpler ternary form related also to sonata form, and the final movement, another variant of sonata form (see table 4.2).

In the opening movement there is alternation between *Largamente* and *Allegro Vivo* before settling into *Andante Moderato*; the time signature changes every few bars. Overall, the whole work repeats sections articulated by distinctive themes and clearly-expressed tonality; at the same time, in this movement there are only two bars of exact repetition, repeated sections being subtly altered. In the repetitions, the original piano part is often maintained, while individual notes in inner string parts are altered, or notes are distributed differently, see examples 4.1a and 4.1b. Note particularly the dynamics in the piano part and doubling of inner parts. Throughout the movement, dynamic and articulation markings vary to such an extent that the implication is that the changes are intentional, neither editorial error nor flippant inconsistency.

---

38 See Blevins, *Ivor Gurney and Marion Scott*, pp. 92–179.

39 Fuller, 'Devoted Attention', p. 95.

40 Programmes Archive, Wigmore Hall, London. The Quintet was performed by the London String Quartet (with either Leopold Ashton or Maddison playing piano).

Table 4.1 Form in Maddison's Piano Quintet, Movements 1 and 2

	Material	**Bars**
Movement 1	A (D minor)	1–79
	B (G major – E♭ major)	80–125
	A2 (D minor)	126–90
	B2 (E major)	191–208
Movement 2	Introduction: X	1–6
	C	7–67
	D	68–83
	Development	84–116
	X2	117–28
	C2	129–82
	Development based on C	183–208
	Coda based on C	209–36

Table 4.2 Form in Maddison's Piano Quintet, Movements 3 and 4

	Material	**Bars**
Movement 3	E	1–43
	F	44–53
	Development	54–108
	E2	109–51
	F2	152–83
	Coda based on E	184–90
Movement 4	Exposition (G) Main Theme E♭ Major Subsidiary Theme B♭ Minor	1–28
	Development (H)	29–91
	Recapitulation (G2) Themes in same keys as Exposition	92–119
	Development (H2)	120–58
	Coda based on (G) Main Theme returns in B♭ Minor – E major – E♭ Major	159–70

Example 4.1a Maddison, Piano Quintet, I, bb. 15–16

Example 4.1b Maddison, Piano Quintet, I, bb. 140–141

Example 4.2a Maddison, Piano Quintet, II, bb. 14–16

Example 4.2b Maddison, Piano Quintet, II, bb. 136–138

Example 4.3a Maddison, Piano Quintet, IV, bb. 7–11, Main Theme and Accompaniment

Rather than develop the material or modulate, these changes serve two purposes: firstly to alter the texture and secondly to alter dynamic climaxes.[41] A similar method is used in the second movement but the changes are less intricate and there is a more obvious thinning of texture with doubled parts missing, compare examples 4.2a and 4.2b where accents and dynamic markings are added, as well as material previously given to the second violin being redistributed in the piano part.

These small variations – together with some obvious errors – might indeed stem from the compositional process: if the composer was working from a skeletal score, or sketch, it is quite likely that she simply transcribed differently each time. But it would then have been a conscious choice not to refer back to the first use of the material. If such was her working method, then it would indicate an eschewing of the need for 'exactness' or too great a punctiliousness, replacing it with a greater freedom and an improvisational attitude to performance. This varied repetition is in contrast to the use of sonata form by Maddison's teacher, Fauré. In his Piano Quartet no.1, for example, the transposed material of the recapitulation is otherwise repeated verbatim.

Despite the subtle changes in the repeated sections, Maddison adheres to fairly standard forms in the first and third movements of the quintet. The fourth movement, however, seems to be a subversion of sonata form and sonata-rondo (the B section does not return in the tonic), which is extended, including repetition of part of the development section within the recapitulation. The first and second themes of this movement are given in examples 4.3a and 4.3b.

While the material of the development section derives from the first theme, so does much of the rest of this movement. The repetition of the development section in the recapitulation has the effect of a dropping of tension, to be built up again as the first theme maintains its dominance at the start of the coda. This, however,

[41] At the same time, the analyst's job is made more difficult by some typographical inconsistencies. For example in Ex. 1 the rhythm in the violin 2 in bars 16 and 141 is expressed inconsistently.

Example 4.3b Maddison, Piano Quintet, IV, bb. 15–21, Secondary Theme and Accompaniment

Example 4.4a Maddison, Piano Quintet, IV, bb. 15–16

Example 4.4b Maddison, Piano Quintet, IV, bb. 106–107

disintegrates into ever-smaller fragments in the final bars and sonata form itself seems to unravel. As with the other movements, repetition is slightly varied, but here rhythm plays a subtle part in the variation, particularly in the second theme, see examples 4.4a and 4.4b. The change in rhythm to a triplet at the end of the first bar could be seen as consolidating an improvisational, free attitude to the performance.

Within this work, therefore, Maddison attempts to maintain the 'intellectual' connotations of the piano quintet while playing with the use of repetition and the legacy of sonata form in the fourth movement. One contemporary critic damned the work with faint praise, and a great deal of condescension:

> Adela Maddison's Quintet for two violins, viola, violoncello, and pianoforte (Curwen) could not possibly be mistaken for great music. I am, however, one who frankly confesses to a partiality for small beer. More potent beverages have their merits and their rights. But surely there is something to be said also for 'the little creature', all modesty and good nature, who will do no harm to man. It is only when small beer bears the label of some famous vintage wine that we feel disconcerted, since we don't know whether the host is conscious of his error or whether he is giving us in good faith what he believes to be something choice and rare. And this Quintet leaves us very doubtful. Unquestionably the composer aims high, and there is merit in hitching one's wagon to a star. But is there not merit also to be won in acknowledging that we are more familiar with the earth than with the stars, and in doing that which we can do with our whole heart rather than in attempting to follow an ideal which evades our grasp?[42]

The waywardness of Maddison's use of repetition and then the 'corruption' of sonata form in the final movement was perhaps too easy to interpret as a shortcoming, especially in the work of a woman composer.[43]

It is significant that although Maddison chose to write in a form with 'masculine' and also 'serious' connotations, she also felt an affinity with freer forms. She was very much in direct competition with male composers for publication, patronage and performance opportunities – even within the female artistic circles of the Princesse de Polignac – and wrote in forms to reflect this. Within traditionally male musical forms, however, she shows a predilection to 'stray' towards the idea of free-form.

Ethel Smyth

Another woman composer who exploited traditional forms was Smyth (1858–1944).[44] She was the most prominent of those who became disillusioned with the

---

42 B.V. 'Chamber Music', *MT*, 66/992 (October 1925): p. 909.

43 To discuss the critics' reception of women's music at this time is beyond the scope of this study. However, for a work which clearly reveals the prevailing prejudices of critics, if of women performers, not composers, see Ellis, 'Female Pianists and their Male Critics' and Lemy Lim, 'The Reception of Women Pianists, 1950–1960' (unpub PhD diss, City University, 2011).

44 The main works relating to Smyth to which this chapter is indebted to are Christopher St. John, *Ethel Smyth: A Biography* (London, 1959); Elizabeth Wood, 'Performing Rights: A Sonography of Women's Suffrage', *MQ*, 79/4 (Winter, 1995): pp. 606–643 and Ethel Smyth's own several volumes of memoirs. These include *Female Pipings in Eden*; *Beecham*

'ready-made' community of women musicians including the SWM composing groups. Smyth was the most successful woman composer of her generation in terms of numbers of performances and publications, both during her lifetime and afterwards, but was one of the most independent and separatist of the women composers discussed. Her career was already underway before the SWM was formed; she joined in 1911 and remained a member until 1914 and some works were played at SWM concerts at this time; she had sporadic contact with the SWM throughout her life.[45] But even during the period of her membership, she had little involvement with the organisation.[46] At this time, however, she assisted Emmeline Pankhurst in the WSPU fight for the vote for women. This included violent acts of protest, a short period in prison and writing compositions used in the protests and rallies. Indeed, her involvement with the WSPU could certainly have contributed to a more distant relationship with the SWM who were trying to separate themselves from the suffrage movement. It might be asserted that she adopted an international rather than parochial brand of feminism; but Smyth was an intensely self-centred woman who showed little concern for the situation of other women *composers* at any point in her life.

Smyth's early training in composition was, typically for a woman of her class, a private one, with the composer Alexander Ewing (1830–1895).[47] She later turned to Europe for her education, to the Leipzig Conservatoire and Carl Reinecke (1824–1910) in 1877, one of a number of foreign women composers to do so before the turn of the century.[48] Grieg, Dvorak and Tchaikovsky were all students at the conservatory; nevertheless, dissatisfied with the structure and teaching methods of the institution, she left to take lessons from the German composer, Heinrich Herzogenberg (1843–1900). She became part of the social circle of Heinrich and his wife Elisabeth (known as Lisl), which included Brahms, Joachim

---

and Pharaoh (London, 1935); *As Time Went On* (London, 1936); *Streaks of Life* (New York, 1924) and *A Final Burning of Boats* (New York, 1928).

45 See Appendix 2 SWM membership list, SWM Archive, RCM, London.

46 SWM Archive, RCM, London box 177, Smyth's relationship with the SWM was at times warm as seen in correspondence to Adine O'Neill.

47 See Appendix 1 for more information on Alexander Ewing.

48 The Leipzig Conservatory was founded by Mendelssohn in 1843. Known as the *Hochschule für Musik*, it attracted many foreign students, including women composers. The index to the *New Grove Dictionary of Women Composers* reveals a long list of these. The American singer and composer, Clara Rogers (1844–1931), was a pupil there from the age of 12. Later, and contemporary with Smyth, were Florence Maud Ewart (1864–1949), who studied the violin there with Adolph Brodsky shortly after 1882 and then tutored there, and the Scottish Helen Hopekirk (1856–1945) who also studied composition with Carl Reinecke (1876–1878), and therefore very likely knew Smyth. Somewhat later were the Swedish composer, Sara Wennerberg-Reuter (1875–1959), who also studied with Carl Reinecke, in 1896–8; the Ukrainian, Anna Maria Klechniowska (1888–1973), who studied with Stephan Krehl, 1906–1908, and her contemporary, the Greek Elena Lambiri (c.1882–1960), whose teacher in 1908 was Max Reger (see entries for all these composers at *Grove Music Online*).

and Clara Schumann; this allowed her to move in musical worlds which would not have been open to her in England, especially considering her unorthodox musical background.

Although Smyth is viewed primarily as an opera and orchestral composer, her chamber music output is considerable. In the early part of her career, while still in Leipzig, she experimented with compositions for string ensemble and strings with piano as well as piano sonatas. After 1887 she ceased to compose for small ensemble and in 1890 returned to London to secure her orchestral debut at the Crystal Palace concert series. Apart from the String Quartet in E minor, 1902–1912 (1914) and several songs, including those connected with the suffrage movement (1910–1920), Smyth's instrumental chamber music output did not flourish until the late 1920s.

On her return to England in 1889, the composer was disappointed with the paucity of performances she received there compared with those in Europe, especially Germany before the First World War. She appears to have blamed this lack on establishment attitudes to her sex and thus showed herself to be concerned with the same issues as the SWM founders some years later:

> When in 1889 I came back to England from Leipzig where I had learned my trade, and where my works had been publicly performed, I found myself up against a brick wall. Chief among the denizens of the Groove at that time were Parry, Stanford and Sullivan. These men I knew personally, also Sir George Grove; Parry and Sullivan I should have ventured to call my friends. Possibly I was too proud, or too shy, to ask directly for help; anyhow not one of them extended a friendly finger to the new comer – nor of course publishers.[49]

While Smyth may have exaggerated the extent of her relationships with the male preserve of the English musical establishment – she was writing over 40 years later – she appeared to encounter difficulties more extreme than were faced by, for example, Thomas Dunhill, Percy Grainger (1882–1961) and Cyril Scott, who had also studied in Germany.[50] Indeed the support network provided by the SWM was not yet in existence. It should also be remembered that Smyth was not a performer and therefore missed the opportunities of composer/performers such as Ethel Barns, Alice Verne-Bredt, Grainger and Scott, who regularly performed their own works in recital.

As has been demonstrated in previous chapters, women were active as composers at this time, but genre and type of musical activity had a crucial

---

[49] Smyth, *Female Pipings in Eden*, p.38. Smyth's phrase 'denizens of the Groove' refers to figures such as Grove, Parry and Sullivan who had adapted their music and careers to conform to an acceptable and strictly defined composer identity. The use of the word denizen may also reflect Smyth's return to England from Germany and the necessary re-definition of her 'foreign' status.

[50] See Appendix 1 for more information on Percy Grainger.

influence on performance opportunities. Smyth had moved to public recitals via private chamber music performances in Leipzig. In London, therefore, she attempted to by-pass the accepted route for women composers of 'At Home's and small-scale recitals of songs and chamber works, moving towards large-scale public performances and publication.

As an alternative mechanism for support – financial and emotional – Smyth exploited her connections with the aristocracy and the upper classes, as she did throughout her life. While she was supported creatively as well as financially by powerful and wealthy women such as the Empress Eugénie and the Princesse de Polignac, her relationships with these women did not appear to increase her sense of collective purpose for women's music.[51] This form of support in no way guaranteed acceptance in musical circles, but it secured performances on the composer's return to England, which were otherwise elusive.

> Eventually, thanks to my neighbour and wonderful friend the late Empress Eugénie, who not only financed me but stirred up the interest of the Duke of Edinburgh, the president of the Royal Choral Society, my Mass was performed at the Albert Hall in 1892. *Reception*: Enthusiastic. *Press*: Devastating. Here at the outset, let it be pointed out that very few girls happen to live next door to rich Empresses of pronounced feminist sympathies. But for this supreme bit of luck, in all probability my Mass would never have been printed, published or performed at all.[52]

Smyth's difficulties in the 1890s were also due, in some respects, to the scale of the works she was attempting to mount and the costs involved in their production. Her lack of connections in England; her chosen genres; her non-performer status – although she did some conducting – the structure of musical society and the process of critical assessment and canon formation: all these combined to produce a considerable barrier to success. To this list could be added the fact that she was a woman composer: while there was some excitement at the discovery that the composer E.M. Smyth was a woman and a certain incredulity that such 'masculine' sounding music could have been conceived by such, the revelation did not lead to regular performances of the larger-scale works.

Smyth's feminist beliefs in some senses contradicted those of Scott and Eggar, as she was determined only to compete on a platform level with male composers. But Smyth had not necessarily formulated her own feminist ideals by 1911 and the birth of the SWM. It appears that she felt guilty that she had not engaged with the suffrage movement earlier. The WSPU had formed officially in 1903, and her

---

[51] See Jane Marcus, 'Virginia Woolf and her Violin: Mothering, Madness and Music', *Mothering the Mind: Twelve Studies of Writers and their Silent Partners*, eds Ruth Perry and M. Watson Brownley (New York, 1984), pp. 180–203 and Sylvia Kahan, *Music's Modern Muse*, p. 155. See Appendix 1 for more information on Empress Eugénie.

[52] Smyth, *Female Pipings in Eden*, pp. 38–9.

biographer Christopher St John argues that Smyth was focused primarily on her own causes: '"I have always been deficient in a group sense" was her subsequent defence.'[53] This aspect of her personality, with which she does not seem entirely comfortable, is consistent with her attitude towards other women composers.

In the context of the chamber music movement, Smyth is even more of an isolationist. This was partly due to her much-reduced chamber output in the period from 1900 as well as her lack of contact with other women composers, except Augusta Holmés and Adela Maddison.[54] 'Though she encouraged solidarity among female musicians, she chose to ignore many women *composers* with whom she was contemporary – with the notable exception of Augusta Holmés (Holmes) – for few had achieved lasting widespread fame, and a lesbian tradition in music was completely unknown.'[55]

Although Smyth had returned to England by the time Adela Maddison had moved to Germany, their works were performed in the same venues and they probably would have been aware of each other's output. While Smyth's support was not always tactful and productive, it is notable that Maddison is one of the very few women composers in whose work Smyth was interested, to the extent that she tried to promote it to Delius in order to obtain a performance for it.[56]

Unlike that of many SWM members, Smyth's interaction with figures in musical society often clashed with Edwardian ideals of how a woman should behave. Edward Sackville-West describes Brahms's categorisation of women as either ladies or tarts; in pre-war England, Smyth was neither. Nor did she fit any other version of femininity.[57] This she projected increasingly not only in her musical output but also her dress and demeanour.

This 'masculinised' projection of Smyth is bound up with her ambiguous sexual identity, although she never explicitly writes about the nature of her relationships with women. Even in the context of her relationship with writer Henry Brewster she is projected as a 'masculine' figure when he praises her for her energy and vigour, whereas he, through their collaboration on *The Wreckers* and in her interpretation of his work, *The Prison*, after his death, is cast in the role of muse to her creative 'genius'.[58] Smyth and Brewster's relationship echoes the themes addressed in *The Wreckers*, especially freedom of the individual and

---

53 St John, *Ethel Smyth: A Biography*, p. 144.

54 The composer Maude Valerie White mentions being visited by Smyth at her house in Sicily in her autobiography, *My Indian Summer*, p. 7 although it is unclear what they discussed. See Appendix 1 for more information on Augusta Holmés.

55 Christopher Wiley, '"When a Woman Speaks the Truth About her Body": Ethel Smyth, Virginia Woolf, and the Challenges of Lesbian Auto/Biography', *M&L*, 85/3 (August, 2004): pp. 407–408.

56 Smyth's lobbying of Delius did not lead to a performance in this case. See Sophie Fuller, *The Pandora Guide*, p. 204.

57 St John, *Ethel Smyth*, p. 252.

58 Wiley, 'When a Woman Speaks the Truth', pp. 408–409.

criticism of the power of the church.[59] These are reflected in their '"true marriage", one that did not need to be sanctioned by the church and that allowed both parties the individual freedom they aspired to'.[60]

It can be argued that not only the supposedly 'masculine' qualities of Smyth's music, but also her transgressive, un-feminine approach to its promotion, caused the musical establishment to eschew performances of her works beyond the novelty of a first hearing. This included her chamber work and songs as well as the large-scale orchestral and operatic works:

> To this market [the English musical establishment], then, I took my wares; short choruses, chamber music, orchestral pieces, and what not. The result was *nil* – not a conductor would accept them; and if occasionally, thanks to a little greasing of the wheels, I got something poked into a programme, that was the end of its career.[61]

Smyth was one of the few women composers in this period who was prepared to confront a male-driven musical culture, although she did not choose to do this through the SWM. She was thus criticised by male critics in the Press for producing 'masculine' music with such force that they were rather fearful of her: 'You scorned sugar and sentimentality; and you were exuberantly ferocious. You booted Elgar contemptuously out of your way as an old woman. And now you say we shrink from you because you are "only a woman". Good God!'[62] Yet this approach seems to have isolated her from other women composers, especially those involved in the SWM. Further, Smyth did not write extensively in the chamber media promoted by these composers.[63]

The String Quartet in E minor is an anomaly in Smyth's catalogue of works, being her solitary chamber work in this English pre-war period. It was completed in the context of Smyth's most politically-aware period which included membership of both the SWM and the WSPU. The first two movements were composed in 1902, in the same year as the start of the opera, *The Wreckers*, but the final two

---

59 See Suzanne Robinson, 'Smyth the Anarchist: *Fin-de-Siècle* Radicalism in *The Wreckers*', *Cambridge Opera Journal*, 20/2 (2008): pp. 149–179.

60 Ibid., p. 167.

61 St John, *Ethel Smyth*, p. 40.

62 Letter from George Bernard Shaw to Ethel Smyth in St John, *Ethel Smyth*, p. 185.

63 Ironically, although Smyth's position caused her frustration, her strategy, in both music and literature, may have allowed her the recognition of future generations. Regarding her literary output, Christopher Wiley argues, 'Smyth's employment of masculine paradigms did serve one crucial function, in ensuring her autobiographies reduced her to a persona appropriate to posterity'. The term 'reduced' has perhaps confusingly negative connotations but Smyth is one of the few composers of either sex to remain in the public consciousness as a historical figure without obtaining high levels of critical attention and continued performance. Wiley, 'When a Woman Speaks the Truth', p. 409.

movements were completed only in 1912. It seems Smyth's experimentation with the genre had occurred particularly in the 1880s while still in Germany, when she wrote two string quartets, a piano trio and a piano quintet; she completed the String Quartet in E Minor over 20 years later. The Quartet, therefore, is a reflection of two neighbouring periods in her life: her exposure to traditional 'masculine' forms and her new-found collective expression of feminist ideals.

Smyth emphasised the importance of the sacrifice of her compositional career during her suffragette years in *Female Pipings in Eden*:

> She, [a cabinet minister's wife] on her side, knew from mutual friends that my life was wholly given to music, and her first words were: O my dear, how can you, of all people, forsake your beautiful art for politics!

This was just the opening I wanted. I asked her to judge by that what the cause meant to us, and pointed out that owing to the circumstances of my career as woman composer I knew more than most people about the dire workings of prejudice.[64]

Smyth did, however, complete the String Quartet, as well as mount a performance of her works including some of the suffrage music at the Queen's Hall in 1911, where it was performed by the London Symphony Orchestra. As St John says: 'Her output as a composer was rather larger [during her suffragist years] than it had been when she was zig-zagging all over Europe fighting for performances of her operas, or indulging to excess her twin passions for sport and friendship.'[65]

Indeed her ambition to become an opera composer was the probable reason for discontinuing the String Quartet ten years before. *Der Wald* was first performed in Covent Garden in July 1902, the year the String Quartet was started. Referring to 1903 in her memoirs, she writes: 'From now onwards nothing existed for me – nor I think Harry [Brewster] – except the coming into being of the libretto of *The Wreckers* – the subject on which we had been meditating all this time.'[66] The score of this work was not finished until 1905.

Smyth did collaborate with the SWM to perform the first two movements of the String Quartet at a SWM concert in 1912, an anonymous critic reviewing the concert in the *Musical Times*, described the part of work presented as 'remarkable for an originality which had no recourse to the eccentric'.[67] This suggests that the later two movements were not completed at this point, although perhaps this

---

64 Smyth, *Female Pipings in Eden*, p. 204.

65 St. John, *Ethel Smyth*, p. 159.

66 Ethel Smyth, *The Memoirs of Ethel Smyth*, abr., intr. Ronald Crichton (Harmondsworth, 1987), p. 259.

67 n.a., 'Chamber Music' (reviews) *Musical Times*, 53/829 (March, 1912): p. 181.

was all that could be presented in the time available to her.[68] The first official performance of the complete work appears to have been given by the London String Quartet (Albert E. Sammons, Thomas W. Petre, H. Waldo Warner and C. Warwick Evans) at the Bechstein Hall on 23 May 1913.[69] This performance occurred in the final months of Smyth's secondment to the WSPU. It became one of her most performed works, as it was later performed by the Philharmonic String Quartet in 1920, became part of the Vienna repertoire of the Rosé Quartet, and was played by the Bohemian Quartet in 1922.

The period of composition of the String Quartet is significant. Elizabeth Wood sees its completion as Smyth's celebration of her return to the world of music after her suffrage sacrifice.

How better to prove, both to herself and the musical establishment, a woman's equal rights in music's body politic, and the power of female desire and creativity to conquer male prejudice and exclusion, than to demonstrate 'mastery' of the supremely mainstream classical string quartet tradition of Beethoven and Brahms in which she was trained?[70]

Smyth chose to compose within the boundaries of sonata form for all the reasons discussed previously; this reveals her desire to sail in the male mainstream. But even if she wished, at least overtly, to be an 'honorary male', musicologists such as Elizabeth Wood have considered whether Smyth treated established forms subversively. Yet within this context the form of the String Quartet is indeed traditional, see tables 4.3, 4.4 and 4.5; compared with Maddison's quintet, Smyth makes much greater use of sonata form, following established protocol.

Table 4.3 Form in Smyth's String Quartet, Movement 1

Material	**Bars**
Exposition Main Theme (E minor) 2nd Theme (E minor) 3rd Theme (E major)	1–82
Bridge	70–82
Development	83–156
Recapitulation (Keys of the themes remain the same as the Exposition)	157–228
Coda	229–37

68 SWM Archive, RCM, London, Notice of 2nd Composer's Conference 1912, box 176.

69 See Appendix 1 for more information on Waldo Warner.

70 Wood, 'Performing Rights', p. 623.

Table 4.4 Form in Smyth's String Quartet, Movement 2

Material	Bars
A	1–39
B	40–66
Bridge	67–73
Development based on A	74–112
A^2	113–51
B^2	152–78
Bridge^2	179–89
Development^2	190–219
Coda	220–38

Table 4.5 Form in Smyth's String Quartet, Movement 3 and 4

	Material	Bars
Movement 3	Exposition Main Theme (C major) Subsidiary Theme (E♭ Major)	1–65
	Development (C)	66–97
	Recapitulation Main Theme (C major) Subsidiary Theme (G minor)	98–159
	Development (C^2)	160–74
	Coda	175–80
Movement 4	Exposition Main Theme (E minor) Subsidiary Theme (A major)	1–98
	Development	99–152
	Recapitulation (Keys of the themes remain the same as the Exposition)	153–232
	Coda	233–68

Example 4.5a Smyth, String Quartet, I, bb. 1–10, Main Theme

Even in this work, however, there is a subtle subversion of the treatment of formal materials. The first movement offers a conventional use of sonata form with considerable use of exact repetition in the recapitulation and sections that are more clearly defined than those in the other movements. Smyth's treatment of themes uses multiple second themes inserted into the texture of the exposition; while this is not so unusual at this time, these themes are always followed by a rhythmical reference to the opening first theme, see examples 4.5a for the main theme, 4.5b for the first subsidiary theme with fragments of the main theme in the lower parts at bar 32 and 4.5c for the second subsidiary theme with fragments of the main theme at bar 52.[71]

The status of the first theme is here being brought to our attention. While this strategy could be interpreted as the dominance of the first theme being constantly asserted, as the listener is reminded of its presence even when other material

[71] Works using multiple second themes in sonata form include Beethoven's Piano Sonatas op. 7 (1796) and 10 (c.1795–1798), Brahms's Piano Quartet in A major (1861) and Dvorak's Quartet no. 1 in D major (1862). Tovey's Trio op. 8 for pf, cl and hn (1905) does not use multiple second themes but the first theme permeates the whole by interrupting the second theme. The first theme is placed after pauses or punctuating chords, however, rather than what occurs in Smyth's closely woven texture.

Example 4.5b Smyth, String Quartet, I, bb. 28–33, First Subsidiary Theme

is introduced, the textures Smyth creates within this movement mean that the first theme's dominance is rather being constantly questioned as other material continually infiltrates its space.

This serves as a preparation for the clearer subversion of the first theme in the last movement. After the work is over, therefore, it seems that this interpretation of the first movement fits better with its overall structure.

The form of the musical material becomes less rigorous as the string quartet progresses. In the second movement – not strictly in sonata form – for example, the coda is based on the first theme but leads to a jolting, quirky presto. In the third movement, the recapitulation material is split differently between the instruments, using additional gestures in the first violin. When the first theme recurs, it offers exact repetition for only two bars before modulating. While the material here is developed, it remains confined within the same number of bars as the exposition.

In the final movement, which combines the two most respected compositional techniques at this time, sonata form and fugue, the traditionally 'main' and 'subsidiary' themes do not occupy clearly defined sections; instead the themes play an equal role, so although the movement ends with a return to the main theme, it is immediately broken down into small fragments from bar 260, see example 4.6, with the semiquaver–semiquaver–quaver motif playing a large

Example 4.5c Smyth, String Quartet, I, bb. 46–53, Second Subsidiary Theme

Example 4.6 Smyth String Quartet, IV, bb. 256–68

part. There is not, therefore, a succinct conclusion with a sense of an ultimately ‘triumphant’ main theme.

Elizabeth Wood sees the interplay between these themes in the final movement in relation to Smyth’s suffrage experience.

> By voiding the assumption in sonata form of thematic duels and tonal certainties and closures, she liberates the form from its rigidly defined and perfomed identities and roles by superimposing upon and around and about them the fluid, provisional inscriptions and inclusive metaphorics of ‘equal’ (‘Suffragette!’) fugal voices performing their democratic rights.[72]

While this is Wood’s subjective interpretation, of course, there is a return to the main theme as might be expected but it enters at a *pp* dynamic. This is not a domination of the main theme over the subsidiary material and from its entry in bar 256 a process of disintegration occurs, see example 4.6. One might argue that, in this work, Smyth is attempting simultaneously to work with a ‘male’ form whilst also referring to female experience. Smyth achieves this, in contrast to Maddison, by altering the relationships between and treatment of the *themes* within the work to create what might be considered a feminist narrative. While still managing to maintain sonata principles, not only the much discussed final movement but the work as a whole has a subtext. There is a journey from the use of continually interrupted subsidiary themes in the first movement and the eventual reassertion of the main theme in the closing bars, to the equalising force of the fugue in the final movement. This path

[72] Wood, ‘Performing Rights’, p. 625.

has parallels in the struggles of the suffrage movement and the distance travelled by the movement in the ten years in which the piece was composed.

Morfydd Owen

The youngest composer in this study, whose career was the least established at the time of the formation of the SWM, is the Welsh composer, Morfydd Owen (1891–1918).[73] After studying composition and piano at University College, Cardiff, under David Evans, she entered the RAM in 1912. Unusually, her principal study was composition, with piano and singing as second studies. This meant she received individual composition lessons with Frederick Corder. She was not a member of the SWM; it is unclear whether Katherine Eggar, who had studied at the RAM herself, was as active as Marion Scott – who was still associated with the RCM Union in this period – in promoting the SWM there. Indeed, of Owen's fellow students from the RAM, including performers Myra Hess, Harriet Cohen, and the Goossens and composers Arnold Bax, Dorothy Howell (1898–1982) and Ethel Bilsand (1892–1982), only Bilsand was a member of the SWM, so it may be that the RAM students were largely unaware of the Society.[74]

Owen had an illustrious career at the RAM, winning the Charles Lucas Medal for composition in 1913 with her *Nocturne* for orchestra as well as the Oliveria Prescott Prize for overall attainment.[75] She went on to have numerous compositions played at RAM student concerts, launched a career as a recital singer, was granted the Goring Thomas Scholarship at the RAM and obtained the position of sub-professor. Corder's glowing eulogy after her early and tragic death not only highlights the esteem in which he held her as a composition student but also the parameters by which he judged her talent:

---

[73] The main works relating to Morfydd Owen are Eliot Crawshay-Williams, 'Morfydd Owen', *Wales*, iv (1958): pp. 50–56; Rhian Davies, *Yr Eneth Ddisglair Annwyl, Never so Pure a Sight, Morfydd Owen (1891–1918): A Life in Pictures* (Llandyssyl, Dyfed, 1994) and 'Morfydd Owen (1891–1918): A Refined and Beautiful Talent' (unpub. PhD Diss, University of Wales Bangor, 1999); also Kitty I. Jones, 'The Enigma of Morfydd Owen', *Welsh Music*, v/1 (1975–1976): pp. 8–21.

[74] See SWM membership list in Appendix 2. In general there were more SWM members with a connection with the RCM than with the RAM. Marion Scott worked for the RCM Union during this time period and had close relationships with many RCM students including Ivor Gurney, Herbert Howells and Sidney Shimmin. Owen started studying at the RAM in 1912 and would have known of Howell who was a student at the RAM 1914–1919 and Bilsand 1909–1913.

[75] For more detail see Rhian Davies, 'A Refined and Beautiful Talent', Chapter 4 (especially pp. 104–34).

> Morfydd Owen was a young woman of nearly 20 when she entered the Academy in 1913 [sic], a B.A. [sic] of Cardiff University, a *petite* yet striking figure of decidedly Spanish rather than Welsh appearance, with an almost overpowering energy allied to extreme feminine beauty and charm. Her abilities were great and various: her general education of a very high order, her knowledge wide and accurate, her musicianship quite unusual for one of her sex. Not only a good pianist and a singer of unique style, her powers in composition (to which she chiefly devoted herself) were proved by the production of some 60 songs of quite remarkable originality.[76]

Owen's Welsh nationality has perhaps differentiated her from other young women studying composition in London and having works performed; these included Jane Joseph, Harriet Cohen and the younger Dorothy Howell. Owen's physical appearance also generated much fascination amongst contemporaries and is often still discussed before her musical output. As is the case with Smyth, Owen's image is bound up with her reception as a composer. Her approach to her image was constantly changing in this period. Whereas Smyth chose an uncompromising mode of dress, Owen flitted between the reserved, the outrageous and the bizarre, see figure 4.1. As Rhian Davies notes her clothes:

> … were always strange and arresting; she would buy yards of cheap cheesecloth which she would dye dark green or tomato red, and make them up into unconventional but effective dresses. She would buy a straw hat for fourpence and decorate it with cherries or radishes or anything that took her fancy.[77]

The image she projected was also connected to the different segments of London society, which she inhabited; she projected her highly feminised and glamorous image within both the London Welsh community and the bohemian Hampstead set. The movement between different areas of society is perhaps a common theme amongst Edwardian women composers but her movement was between communities with strict and separate definitions of acceptable behaviour and demeanour. This difficult balance was disrupted by her secret marriage to the psychoanalyst Ernest Jones (1879–1958) in February 1917.[78] Jones was a disciple of Freud, and was a domineering husband. The freedom and time to devote to composition, which Owen had previously enjoyed, ceased and her allegiance to the London Welsh Presbyterian community evaporated.

In the period leading up to and shortly after her marriage, Owen's teaching and singing activities increased, while her compositional output from 1916 was much

---

[76] Frederick Corder, Scrapbook, RAM, uncatalogued, 1922, in Rhian Davies, 'A Refined and Beautiful Talent', p. 109.

[77] Bethan Jones, 'Letter of 30th May 1976', *Welsh Music*, 3 (Summer, 1976): p. 100 cited in Rhian Davies, 'A Refined and Beautiful Talent', p. 198.

[78] See Appendix 1 for more information on Ernest Jones.

Figure 4.1 Morfydd Owen

more limited, consisting of a small number of songs. Certainly the promotion of her works ceased after she met Jones and she had very few professional performances. It appears she did not ally herself with the community of women composers represented by the SWM. Rhian Davies claims that she was ambivalent about the women's movement:

> She never claimed herself to be a special or different case, and she never described herself specifically as a woman composer. Morfydd's position on women's rights would hardly have impressed Ethel Smyth. 'I do hate these silly suffragettes!', she wrote to Eliot Crawshay-Williams in 1912. She resented the convention of being chaperoned as an unmarried young woman but the only time she went on record to express any real frustration at not being a man was when this restricted her opportunities to go camping.[79]

It is debatable whether Owen held this view throughout her short life and it is possible she was merely saying what she thought Crawshay-Williams wanted to hear, but it is certainly true that she did not actively ally herself with suffrage groups or the SWM.

[79] Davies, 'A Refined and Beautiful Talent', p. 449.

One of the most substantial of Owen's works, written at the peak of her compositional career at the RAM in 1915, was the Piano Trio, whose two movements were entitled 'The Cathedral at Liège' and 'The Cathedral at Rheims'. It was written under the pseudonym, 'Lenavanmo' and remains unpublished. Davies surmises the work was written as a competition submission at the RAM for 'the composition of a short slow movement and an allegro for violin, cello and piano' and that Lenavanmo was a pseudonym she used more than once.[80]

The cathedrals at Liège and Rheims had tragic histories, both being bombed by the Germans during the first days of the First World War.[81] Liège's original Cathedral of Our Lady and St. Lambert was demolished by revolutionaries in 1794 when the town was still French territory and consequently the church of St. Paul had its ecclesiastical status raised to 'cathedral'. Liège became part of Belgium in 1830 and was bombed by German zeppelins during the battle of Liège in the First World War during August 1914. In September 1914 Rheims Cathedral was virtually destroyed as part of a two-day German offensive on the city. There was an outcry in the allied press over the tragedy of such a building being a target, forcing the German authorities to issue a statement as reported in the *New York Times*, 'We regret the necessity, but the fire of the French came from that direction. Orders have been issued to save the cathedral'.[82]

The fate of both cities had heavy press coverage in 1914 and it seems likely that Owen was aware of this. Perhaps surprisingly, as Davies points out, much of the musical material used in the Trio emanates from earlier piano works, *Prelude in the Manner of J.S. Bach, Little Eric* and the vocal work, *Pro Patria*.[83] However, in no way does this detract from its patriotic sentiments, given the timely significance of its titles, inseparably linked to the events of 1914.

A work in two movements, it establishes from the first its separation from traditional forms. The structure of the first movement, 'Liège', is basically ternary, whereas the second movement, 'Rheims', can initially be classified as in sonata form but the recapitulation is based on material from both movements. The main

---

80 Ibid., p. 221. The competition prize was awarded to William Braithwaite Manson, who was a composition student at the RAM. He received the Charles Lucas Medal for composition and the Oliveria Prescott Prize for composition in 1915. He was a private in the London Scottish Regiment and died at the Somme in 1916. Although Owen would have known Manson there is no evidence that they were friends; however the numbers of RAM students fighting in the First World War may have contributed to Owen's references to the war in the Piano Trio. The RAM's new music ensemble remains 'The Manson Ensemble', named in his honour.

81 Information on Liège and Rheims see 'Liège', *Merriam-Webster's Geographical Dictionary*. <www.credoreference.com/entry/mwgeog/li%C3%A8ge> [accessed 17 August 2009] and 'Rheims', *The Columbia Encyclopedia* <www.credoreference.com/entry/columency/reims_or_rheims> [accessed 17 August 2009].

82 G.H. Perris, *New York Times*, September 21, 1914.

83 Davies, 'A Refined and Beautiful Talent', pp. 475–7.

Table 4.6 Form in Owen's Piano Trio

	Material	Theme	Bars
Movement 1	A	M (D minor)	1–28
	B	L (D minor)	29–61
	A	M (D major)	62–89
	Coda	M (D minor)	90–94
Movement 2	Exposition	F (A minor) b.33 C (C minor)	1–39
	Development	F (A♭ major) b.93 C (A major)	40–113
	Recapitulation	F (A minor) b. 127 M (A major) b. 129 D major	114–42
	Coda	M (D major)	142–46

theme returns in the tonic for the recapitulation, however, first movement material is then re-introduced and the movement ends in the relative major of the first movement, see table 4.6.

The work is based on four different themes, labelled here as military theme (M), lyrical theme (L), folk theme (F) and chorale theme (C); see examples 4.7a, 4.7b, 4.7c and 4.7d. As with Maddison's Quintet, there is only a small passage of exact repetition within the work.

Example 4.7a Owen, Piano Trio, I 'Liège', Military Theme, bb. 11–15

Example 4.7b Owen, Piano Trio, I 'Liège', Lyric Theme, bb. 31–38

Example 4.7c Owen, Piano Trio, II 'Rheims', Folk Theme, bb. 1–9

Example 4.7d Owen, Piano Trio, II 'Rheims', Chorale, bb. 33–39

Owen's work, however, contains a much more pronounced variety of material than does Maddison's. Indeed the subsidiary themes – lyrical and chorale themes – have a less prominent role than in Smyth's Quartet. The lyrical theme does not return in the second movement and maintains the tonic rather than moving to the dominant. The chorale recedes so that the climax of the Trio is a competition between the military and folk themes. They unravel in the final bars of the piece, however, as the military theme is reduced to a rhythmic fragment.

Owen's use of a folk tune in this work reflects her interest in both Welsh and Russian folk music. Indeed in 1915 she applied for a fellowship at Cardiff University to travel to Russia to study folk music.[84] The military-style motifs in this work, which undoubtedly invoke the Great War, contrasts with much of her opus, particularly the published vocal pieces. She appears to be experimenting with silence here. This isolates and emphasises particular moments within the work: in the first movement, for instance, silence suddenly halts the progress of the lyrical theme, while in the second where the texture is more sparse, silence

[84] Ibid., pp. 213–217. Davies suggests Owen's relationship with Alexis Chodak led to her increased interest in Russian culture, pp. 212–213. His full name appears to have been Henry Alexis Chodak Gregory from Tashkent in Russia, being the only surviving member of his family who were murdered in 1904. He trained in Medicine at Edinburgh University and the London Hospital and married Dr Hazel Chodak-Gregory who was a specialist in women's medicine in 1916. See Gill Gregory, 'Dr Hazel Chodak-Gregory' <http://hle.org.uk/history.html> [accessed 8 January 2011] and Gill Gregory, *The Sound of Turquoise* (London, 2009).

adds impact to the *ff* entry in b. 45. It also halts the progress of the A theme at b. 108 and again in b. 113.

The use of silence in the work also contributes the sense of narrative running throughout. The Trio is the only one of the works analysed here with titled movements. As Byron Almén argues, narratives in music do not necessarily need text or titles, that is programme music, but rather narrative can be found in multiple elements within a piece of absolute music. 'For the individual, then, narrative patterns are psychological templates illustrating possible responses to conflict. For society they represent paths to visualise and confront structures of power in constructive and/or critical ways.'[85] If, however, the listener should approach the Trio without the stimulus of the titles, the strongly evocative musical features of the themes would still allow a narrative reading.

In the first movement, although the military and the lyrical theme are not tonally distinctive, they do not flow into one another, see figure 4.2. The lyrical theme is introduced with a *subito pp*, is interrupted by the less-than-lyrical dotted rhythms in its final bars and the military theme is only introduced again after a general pause. It is as if these two musical aspects are operating in different spheres unconcerned by one another, see table 4.7.

Table 4.7 Progression of Themes in Morfydd Owen's Piano Trio

Bar	Theme	Notes
First Movement		
1	Military	
31	Lyric	Introduced in sudden change to *pp* through ostinato pattern bb 29–30 used as connecting
61	Military	Re-introduced after general pause
Second Movement		
1	Folk	Introduced start of second movement
33	Chorale	Introduced with upbeat in piano
40	Folk	Chorale finishes on a semiquaver at the beginning of the bar acting as the start of the folk theme in the cello
93	Chorale	Chorale enters *fff* after sustained diminuendo chord in cello in b.92 – other instruments in silence
114	Folk	Introduced after general pause
126	Military	Introduced after crotchet general pause

[85] Byron Almén, *A Theory of Musical Narrative* (Bloomington, Indianapolis, 2008), p. 27.

More pronounced in the second movement is the halting of the folktune when the choral is introduced, the two very different characters of the themes indicating something darker below the surface. There are similar techniques in Dukas's *The Sorcerer's Apprentice*, 1893 as analysed by Carolyn Abbate, where she describes 'a strange passage in the midpoint of the piece at which the entire musical progress comes to a full stop'.[86]

When the music does regenerate itself, it does so in a disturbingly incessant repetition of notes. In the Owen work the sense of unease is also intensified with two bars of silence at bar 44, the sudden silence perhaps alluding to the aerial bombing of the cathedral and the moment of silence as the bombs are released. The folk tune then is no longer stable, getting stuck in repeated fragments continually, see example 4.8 until it recovers itself in bar 62, towards a climactic point.

At bar 125 the folk theme is cut unceremoniously, again followed by an ominous silence and an upbeat chord into the bugle-like signal in bar 127, which indicates the return of the military theme. This has two purposes; firstly to surprise the listener with an unexpected recurrence and, secondly to bind the two movements and the two cathedrals together. Although there is some incorporation of folk elements within the chorale, in general the themes do not interact with one another. The military theme especially is introduced using general pauses, and is indeed victorious at the end of the piece with a jubilant return in a major key. It is as if the piece is a statement about the inevitability of the war impacting on all areas of life. Owen wrote to her friend Kitty Lewis on 8 September 1914, just after the attacks on the cathedrals: '[O]ne feels there isn't time for anything on the "gorgeous" side of life these days. Everything is awful and ghastilly [sic] horrible – it seems so un-Christian that the most cultured nations in the world, treat one another so.'[87]

Davies claims that composing chamber music appears to have been a complex process for Owen and something that did not come naturally:

> She had little instrumental experience and, although she accompanied occasional violinists and brass players, there is no evidence that she ever played in an ensemble. Consequently, chamber instrumental music always required more struggle and graft than other areas of composition, and those few works which survive in this category were written to fulfil the requirements of Cardiff coursework or Academy competitions.[88]

Indeed, as a 'Welsh' composer – for whom vocal/choral music was often the pinnacle – let alone a woman, she was not expected to excel in instrumental music;

---

[86] Carolyn Abbate, *Unsung Voices: Opera and Musical Narrative in the Nineteenth Century* (Princeton, 1991), p. 30.

[87] Letter from Morfydd Owen to Kitty Lewis, 8 September 1914 cited in Davies, 'A Refined and Beautiful Talent', p. 177.

[88] Davies, 'A Refined and Beautiful Talent', p. 472.

Example 4.8 Owen, Piano Trio, Rheims, bb. 50–61

therefore this review from *The Western Mail* in 1949 referring to her earlier piano trio is perhaps unusual praise. 'Her piano music, for all its promise and interest, was never wholly satisfactory; few Welsh composers have ever acquired quite the art of writing effectively for the piano. On the other hand, her piano trio, written in 1912, well merits the attention of chamber music players.'[89]

In her later piano trio, she was developing forms with which she had started to experiment as an undergraduate. And while the SWM could have provided performers and opportunities to try out work, Owen was still at the RAM and thus benefiting to some extent from their support.[90] Indeed in this period it was becoming less difficult for women to enter conservatoires to study composition, and, as RAM programmes show, works by female students were included in student concerts, although these tended to be vocal and piano works.[91] This may have contributed to low numbers of RAM students in the SWM membership, with a rise in these when the conservatoire's facilities were no longer available after graduation. Indeed older SWM members were felt to be unapproachable by younger composers/performers, as the pianist Kathleen Dale notes:

> As long ago as 1916 I had met Marion Scott at the Society of Women Musicians, but in those early days a wide distance separated us – not only her seniority in years. She was the co-founder of the Society, of which I was an untried new member. She was the heart and soul of the Royal College of Music, while my own loyalties were to the Royal Academy; she was a string player and I a pianist … I stood in awe of her.[92]

Although Owen was younger than Maddison and Smyth, and was not able to mature as a composer due to her tragic death at the age of 26, the Piano Trio represents one of her most complex and large-scale works. Despite this she exhibits similarities with the two older composers both in her situation as a woman composer and in

---

89 S. Northcote, *Western Mail*, 14 March, 1949. G44 Papers of Eliot Crawshay-Williams, National Library of Wales. Morfydd Owen composed another Piano Trio in Cardiff in 1912, but the manuscript has not been uncovered.

90 RAM student concert programmes indicate that Owen's songs *By the Lone Shore and Beautific Sea* were sung by Mary Purcell at the Student Orchestral Concert, Queen's Hall on 19 March 1913, *In Cradle Land* and *The Fairie's Wedding* were sung by Owen at the Student Orchestral Concert, Queen's Hall, 27 June 1916 and *An Irish Lullaby* and *Pitter Patter* were sung by Owen at the Student Orchestral Concert, Queen's Hall, 22 June 1917. Owen was the female student with the most works performed in these years but her instrumental music was not performed. Programmes of student concerts 1910–1920, RAM Archive, London. Her orchestral works were performed at outside venues in London and Wales.

91 Programmes of student concerts 1910–1920, RAM Archive, London.

92 Kathleen Dale, 'Memories of Marion Scott', *Music and Letters*, 35/3 (July 1954): p. 236.

her approach to composition. Hers deals directly with conflict as does Smyth's, but the latter evokes Smyth's suffrage experience. Both openly manipulate their thematic material in the service of this conflict, and in the case of Owen, texture contributes too. Maddison also uses similar scenarios, presenting conflict though texture and dynamic variation.

Owen's identity as a Welsh composer was an integral part of her composition and she even added a middle name 'Llwyn' to her own surname on manuscripts and letters in 1912 and 1914, and then on published music from 1916, to appear more intensely Welsh.[93] It is no wonder then that she did not engage with issues of 'Englishness' in music, which may have been another reason not to join the SWM.

For established women composers with an international outlook such as Smyth and Maddison, the SWM did not provide the most needed type of patronage such as assistance in publication, international performances or, in the case of Maddison, basic living support on her return to England. Smyth in particular acknowledged that she had an individual approach to composition and did not want to engage with a collective approach. For the younger and less established Owen, the support the RAM provided was perhaps sufficient during the period when the Trio was being composed. Yet what the RAM could not have provided was a sense of solidarity amongst its female composers, as there were very few, with no female composition tutors at this time.

Between 1912 and 1916, while in London, each of the three composers under consideration here chose to write instrumental chamber music. In each case it was not a genre with which she had extensively engaged previously and actually accorded with the SWM's exhortations. For none of the three, however, did chamber music represent the 'step-up' from smaller forms that it was for many other women composers.

While, of course, on the Continent, many male composers were eschewing sonata form altogether, British composers in general were not. Maddison, Smyth and Owen, like their male colleagues, Hurlstone and Scott, still retained some allegiance to it. The fact that the second themes of the works in question by Smyth, Maddison and Owen are generally more lyrical than are the first themes underlines the traditional outlook of these composers: their conformity to the norms of an earlier generation, at least in this regard. Smyth and Owen deviate from this arrangement of themes, however, as the second theme in Smyth's fourth movement would not fit this description and Owen's chorale theme is forceful, with an *fff* entrance, punctuating the main theme. It would be wrong to argue that this is either exclusively a female trait, or even primarily one. Subversion of the character of the themes is present in the work of other contemporary composers such as in the piano trio by William Hurlstone – see the themes of the first and fourth movements.[94] Maddison, Smyth and Owen all create main themes with striking rhythm; both Maddison and Owen use this characteristic to connect to the

93 Davies, 'A Refined and Beautiful Talent', p. 175.

94 William Y. Hurlstone, Trio in G (London, 1907).

second themes. The themes do not, however, flow into one another as advocated by Macpherson.

In Smyth's string quartet the collection of 'subsidary' themes in the first movement can all be described as more lyrical than the main theme, and they all transform into one another, creating fluidity rather than conflict. In the fourth movement the second theme is not lyrical and does not flow from the main theme; however, it is broken down into small fragments, before the first theme quietly reasserts itself.

While the contrast between themes is greatest in the Owen trio as seen in see example 4.7 previously, in the first movement they are linked by their rhythmic characters, and although they do not flow into each other they are connected by an ostinato figure in the piano. There is a changing texture at b. 29, into a piano 'vamp' pattern, which emphasises the different characters of the themes. In the second movement the fast, dynamic folk theme is interrupted by the chorale, which maintains flow on its first entry but then operates almost in a different sphere, separated by general pauses. The sense of drama is greater than in the Smyth and Maddison works as the two main themes return at the end of the second movement.

The issue of the location of the climax of a sonata form movement has been much debated amongst feminist musicologists, and offers another aspect of the form, which could prompt gendered responses from composers. Susan McClary suggests that the end of the development section in classical sonata form is an event of power and violence with the masculine theme forcefully returning.[95] Stanford concurs, to the extent that he recommends that the climax should be within the development section before a subsidence into the recapitulation.[96] Liane Curtis counters this by observing that Clarke's sonata has the climax in the *middle* of the development, that the recapitulation does not start in the tonic and the cadenza contains a more triumphant return of the second theme.[97] Webster, on the other hand, considers the coda (as opposed to the recapitulation), to be the most likely place for climax in the late nineteenth century version of the form.[98]

In Sally Macarthur's reading of Clarke's Piano Trio (1921), she argues that the climax would be expected to be around the golden mean (approximately 0.618) wherever that occurs in the music; instead 'the movement seems to make a feature of the halfway mark'.[99] She goes on to argue that 'it is possible that a female composer, inhabiting a female body, conceives of her musical proportions differently than does a male composer'.[100]

95 McClary, *Feminine Endings*, p. 15.

96 Stanford, *Musical Composition*, p. 90.

97 Curtis, 'Rebecca Clarke and Sonata Form', p. 400.

98 Webster, '19th Century/Romantic Sonata Form', p. 695.

99 Macarthur, *Feminist Aesthetics in Music*, p. 96.

100 Ibid.

Smyth is most consistent with Stanford (and McClary), while the fourth movement of the Maddison work has climactic points in both the development and the repetition of the development but the main point of climax is delayed until the coda. In both movements of the Owen work, the climax is delayed until the end. None of the sonata form movements, however, places a climax at the end of the development going into the recapitulation – even in the Maddison there is a subsidence before the recapitulation – thus avoiding highlighting the return of the first theme. None of the works has a climax at the golden mean. In 'Liège', bar 58 – which is where the golden mean occurs – follows a general pause and marks the start of the second half of the movement. This is too small a sample, however, to infer that female composers may have a different sense of proportion, especially as the climaxes of each piece occur at very different points proportionally.

Maddison's, Smyth's and Owen's use of sonata form is, therefore, consistent with the late-Romantic vision of the form, using the same practices as their male contemporaries. Indeed some aspects, such as Maddison's and Owen's use of themes are particularly conventional. Yet Smyth's treatment of themes, Maddison's subtlety of recurrence and rejection of sonata form for the first movement, as well as Owen's repetition of the previous movements' themes, suggest individual explorations of the possibilities of the form.

Chapter 5
The Early Twentieth-Century Phantasy

While the previous chapter discussed works by three women who did not have close relationships with the SWM, works by Ethel Barns (1873–1948), Alice Verne-Bredt (1868–1958) and Susan Spain-Dunk (1880–1962), who were involved with the SWM or their members, will form the focus of this chapter.[1] Barns and Spain-Dunk, part of the second, more political generation of women under discussion, went on to be members of the SWM and were active string players. Verne-Bredt was older and, while she did not join the SWM herself, she had works performed by female players many of whom were connected to the SWM.

The issue of following in the footsteps of male composers is rather complicated by a new trend at this time: many pieces of chamber music written in the pre-First World War period are designated 'phantasies'. The genre is often seen as a departure from sonata form but it is not always the case. Why did composers choose to write phantasies? How did they engage with the structure and possibilities of the genre? How did the relationship of women composers with the SWM and other women musicians affect their contribution to this genre? This chapter will firstly describe the growing popularity of the phantasy in early twentieth-century Britain and then offer introductions to phantasies by Barns, Verne-Bredt and Spain-Dunk, before comparing these works with those by male contemporaries.

'Fantasia' was a term first used in the Renaissance to describe a composition 'whose form and invention sprang "solely from the fantasy and skill of the author who created it"' (Luis de Milan, 1535–1536).[2] This is not to suggest that a fantasia necessarily lacked formal structure, only that its form was not prescribed. Sixteenth-century English as well as Spanish and Italian fantasias were technically demanding and included some of the most florid writing of the period. In practice, they usually consisted of a number of sections whose floridity and difficulty increased as the work progressed. Elizabethan composers known for writing lute fantasias included John Dowland, while William Byrd excelled in the fantasia

---

[1] Ethel Barns and Susan Spain-Dunk were married to Charles Phillips and Henry Gibson respectively but used their maiden names for publication and performance. Spain-Dunk is sometimes referred to as Mrs Henry Gibson in SWM papers. Alice Verne-Bredt was married to William Bredt and combined her names for professional use.

[2] This and the following general information on the Fantasia is taken from Christopher D.S. Field, et al. 'Fantasia', *Grove Music Online, Oxford Music Online* <www.oxfordmusiconline.com> [accessed 3 May 2009]. Other variations on the term fantasia include Fancy, Fancie, Fansye, Fantasy Fantazia, Fantasie, Fantazie, Phantasy, Phantasie, and Phansie. The term was also used interchangeably at various times with ricerar and caprice.

for keyboard. The genre allowed composers considerable freedom if they were technically assured enough to exploit it.

The phantasy became, in the early twentieth century, a short piece of instrumental music that, in one movement, progressed through a variety of tempi and styles, with an equality among its instrumental parts. At its most extreme it differed from sonata form in the following ways. The phantasy was often more sectional than the sonata and most examples did not employ strict sonata form. Phantasies generally contained several themes, which often had similar features, therefore, the duality of the main and subsidiary themes of sonata form was not present. By omitting a return to previous material, the phantasy allowed more freedom in form and tonality. The phantasy was also concerned with the imagination: 'Its earliest appearances in a musical context focus on the imaginative musical "idea".'[3] The explosion of phantasy writing in the early twentieth century, as mentioned previously, was primarily due to its promotion by Walter Willson Cobbett. 'Phantasy' implied a particular attitude to form – even if the details were rather vague – indeed, Cobbett stated that composers should give free reign to their imagination. In this sense, the phantasy could be considered antithetical to the structural clarity – and, some would argue, the intellectual discipline – of sonata form.

Members of the musical establishment, however, were insistent that the musical phantasy should also have some defined basis. As Stewart Macpherson writes, they were reluctant to endorse free-form composition:

> [I]t may be that we, in these latter days, are on the eve of another overthrow of time-honoured landmarks in more than one direction. 'Who lives will see'; but it is certain that, whatever new developments may await us, the element of Form must of necessity hold an important place.[4]

Yet, in a period where writers such as Prout, Macpherson and Scott were highlighting the need for logic and flow, the phantasy seemingly fulfilled these criteria more closely than multi-movement works. Herbert Howells sees the relationship between the sonata and the phantasy thus: 'It [the Cobbett Fantasy] can also be thought of as a condensation of the three or four movements of a sonata into a single movement of moderate dimensions.'[5]

Indeed, it appears that Cobbett could not ignore the sonata and announced, in 1909, a competition for a violin sonata rather than a phantasy. He comments on the phantasy's relationship to the sonata:

> The major number of the Phantasies so far composed have consisted of a sort of condensation of the scope of four movements, treated not less organically than in sonata form. In place of the development section a movement of slower

---

3 Ibid.

4 Macpherson, *Form in Music*, p. 259.

5 Christopher Palmer, *Herbert Howells: A Celebration* (London, 1996), p. 59.

tempo is sometimes introduced, and this again may embody a movement of a *scherzando* type. In any case the music is continuous, and a logical connection is maintained. A return to the characteristics of the first part of the movement is made, but not necessarily a definite repetition, and a developed coda is added, which as regards style and tempo might suggest the usual *Finale* of a four-movement work. Thus the essential characteristics of an ordinary chamber work may be embodied in one movement of moderate length.[6]

Stanford, however, is suspicious of the phantasy:

This tabloid preparation of the three or four movements of a sonata must contain all the ingredients of the prescription, and yet not exceed the proportions of any of them. Then, again, the themes must be clear and intelligible to the hearer, and this needs what is termed 'spacing'. The difficulty of ensuring this, without loss of breathing room when they are concentrated into the smallest possible space, must be obvious ... The subject, therefore, must be conceived in miniature so as to ensure their proportion to each other and the whole design. A composer cannot set himself a more exacting problem.[7]

While music critic John Fuller Maitland (1856–1936) also suggests that it is 'recommended, that the development section of the sonata form is replaced by a movement in slow tempo, which may include also a scherzando movement', Ernest Walker argues that very few phantasies follow the guidelines set by Stanford or Fuller Maitland, especially those composed post 1910.[8]

Despite Cobbett's assertion that composers should be given 'free reign', the phantasy had close links with sonata form not least because commentators such as Prout, Macpherson and Scott refer to the development section of sonata form as the 'free fantasia'. Prout, in general saw the fantasia as 'almost any kind of composition without a clearly defined form'.[9] He goes on accurately to predict:

The fantasias of more recent composers generally consist of a series of movements following one another without a break, in various keys, not always ending with the same tonic with which they begin ... These, however, may be regarded as exceptional cases; in the majority we find the usual law of tonality ... adhered to.[10]

---

6 W.W. Cobbett, 'British Chamber Music', *MT*, 52/818 (April, 1911): p. 243.

7 Stanford, *Musical Composition*, pp. 163–4.

8 John Fuller Maitland quoted in Ernest Walker, 'Cobbett Competitions', *Cobbett's Cyclopaedic Survey of Chamber Music*, vol. 1, p. 286. See Appendix 1 for more information on John Fuller Maitland.

9 Ebenezer Prout, *Musical Form,* 4th edn (London, 1893), p. 2.

10 Ebenezer Prout, *Applied Forms*, p. 238.

Cobbett's attendance at the Gresham lectures by Sir Frederick Bridge, where he heard fancies by Ravenscroft, Deering, Ward, Lawes, Crawford and Locke, proved an illuminating experience and resulted in an almost obsessive preoccupation with the genre:

> They [the fancies] contain striking little adumbrations of modern harmony and string effects which would not have shamed one of the great writers of a later century. That they were full of naiveties of construction and tonality, rarely finishing in the initial key, and that development was absent for the most part, is not surprising considering the period when they were written, but as centuries-old native productions they were so interesting that I was moved to give commissions to 12 different composers of the younger generation to write so-called Phantasies for various combinations of instruments used in chamber music, works which may be described as the present-day analogues of the fancies, conceived of course in modern idiom, and without their structural defects.[11]

As will be seen later, Cobbett's drive and enthusiasm for the genre led to his commissioning phantasies for his publication series and the instigation of competitions for the composition of phantasies.

By the 1907/08 season, the phantasy had a significant presence on the London concert scene, as shown by the numbers of reviews in the *Musical Times*. This is especially accentuated by the decision of the London Trio (Amina Goodwin, Achille Simonetti and William E. Whitehouse) to play three prize-winning phantasies over a series of concerts in 1908 and 1909. Those by John Ireland (1879–1962) and James Friskin (1886–1967) received extended reviews in the *Musical Times*, the former being played again along with one by York Bowen in a Langley-Mukle series concert at 19 Grosvenor Square, with many more subsequent performances.[12] In the 1910s it became practically a rite of passage for younger English composers to gain a prize for a phantasy at a Cobbett Competition.[13]

An inconspicuous announcement in *The Musical Times* in July 1905 advertised a competition for a 'short piece of Chamber String Music';[14] this was followed by a more extensive explanation of the structure and requirements of the competition in December 1905:

> The composition of a short 'Phantasy' in the form of a String Quartet for two violins, viola, and violoncello. The parts must be of equal importance, and the duration of the piece should not exceed 12 minutes. Though the Phantasy is to

[11] W.W. Cobbett, 'The Beginnings of British Chamber Music', *Chamber Music*, 13 (March, 1915): p. 50.

[12] See Appendix 1 for more information on Friskin, Ireland and York Bowen.

[13] See Appendix 6 for a catalogue of Phantasies produced between 1905 and 1920.

[14] n.a.'Front Matter', *Musical Times*, 46/749 (July 1905): p. 430.

> be performed without a break, it may consist of different sections varying in *tempi* and rhythms.[15]

At this first Cobbett competition for a 'phantasy string quartet', William Hurlstone, who was to die prematurely shortly afterwards, was awarded first prize.[16] The competition was adjudicated by Cobbett, Sir Alexander Mackenzie, Alfred Gibson and Hermann Sternberg.[17] While neither the competition announcement nor the report of the results indicates if the entries were judged anonymously, in his *Cyclopaedic Survey of Chamber Music* published in 1929, Cobbett describes his surprise during the first competition when he opened the envelope revealing the name of Hurlstone, as he had thought he knew the composer's work well.[18] This suggests that the compositions were submitted anonymously, although in practice the judges would have had detailed knowledge of the compositional styles and manuscript of many of the competitors.

The other winning phantasies in 1905 were by Frank Bridge (2nd); James Friskin (3rd); Joseph C. Holbrooke (4th), H. Waldo Warner (5th) and Haydn Wood (6th).[19] By the 1907 competition for phantasy piano trio, there were 67 anonymous entries and the positioning of prizes was as follows: Frank Bridge (1st), John Ireland (2nd) and James Friskin (3rd).[20] But now there were also supplementary prizes; these were awarded to Alice Verne-Bredt, Susan Spain-Dunk, J.A. Harrison, 'Dr Blair', Sidney Goldsmith, Harold R. White and Ernest Halsey.[21] It is not clear exactly how the judging process proceeded; in 1907 the *Musical Times* stated that the judges included Dr Cummings but did not give detailed information on the other judges.[22] The competition announcement for the 1915 contest is more

[15] n.a. 'Front Matter', *Musical Times*, 46/754 (December 1905): p. 791.

[16] Hurlstone died in 1906 of asthma.

[17] Alfred Gibson taught Susan Spain-Dunk violin at the RAM between 1902 and 1905. He does not appear to be related to her future husband Henry Gibson. Student Record for Susan Spain-Dunk, RAM Archive, London. For more information on George Alfred Gibson see n.a. 'George Alfred Gibson', *MT and Singing-Class Circular*, 41/686 (April, 1900): pp. 225–8.

[18] W.W. Cobbett, 'Chamber Music Life', *Cobbett's Cyclopedic Survey of Chamber Music*, vol. 2, p. 261.

[19] See Appendix 1 for more information on Holbrooke and Wood.

[20] There is some discrepancy between sources: some state that Ireland won 2nd prize and Friskin 3rd, others that Friskin won 2nd and Ireland 3rd. James Friskin was the future husband of Rebecca Clarke. (Notoriously, until the Grove Dictionary of Women Composers, 1994, she was represented there only in the entry for him.)

[21] Spain-Dunk had further success at the Cobbett competitions with her Sonata for violin and piano when she won 4th prize in 1910. See Appendix 1 for more information on Halsey and White.

[22] W.W. Cobbett, 'British Chamber Music', *MT*, 52/818 (April, 1911): p. 243. Dr Cummings is likely to be William Hayman Cummings (1831–1915) who founded the Purcell Society and was Principal of the Guildhall School of Music 1896–1910.

specific; 'Mr Cobbett will himself examine the manuscripts, selecting a few to be performed for a small select audience, who will make the ultimate adjudication by vote'.[23]

The early Cobbett competitions stipulated a particular ensemble such as a piano trio or string quartet. Later, greater freedom with regard to choice of ensemble was allowed, but the designated work remained a 'phantasy'.[24] Cobbett declared that it was 'the counterpart of the chamber quartet and trio of the present day'.[25]

While Cobbett showed reluctance to accept total responsibility for its choice, for composers and the musical public, he and the genre were inseparable. The musical establishment was sometimes critical of Cobbett's apparent directive power; he, somewhat defensively, responded:

> It has been said of me, the initiator of these musical adventures, [the phantasy competitions] that I arrived at supplanting the sonata form. No such idea ever crossed my mind. Sir Charles Stanford once spoke of 'this tabloid preparation of the three or four movements of a sonata'. This was nearer the truth, for I doubt if there will ever be evolved a successful form which does not owe its origin to some period of the sonata. But his words imply some sort of design on my part to impose conditions upon competitors, whereas they were asked simply to give free play to their imagination in the composition of one-movement works, to write what they liked – in any shape – so long as it was a shape.[26]

Indeed Cobbett did not want to contest the status quo or appear too radical. He comments further:

> Sonata [form] will always remain to lovers of absolute music the most serviceable of musical structures. I would rather say that a new convention is wanted to stand side by side with the old one; which, though conceived on a less ambitious scale, is yet deemed worthy of academic sanction.[27]

How did composers, therefore, react to this challenge? The English composer was seen as measured and serious; a 1916 *Musical Times* article, for instance, wished

---

23 n.a. 'Occasional Notes', *MT*, 55/855 (May, 1914): p. 305.

24 The instrumental combinations were as follows: 1905 Phantasy for String Quartet, 1907 Phantasy Trio, 1909 Sonata for violin and piano, 1915 String Quartet in sonata, suite or fancy form, 1917 Folksong Phantasy, 1919 Dance Phantasy, 1921 Phantasy Duo. In the 1920s prizes for chamber music composition including phantasies were focused on composition students at the RCM.

25 Cobbett, 'Phantasy', *Cobbett's Cyclopedic Survey of Chamber Music*, vol. 2, p. 217. The Gresham lecturer referred to by Cobbett was Sir Frederick Bridge. Gresham College in London has given free public lectures in a variety of disciplines since the sixteenth century.

26 Ibid.

27 Cobbett, 'British Chamber Music', p. 242.

English music to 'stand for clearness of conception and purity of style, sanity of mind, and temperateness of spirit'.[28] Significantly, a chamber work by Thomas Dunhill, played in a RCM Patron's Fund concert on 13 December 1905, was praised by the reviewer of the *Musical Times* for being 'sanely imaginative'.[29] The phantasy provided some relief; indeed James Friskin's Phantasy Quartet was commended for 'the quality of its humour –a sense that is not greatly possessed by most young English composers, judging from the lugubrious products of their pens'.[30]

By 1919, composers such as Herbert Howells were reacting against the phantasy, perceiving that the concert community was growing weary of this form: 'I began this morning by changing the Sonata's name. By deed poll I have dropped "Phantasy" from it: the word has begun to frighten onlookers at British Music!'[31]

Jung and Freud contrast the concept of the 'phantasy' with that of the 'dream' in that the basis in reality of the former is absent from the latter. Jung describes the phantasy in terms of psychological types as:

> [F]or the most part a product of the unconscious. It does indeed contain elements of consciousness, but for all that is a special characteristic that it is essentially spontaneous, and quite foreign to the conscious content. It shares this quality in common with the dream, though the latter is wholly involuntary and far more bizarre in character.[32]

The 'psychological' phantasy revealed the unconscious and some musical phantasies also had a 'darker' element; yet the genre was considered, perhaps because of its brevity, less serious than multi-movement forms. Indeed the manuscript of Alice Verne-Bredt's Phantasy Trio bore the motto, 'under the light there is darkness', though this was not included in the published version.

Jung sees the propagation of phantasies as dependent on society as well as the individual. The 'spirit of the age' of Edwardian London was one of release, a reaction to Victorian propriety and social behaviour, and the musical phantasy reflected this. Indeed if a composer wanted to present a 'serious' phantasy it was sometimes necessary to suggest this in its title, such as the *Fantasie Sérieuse* by Greville Cooke presented at the Queen's Hall in 1911.[33] In the latter half of the decade, though, the number of phantasies by composers of both sexes dropped: it seems that the First World War was not conducive to the composition of such works; in any case, there was a general decrease in compositional activity.

---

28 Colin McAlpin, 'Britain: Her Music', *MT*, 57/884 (October, 1916): p. 447.

29 n.a. 'Review', *MT*, 47/755 (Jan, 1906): p. 44.

30 n.a. 'Review', *MT*, 47/761 (July, 1906): p. 489.

31 Palmer, *Herbert Howells*, p. 74.

32 Carl G. Jung, 'Psychological Types', in *Collected Papers on the Psychology of Phantasy*, ed. Dr Constance Long (London, 1920), pp. xi–xii.

33 n.a. 'London Concerts' (reviews) *MT*, 52/826 (December, 1911): p. 806.

Table 5.1 Phantasies Written by Women c.1905–1920

Composer	Phantasy	Instrumentation	Notes
Ethel Barns	Phantasy Trio	2vns 1piano	Published by Schott in 1912 as no.4 in Cobbett series
Ruby Holland	Trio in one movement	vn, vc, piano	Probably in phantasy form, unpublished n.d.
M.E. Marshall	Dance Phantasy Trio	unclear	n.d. MS
Susan Spain-Dunk	Phantasy Quartet	2vns, va, vc	Published by Goodwin and Tabb 1915
Susan Spain-Dunk	Phantasy Trio	vn, vc, piano	Cobbett 5th prize 1907
Alice Verne-Bredt	Phantasy Trio	vn, vc, piano	Cobbett Supplementary Prize, Published by Schott 1910
Alice Verne-Bredt	Phantasy Piano Quartet	vn, va, vc, piano	n.d. MS
Alice Verne-Bredt	Phantasy Piano Quintet	2vn, va, vc, piano	n.d. MS

Indeed women composers' involvement with the phantasy was in the context of the general debate on form. Ironically Cobbett himself appears to be calling for a female aesthetic when he writes:

> Certain feminine [*sic*] writers of chamber music show no lack of vitality. In fact they set themselves the task of emulating men in this respect, but the composer destined to achieve greatness in the future is more likely to be simply – herself; not woman pranked in male garb, but woman true to her own nature, woman of whom poets have sung, and whom, strange to say, composers of the opposite sex have best succeeded in interpreting in terms of music.[34]

There were not large numbers of women choosing to compose in this genre, however, it was important in the development of women composers, and highlights many of the challenges both practical and musical facing them when placed in direct competition with men, in one of the first British competitions outside the music college environment. To do so women composers responded positively to the notion of a phantasy; notably, it freed them from an almost exclusively male tradition. Table 5.1 shows the phantasies written by women c.1907–1915. Women composers and performers also acted as judges, although not in as large numbers as male musicians, see Appendix 7.[35]

---

34 Cobbett, 'Women Composers', *Cobbett Cyclopaedic Survey of Chamber Music*, vol. 2, p. 593.

35 Women also contributed to entries for *Cobbett's Cyclopaedic Survey of Chamber Music*; of 139 writers, 13 were female.

Ethel Barns

The *Fantasie* by Barns – a trio for two violins and piano – was commissioned by Cobbett, rather than being written for a Cobbett competition, and was part of a series published by Schott and funded by Cobbett, where several composers were asked to write a phantasy for varying string and piano combinations.[36] Barns was extremely active within the community of women composers. She had studied composition with Ebenezer Prout, as well as violin firstly with Prosper Sainton (1813–1890) and then Emile Sauret (1852–1920) at the RAM, and produced many short works for violin as well as a Concertstück and chamber music.[37]

She performed professionally with Sauret as well as playing his solo works, although a review of Sauret's Suite for unaccompanied violin as having 'little to recommend it for public performance' suggests that she was the more accomplished composer.[38] She continued to compose after her marriage to Charles Phillips, 30 of her works being published, mainly by Schott and Co. She also managed a professional career as a violinist. With Phillips she founded the Barns-Phillips concert series at the Bechstein Hall for chamber music and especially her own compositions. Of the women composers in this study, Barns was the most commercially successful, and (partly due to) her organisation of her concert series, she was one of the more visible women composers of the period. When she died her beneficiaries deposited all her manuscripts in the British Library, which has ensured her presence in modern discourse on women composers even though her works have become little-played.

Katherine Eggar's comments on Barns's standing as a composer, published in *Cobbett's Cyclopedic Survey of Chamber Music* in 1930, are as follows:

> The above works [2nd and 4th violin sonatas and the Fantasie Trio] bear the stamp of the executant rather than the contemplative musician. The violin parts are the work of a skilled player who knows the legitimate capacities of the instrument, and conceives passages which lie well for fingers and bow. The piano, too, is in sympathy with its more brilliant qualities, the chief resource being resonant chords and wide ranging arpeggios. The harmony is strong in six-fours and dominant sevenths with frequent modulations, the composer's favourite device being to shift a passage by semitones from one key-plane to another ... In the trio, the writing for the two violins shows constructive care, and the two parts are of equal interest.[39]

---

[36] Between 1910 and 1912 composers who received a Cobbett commission included: Frank Bridge, James Friskin, Benjamin Dale, Thomas F. Dunhill, James McEwen, Ethel Barns, Ralph Vaughan Williams, Richard Walthew, B. Walton O'Donnell, Donald Tovey, and Edwin York Bowen. While some remained in manuscript, others were published by Augener, Stainer and Bell or Schott.

[37] See Appendix 1 for more information on Sainton and Sauret.

[38] n.a., 'Other Recitals' (reviews) *MT*, 53/829 (March, 1912): p. 181.

[39] Katherine Eggar, 'Ethel Barns', *Cobbett's Cyclopedic Survey of Chamber Music*, 1, pp. 59–60.

Eggar's comments were seen by Cobbett as lacking, to the extent that he added his own entry (below Eggar's) in the *Cyclopedia*, including other works by Barns as well as those mentioned by Eggar. Of the above work, Cobbett writes, 'Her phantasy trio was frequently played by the composer with the late Emile Sauret, always with great success'.[40] Indeed the first performance of the Fantasie was with Sauret and pianist Percy Waller at the first Barns-Phillips concert of the season on 4 November 1911, on this occasion the work was described as having 'all the gracefulness and pleasing sentiment characteristic of the composer's best work'.[41]

Dedicated to Sauret, the *Fantasie* was written at the peak of Barns's compositional output. She had been writing for increasingly large forces from around 1904 including Concerto no. 2 in G minor (1904) and a Concertstück in D minor (1908) both for violin and orchestra. When Barns's marriage broke up in 1913–1914 she produced new works far less frequently and the number of performances of her works sharply declined. Barbara Engelsberg suggests this was because Phillips and Barns had moved in society rather than musical circles and Barns did not have a musical support system.[42] The Fantasie was premiered a few days before the first full meeting of the SWM on 11 November 1911; Barns's was one of the Society's initial members but ceased membership in 1914, another avenue of support thus being lost.

The form of the Barns's *Fantasie* is a series of continually evolving sections, see table 5.2.[43] The *Fantasie* is a departure from the simple ternary structures of Barns' songs, piano and violin works such as the one-movement piano trio, *Adagio*, which moves from A♭ major (bb. 1–34) to G♯ minor (bb. 35–58) then back to A♭ major (bb. 59–end), all the while in 4/4. In contrast the *Fantasie* is sectional with brief interludes between sections, often using repeated patterns in the piano or sustained chords in the piano and strings. These passages, though superficially implying continuity, actually provide clear punctuation marks, underlining the sectional nature of the piece.

In this way Barns's *Fantasie* recalls the strongly articulative nature of nineteenth-century sonata-form pieces. Although Barns allows at least one instrumental line to span the sections, this does not prove a sufficient link, since, as at for instance, bb. 128–9, the self-conscious intervening material is actually divorced from what precedes and follows it by pauses and clear textural changes, see example 5.1. This is also the case in other passages in the work such as at bb. 216–22, although in general, such material is followed, rather than preceded, by a pause, see example 5.2.

While there is a return to the A material at bar 222 – as can be seen in table 5.2 previously – this is a variation of what occurred earlier in the work and the theme is not allowed to reassert itself; thus there is no grand return to the main theme. Each section is distinct from, but related to, what has come before, for example, in section G there is a 2-bar repetition of material from D with a different distribution of it between the instruments and then the music evolves, see example 5.3(a) and (b).

40 W.W. Cobbett, 'Ethel Barns', *Cobbett's Cyclopedic Survey of Chamber Music*, 1, p. 60.

41 n.a., 'London Concerts' (reviews) *MT*, 52/826 (December, 1911): p. 806.

42 Englesberg, 'The Life and Works of Ethel Barns', p. 24.

43 Interestingly Barns reverts to French spelling using *f* rather than *ph* in Phantasy.

Table 5.2 Form in Barns's *Fantasie*

Bar	Tempo	Key	Time signature	Materials
1–116	Andante con moto	D major–E♭ major (b.41)	3/4	A–B (b.41) – Development based on A and B (b.80)
117–47	Meno Mosso–Allegro Moderato (b.130)	D major–D minor (b.30)	4/4	C–D (b.130)
148–71	Poco Meno Mosso	A major	3/4	E
172–85		D major – D minor (b.179)	4/4	F–G (based on A) (b.179)
186–238	Poco Meno Mosso–Tempo I° (b. 222)	E♭ minor–A♭ minor (b. 196)–E major (b.222)	3/4	H–I (variation of E) (b. 196)–A² (222)
239–72	Allegro–Allegando (b.262)	Transition to B♭ major–F major–ends in D major	4/4–9/8 –6/8	Coda (opening based on D)

Example 5.1 Barns, *Fantasie*, bb. 127–130

Example 5.2 Barns, *Fantasie*, bb. 216–222

Example 5.3 Barns, *Fantasie*, bb.130–132, Section D (a) and 179–181, Section G (b)

(a)

(b)

The work uses the greatest amount of constantly changing material of all the phantasies examined, with the exact repetition of, at most, two bars at any one time.

Alice Verne-Bredt

The *Phantasie* for violin, violoncello and piano by Verne-Bredt is a work that was disseminated in her lifetime through performances and publication.[44] The review by Marion Scott and Katherine Eggar in the Chamber Music supplement to the *Music Student* is complimentary. 'There is great freedom of rhythm already evinced by the first subject being cast in 5/4 time. This is a form of emancipation, which always seems a little artificial in composers of Western Europe, but in the present case it is interesting as showing a widening of the imagination.'[45] Eggar and Scott even forgive one apparent shortcoming. 'That the second subject should go into 6/8 with a rather obvious arpeggio accompaniment, must be regarded not merely as inability on the composer's part to sustain the more complicated rhythm, but as commendable feeling for contrast.'[46]

Verne-Bredt indeed displays considerable technique, which is all the more surprising from a composer who did not study at a music college or indeed have a formally structured musical education.[47] However, the sixth of ten children of German immigrants from Oberdorf who grew up in Southampton and then London, she was the daughter of musical parents: her father was an instrumental teacher, specialising in violin, organ, piano and zither, and her mother was an accomplished violin player. While her sister Mathilde was a pupil of Clara Schumann, Alice would receive occasional piano lessons from Marie Schumann when she was visiting London. In a letter to Mathilde, Marie Schumann comments, 'For a girl who has never had lessons, Alice plays remarkably well and technique comes to her naturally'.[48] It is likely, therefore, that Alice received a patchwork of musical instruction from various members of her family. Her sisters recall Alice improvising from an early age:

> We children were often allowed to play the voluntaries and I remember my sister Alice even as a small child always extemporised them. When asked what she had played, it was obvious that most people did not believe her when she told them that they were her own improvisations, so she adopted the plan of attributing them to any well-known composer whose name came into her head.[49]

---

44 As with Barns, Verne-Bredt uses an alternative spelling, choosing 'Phantasie'.

45 Eggar and Scott, 'Women's Doings in Chamber Music: Women as Composers of Chamber Music Third Paper', p. 97.

46 Ibid.

47 The following information on Alice Verne-Bredt is taken from Mathilde Verne, *Chords of Remembrance* (London, 1936).

48 Ibid., p. 43.

49 Ibid., p. 27.

While she was, like her sisters Mathilde and Adela, a talented pianist, she had ambitions to become a light-opera singer; however she contracted typhoid, which ruined her voice.[50] After marrying William Bredt, an amateur conductor, she taught at the Matilde Verne Piano School in London, pioneering techniques for group-teaching of young children. Her compositions were often used as educational materials but also included chamber music, for instance, three Phantasies for piano trio, piano quartet and piano quintet.

However, the democratic part-writing in the *Phantasie* (she played both violin and piano) was not considered by Scott and Eggar to be replicated in the Phantasy Quintet:[51]

> A Quintet (MS) for piano and strings naturally makes more demand [than the trio] upon the composer's experience, and it cannot be said that Mrs Bredt has been altogether successful in this combination. The layout is scrappy. No instrument, not even the piano, has a rich part, and there are long silences for one or other voice which have a leaden rather than golden suggestion. There is perhaps more attempt to free the strings than in the other two compositions, but the effects are often thin and the construction halting. In its suaver passages the work reminds one of the style of Edward Schütt's charming *Walzer-Märchen* Trio, but one feels that the work as a whole is not the composer's favourite child—that not much love was lost in the writing.[52]

While no score is currently available to appraise the opinion of Eggar and Scott of the quintet, the Phantasie Trio appears to have been an artistic and commercial success for Verne-Bredt; it was performed on 25 January 1912 by Mathilde Verne, A.E. Sammons and C. Warwick Evans as part of a London String Quartet concert at the Æolian Hall as well as on 30 April 1914 by the Colanri Trio at the Bechstein Hall.[53] The Phantasy Piano Quartet was also played at the '12 o'clock' concert series at the Æolian Hall in January 1907 by Mathilde Verne (the composer's sister), Beatrice Langley, May Mukle and Cecilia Gates.[54] The Phantasy Trio is one of the shortest examined, probably because it was a competition piece. It contains complete repetitions of whole sections.

---

[50] Ibid., p. 67. Mathilde Verne studied piano with Clara Schumann and founded the Mathilde Verne Piano School in London. Among Mathilde's first pupils when living in Denmark Hill were the Deneke sisters. See Chapter 3 for Marga Deneke and the Oxford Ladies Musical Society. See Appendix 1 for more information on Adela and Mathilde Verne.

[51] This quintet was not published and its manuscript has not been located.

[52] Eggar and Scott, 'Women's Doings in Chamber Music: Women as Composers of Chamber Music Third Paper', p. 97.

[53] n.a., 'Chamber Music' (reviews) *MT*, 53/829 (March, 1914): p. 181.

[54] 'London Concerts' (listings) *MT*, 48/769 (March, 1907): p.181. The score of this work has not been recovered. Alice and Mathilde were not members of the SWM but the rest of the Quartet were for a number of years (Langley 1911–1917, Mukle 1911–1919 and Gates 1917–1918).

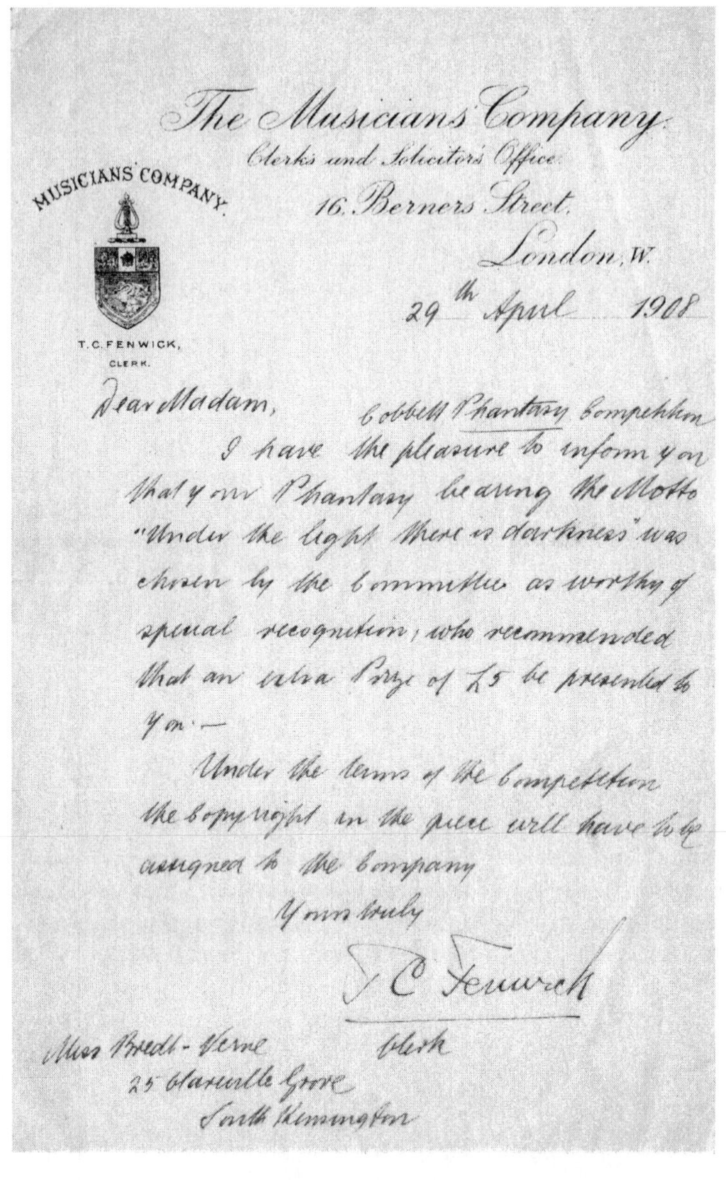

The Musicians' Company.
Clerks and Solicitor's Office.
16, Berners Street,
London, W.

MUSICIANS' COMPANY
T.C. FENWICK,
CLERK.

29th April 1908

Dear Madam,

Cobbett Phantasy Competition

I have the pleasure to inform you that your Phantasy bearing the Motto "Under the light there is darkness" was chosen by the Committee as worthy of special recognition, who recommended that an extra Prize of £5 be presented to you.—

Under the terms of the Competition the Copyright in the piece will have to be assigned to the Company

Yours truly

T C Fenwick

Clerk

Miss Bredt-Verne
25 Clareville Grove
South Kensington

Figure 5.1 Letter to Alice Verne-Bredt from T.C. Fenwick, Clerk Musicians Company, 29 April 1908

Table 5.3 Form in Verne-Bredt's, *Phantasie* (divided by tempo indications)

Bars	Tempo	Key	Time	Structure
1–33	Moderato	C minor	5/4	A
34–66	Andante Cantabile	E major	6/8	B
67–134	Allegretto	E major	2/4	C
135–38	Maestoso	C minor–E♭ major	5/4–4/4 b.(137)	A^2
139–89	Adagio doloroso	C minor	3/4	D
190–207	Andante Cantabile	F major	6/8	B^2
208–49	Allegretto	F major	2/4	C^2
250–70	Maestoso–Andante	C minor	5/4–4/4 (b. 256)	A^3

Of Verne-Bredt's three phantasies only that in C minor for piano trio was published by Schott.[55] It appears publication was not always guaranteed through the competition process; in a letter to Verne-Bredt from the Musicians Company in 1908 informing her that she had won an extra prize of £5 for her Phantasie Trio, she is informed that 'under the conditions of the competition the copyright of the piece will have to be assigned to the company', suggesting publication, see figure 5.1.[56] Her reply, however, is not known, but in a further letter, Verne-Bredt is informed that the 'committee does not propose to publish your Phantasy, at any rate, for the present'.[57] Indeed publication did not occur until 1910.

The Phantasie Trio follows the conditions set for the Cobbett competitions, lasting 10 minutes and moving through a series of time signatures, keys and styles with a structure shown in Table 5.3. Similarly to Barns's work, this piece is sectional with short transitional passages into each new section. It, too, therefore, evokes the dialectic of sonata form in its clarity of structure. The linking passages, again serving as punctuation, use sustained chords over a piano pattern, or as is the case when moving from B to C, a V^7-I cadence, see example 5.4. Unusually in the phantasy genre, Verne-Bredt repeats material verbatim. While the 2nd and 3rd themes (B and C) are transposed at their return, theme A is repeated exactly. This is noteworthy because most composers of the genre tended to vary endings or even individual bars during passages of exact repetition. In many ways this piece offers the clearest formal structure of any to be discussed here.

---

55 The Summerhayes Piano Trio has recorded the work: Summerhayes Piano Trio, *English Romantic Trios*, Meridian Records, 2005, CDE 84478.

56 Letter to Alice Verne-Bredt from T.C. Fenwick, Clerk Musicians Company, 29 April 1908.

57 Letter to Alice Verne-Bredt from T.C. Fenwick, Clerk Musicians Company, 6 May 1908.

Example 5.4 Verne-Bredt, *Phantasie*, bb. 65–67

Susan Spain-Dunk

Spain-Dunk's Phantasy Quartet in D minor was published in 1915 by Goodwin and Tabb, but it is unclear whether it was written for a specific competition. Spain-Dunk was a prolific phantasy composer; there is evidence she wrote another phantasy quartet as well as a phantasy trio, but neither was published. She had studied at the RAM, with violin as her first study and piano as her second.[58]

She was taught harmony by Stewart Macpherson, winning the Charles Lucas Medal for composition and, as mentioned earlier, was a friend of Cobbett, playing viola in his private string quartet. She became a member of the SWM in 1914 as she was writing the Phantasy Quartet and was married to Henry Gibson who also composed music; therefore she was very much at the centre of the group of British women developing composition skills through chamber music.[59]

Spain-Dunk went on to compose an increasing amount of orchestral music as well as chamber music, conducting her works at the Proms concerts between 1924 and 1927. Similarly to Ethel Smyth, Spain-Dunk frequently conducted when her works were included in programmes in the 1920s and 1930s. She seems to have often been programmed alongside Smyth in concerts including at the Bournemouth Festival and the Folkestone Festival, although there is no evidence that the women were particularly supportive of each other.[60] Works by Spain-Dunk, especially those for clarinet and orchestra, were also performed at student

[58] Student Record for Susan Spain-Dunk, Student Entry Records 1902, RAM Archive, p.426.

[59] See Appendix 1 for more information on Henry Gibson.

[60] F.S.H., 'Bournemouth Festival (review) *MT*, 68/1012 (June, 1927): p. 552 and n.a. 'The Folkestone Festival' (review) *MT*, 71/1053 (November, 1930): p. 1035.

concerts at the RAM (where Spain-Dunk was professor) and at Trinity College in the early 1930s.[61]

Despite having gained recognition as the first woman to conduct a regimental band, towards the end of her life, Spain-Dunk's music was much less performed than in previous decades.[62] In an article in 1957 for the *Musical Times* on Broadcast Music, the critic Stanley Bayliss dismisses Spain-Dunk without even mentioning the title of the work broadcast, Evergreen, 'is often stretched in meaning to cover works by such composers as Susan Spain-Dunk, whose music used to be an annual feature of Prom prospectuses, but has never become popular or evergreen'.[63] Yet in his role as chairman for a session by Richard Walthew on String Quartets for the Royal Musical Association in 1916, Cobbett included Spain-Dunk alongside Bridge, Dunhill, Holbrooke, Walthew, Goossens, York Bowen, McEwen and Stanford as a string quartet composer of note.[64]

Spain-Dunk's Phantasy Quartet, whose form is given in table 5.4, has no passages of exact repetition; neither does it possess as many key and tempo changes as Barns's phantasy. This Phantasy Quartet combines some sonata-form principles, such as a return of the main theme in the original key and the use of main and secondary themes, with a more phantasy-like manipulation of previous material at bar 177. The slower, central *Andante moderato* section can also be considered a condensed slow movement of a three-movement sonata. The double bars between bb.90 and 91, as well as bb.176 and 177 indicate the most significant structural pauses. The secondary theme, however, does not move to an alternative key and as a whole the work does not shift tonally as much as do many phantasies by other composers. Spain-Dunk's earlier Phantasy Trio, which won a supplementary prize in the Cobbett Competition in 1907, was dismissed along with Verne-Bredt's by the critic Ernest Walker:

> These two trios [Spain-Dunk's and Verne-Bredt's] stand in a somewhat special position of their own: They were granted supplementary prizes in Mr Cobbett's second competition as examples of what may be called high-class salon music. They fulfil their own functions in capital fashion, but they do not exactly enter into rivalry with the rest of the Phantasies. The former is the more vigorous and impulsive of the two. It consists of an *allegro con brio* in ordinary 'sonata-form', except that in place of a development section there is an *adagio*, the main

---

61 n.a., 'Royal Academy of Music', *MT*, 72/1058 (April, 1931): p. 357 and n.a., 'Trinity College of Music', *MT*, 72/1066 (December, 1911): p. 1128.

62 Spain-Dunk conducted the Royal Artillery Band in a performance of her overture *Andred's Weald* at the Royal Artillery Theatre in Woolwich in March 1932 (Ethel Smyth had already conducted military musicians but not an artillery band), see n.a. 'A Woman Composer', *The Sydney Morning Herald*, 21 March 1932, p. 3.

63 Stanley Bayliss, 'Broadcast Music', *MT*, 98/1373 (July, 1957): p. 375.

64 Richard, H. Walthew, 'String Quartets', *Proceedings of the Musical Association, 42nd session (1915–1916)* (June, 1916): p. 162.

Table 5.4 Form in Spain-Dunk's Phantasy Quartet

Bar	Tempo	Key	Time Signature	Section	Themes
1–54	Allegro con Fuoco	D minor	4/4	A	Main theme
55–90		D minor	4/4		Secondary theme
91–176	Andante moderato	B♭ major–G minor	3/4	B	Condensed slow movement
177–201	Allegro con Fuoco	C minor	4/4	A	Main theme/ development
202–14		F major	4/4		
215–46		D minor	4/4		
247–71		D minor	4/4		Main theme
272–98		D major	4/4		Secondary theme
299–333	Piu Tranquillo	D major	4/4	Coda	

> theme of which is repeated, in grandiose fashion, in the coda. The second trio is perhaps slighter in material, while rather defter in craftsmanship. It includes several short sections in different *tempi*, repeated from time to time, so as to form a neatly balanced structure. Both works are of only moderate technical difficulty, and effectively written for both instruments.[65]

Spain-Dunk went on to win fourth place in the International Cobbett Competition for a violin sonata.[66] It appears that, by the time of writing the quartet in 1915, she had developed her phantasy-writing style, which was becoming more through-composed and less reliant simply on sonata form and exact repetitions of main themes. The sections are much more clearly defined than those in the Barns Fantasie and thus this quartet is a series of segments rather than a seamless, continuous work, see example 5.5. This work is one of the most democratic of those studied here in its distribution of material between the parts. Marion Scott commented on this feature, 'Each of the four parts has an individuality, and there is significance in all the phrases which marks a great advance in musical thought'.[67] Spain-Dunk's

---

65 Ernest Walker, 'The Modern British Phantasy', *Chamber Music*, 17 (November, 1915): p. 26.

66 Anon. 'Foreign Notes', *MT*, 51/804 (February, 1910): p. 116. For this competition the judges were Baron Frédéric d'Erlanger, William Shakepeare, Paul Stroeving and Cobbett. The prizes were: John Ireland (1st), Eric Gritton (2nd), O'Connor Morris (3rd) and Susan Spain Dunk (4th). Ireland and Gritton had both studied with Charles Stanford.

67 Katherine Eggar and Marion M. Scott, 'Women's Doings in Chamber Music: Women as Composers of Chamber Music Third Paper', *Chamber Music: A Supplement to*

Example 5.5 Spain-Dunk, *Phantasy*, bb. 29–37

enthusiastic creation of phantasies may indeed be due to her personal relationship to Cobbett. Her growing success as a composer can be mapped through reviews (even if the scores are not extant) as can her shifting compositional style.

Phantasies written for Cobbett competitions, commissioned by Cobbett for the Cobbett series, and others written independently, generally concur in their structures, use of repetition, sonata characteristics and use of themes. Table 5.5 shows examples of phantasies written between 1905 and 1915 written for a variety of reasons and published by five different companies, see also Appendix 6.

Those phantasies commissioned for the Cobbett series, such as Barns's Fantasie for two violins and piano and Richard Walthew's Phantasy Quintet for violin, viola, cello, double bass and piano, employ less conventional combinations of instruments, but all are for strings and in some cases include piano. While those works included in table 5.5 eschew sonata form, they do exhibit, to varying extents, a return of previous material.

In its use of a series of thematically-related small sections (almost) without exact repetition, the Barns *Fantasie* is similar to the through-composed Phantasy String Quartet of William Y. Hurlstone, which won first prize in the first Cobbett

---

the Music Student, 9 (July, 1914): p. 98.

competition of 1905. In both of the works by Barns and Verne-Bredt, however, there is some attempt to maintain a continuous line between sections, whereas Hurlstone uses double bar lines to indicate sections and deliberately introduces pauses – sometimes occurring within sections – producing an unapologetically sectional work. The Bridge Phantasy, on the other hand, employs pauses between sections.

The Hurlstone Phantasy, a condensed sonata, was described in the *Musical Times* as 'a composition of distinct merit in its musicality and pleasure giving qualities. Its three movements are deftly connected by a metamorphosis of two themes, and as the entire work is commendably concise it is a welcome example of linked sweetness *not* drawn out'.[68]

Table 5.5 Phantasies Composed 1905–1915

Composer	**Instrumentation**	**Date**	**Publisher**	**Conditions of Composition**
Ethel Barns	2 vns, piano	1912	Schott	No.4 in Cobbett series
Frank Bridge	Vn, vc, pf	1908	Augener and Novello (1909)	Independent?
Thomas F. Dunhill	Vn, va, pf	1912	Stainer & Bell	No.6 in Cobbett series
William Y. Hurlstone	2 vns, va, vc	1905	Novello, pub.1906	1st prize, Cobbett Competition
Susan Spain-Dunk	2 vns, va, vc	1915	Goodwin & Tabb	Independent?
Alice Verne-Bredt	Vn, vc, pf	1908	Schott pub.1910	Supplementary Prize, Cobbett competition
Richard Walthew	Vn,va,vc, d.bass, pf	1912	Stainer & Bell	Cobbett series

It also has structural similarities to the Spain-Dunk work, as it combines a condensed sonata with the sectional features of the phantasy, though Spain-Dunk uses movement of material between instruments and texture to a greater extent. Hurlstone uses recurrence of fragments of the themes, generally lasting no more than two bars before the theme evolves, and lengthening of themes especially in canon, the only exception being a ten-bar repetition of theme 2 with differing accompanying material towards the end of the piece at b. 229. The same technique occurs extensively in Dunhill's Phantasy Quartet and Walthew's Phantasy Quintet, as does octave transposition of material before it evolves.

The Hurlstone *Phantasie* does not have a triumphant return to the main theme at the end of the work; similarly to the Spain-Dunk, it ends in the relative major

68 n.a. 'Prize Phantasies', p. 489.

Example 5.6. Verne-Bredt, Phantasie Trio, bb. 129–136

key. Similarly to Barns, as will be discussed later, the Hurlstone work manipulates several themes rather than using a main and a subsidiary theme, as occurs in both Spain-Dunk and Verne-Bredt.

As far as their orchestration is concerned, all the phantasies with piano treat the instrument as a unit separate from the strings, often with themes being passed from the strings to the piano. The Walthew Phantasy is at the extreme of this, with 71 of its 297 bars allotted to strings or piano alone: the latter rarely introduces themes and generally acts as an accompanying device. While in most examples of the genre the violin introduces the themes, in the Bridge Phantasy, the cello introduces the theme in the B section, and in the Verne-Bredt Phantasie, the cello introduces both A and B themes. Canonic devices are exploited in both the Walthew and Dunhill, especially amongst strings and to a lesser extent between the piano and strings. This is not the case in the other phantasies and may reflect the kind of musical training each composer received.

A number of works move through chromatically-related keys, modulating by chromatic shifts or pivots, as in the Dunhill and Walthew; in the latter, for example, they may also move without warning from major to minor tonic. The Verne-Bredt Phantasie, moving initially from F major to C minor, uses a downward chromatic scale in violin and cello against an upward shift in the piano, gradually adding chromatics for more fluid modulation, see example 5.6. This technique is also exploited in the Barns phantasy. Verne-Bredt, who had not formally studied composition, produced the least free-form phantasy of the three women. The form of the Verne-Bredt work, however, resembles the phantasy trio by Dunhill (A–B–C–A–B–Coda) whereas phantasies such as the quartet by Bridge have an arch form (A–B–C–B–A–Coda). Compared to the rest of their compositional output, the structures of the Barns and the Spain-Dunk works are, however, unusual as even their orchestral works display more conventional form.

Thematic materials in the phantasies of Barns, Verne-Bredt and Spain-Dunk reflect traditional sonata-form characteristics, as discussed in the opening to this chapter: the second themes tend to be more lyrical and the first, more dynamic. The phenomenon also accords with the 'non-phantasies' of Maddison, Owen and Smyth, as discussed in chapter 4. This perhaps reflects the composers' backgrounds, as Barns had studied with Prout and Spain-Dunk with Macpherson. While the Phantasy Quartet of the latter shows a conventional use of first and second themes, see examples 5.7a, 5.7b and 5.7c, in Verne-Bredt's work, the first theme enters much more lyrically before becoming more articulated and dynamic; the second theme is marked andante cantabile. Verne-Bredt's treatment of the two main themes is significant in establishing a darker undercurrent to the work. As mentioned previously, this phantasie originally bore the sub-title, 'Under the light there is darkness'. This is illustrated in the subdued first entrance of the main theme in C minor and especially at the return of the main theme at b.135, after the second theme and quirky interlude in E major, see example 5.8. Here the main theme returns triumphant in the original key but dissolves into melancholy. Unlike the other phantasies there is not jubilant finale but, rather, descending fragments from the main theme, as the violin and cello give way to the lower range of the piano, see example 5.9.

Example 5.7a Spain-Dunk, *Phantasy*, Main Theme, bb. 1–13

Example 5.7b Spain-Dunk, *Phantasy*, Secondary Theme, bb. 36–40

Example 5.7c Spain-Dunk, *Phantasy*, Theme from Andante Moderato Section, bb. 90–97

Andante Moderato

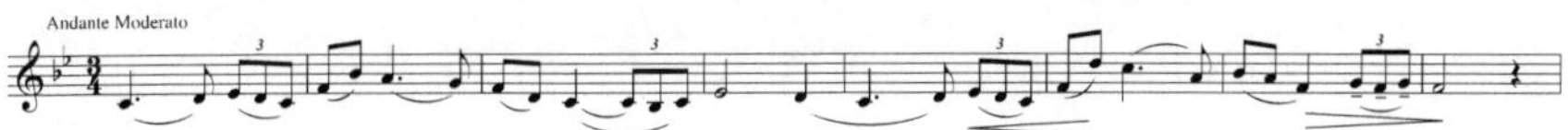

Example 5.8 Verne-Bredt, *Phantasie*, bb. 131–9

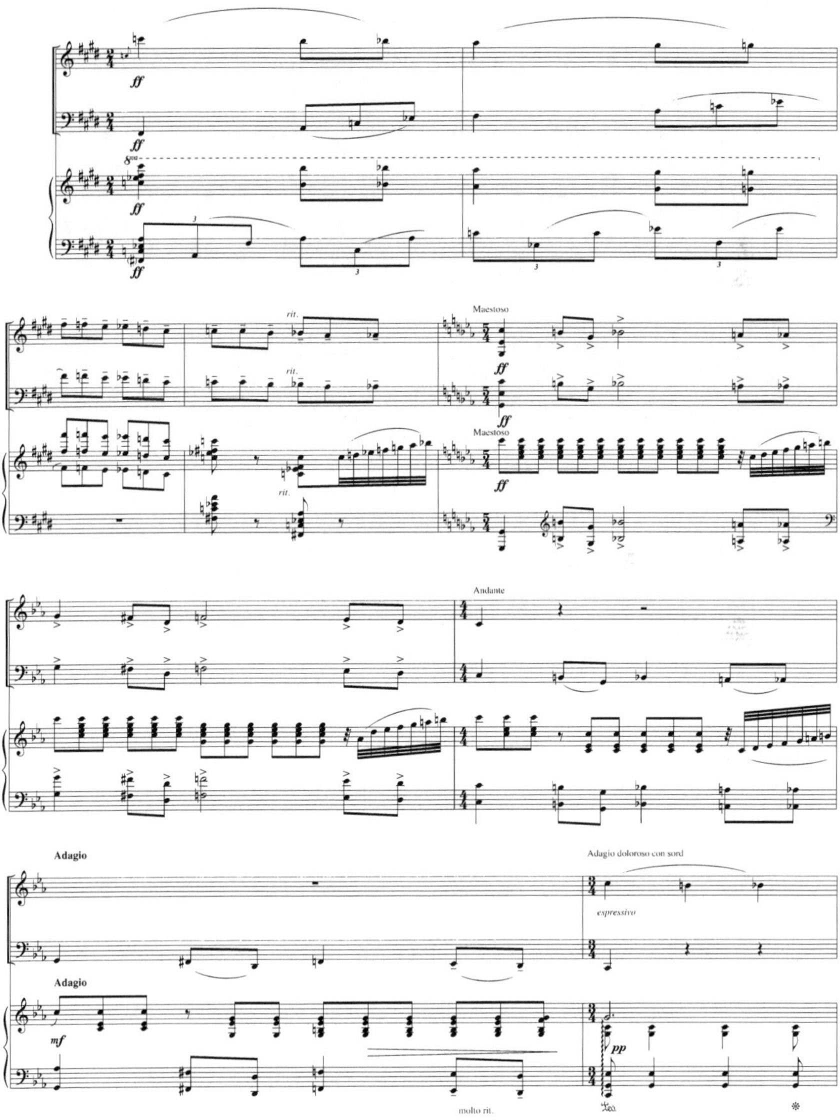
ff
rit.
Maestoso
Andante
Adagio
Adagio doloroso con sord
espressivo
mf
pp
molto rit.

Example 5.9 Verne-Bredt, *Phantasie*, bb. 163–70

The Barns *Fantasie* contains four themes comparable to the Owen work; however, these themes do not have such distinguishing characteristics. While the first theme has a more sweeping range than the second and third, there are rhythmic similarities in the use of triplets and syncopation. As is the case also in the Hurlstone *Phantasy*, it is the fourth theme that contrasts most with the others, in rhythm, articulation and range of dynamics.

Indeed, while large numbers of women composers, still in the thrall of the male tradition and their own education, wrote piano trios and string quartets, others, including Swepstone, Eggar, Verne-Bredt and Dorothy Erhardt – still considered minor composers, to be sure – chose the phantasy as a way to gain publication, performance and competitive success. There appears to have been a divide between those women, such as Smyth and Maddison, who had international careers/educations and who did not engage with the phantasy and those women who were more closely involved in London's musical circles, who often produced a series of phantasies. Ironically Verne-Bredt, who was not a member of the SWM, seems to have benefited most from the support of other women musicians, who played her phantasies, including as part of a SWM concert in February 1913.[69] Later that year the SWM hosted a study afternoon on phantasies, with presentations by Cobbett and Rutland Boughton, as part of its composer conference.[70]

Of course many British male composers also chose to write phantasies, as a means of gaining recognition and publication with Cobbett's encouragement and promotion of what was seen as a 'British' genre. Donald Tovey commented in 1916 that one of the reasons that the Cobbett competitions were supported by young composers was that many other competitions had a 'natural tendency to foster a style that makes primarily for safety' whereas here the 'art-form required was, while clearly and adequately defined, both new and entirely under the control of each individual competitor'.[71] However, the fact that some women composers chose to experiment with the genre, and that even those who did not (such as Maddison) showed tendencies towards the style in their chamber works, indicates that the (male) tradition of composition was indeed being challenged.

---

69 SWM Archive, RCM, London, SWM 2nd public concert, Æolian Hall, London, 24 February 1913, box 176.

70 SWM Archive, RCM, London, Notice of 2nd Composer's Conference, 1913, box 176.

71 Donald Tovey, 'Frank Bridge: Phantasy in F♯ Minor for Violin, Viola, Violoncello, and Pianoforte', in *The Classics of Music: Talks, Essays, and Other Writings, Previously Uncollected*, ed. Michael Tilmouth completed David Kimbell and Roger Savage (Oxford, 2001), p. 85. See Appendix 1 for more information on Donald Tovey.

Epilogue

This study has investigated six chamber works by women from a range of backgrounds and has offered an insight into the production of women's music in the early twentieth century. The works have divided into phantasies and other kinds of chamber music. The phantasies have been an interesting case because of early twentieth-century notions of the phantasy as a 'new' genre, even if this was not actually the case. In some senses then, the phantasy provided a more level arena in which women could compete with male composers. This was due not only to Cobbett's inclusive attitude, but also to each composer having to find his/her own definition of the genre. This perhaps led to greater scope for the possibility of a female aesthetic than those non-phantasy chamber works, which engaged with sonata form to varying degrees. Despite the disappearance of Susan Spain-Dunk's other phantasies, the contemporary commentary on these pieces suggests her developing sense of what the phantasy should be. Pertinently she moved away from a more rigid condensed sonata form to a freer style, which was also employed by Barns and to a lesser extent Verne-Bredt.

It seems, as discussed in Chapter 5, that commentators such as Stanford and Fuller Maitland viewed the phantasy as a problem that needed to be solved, evident in the advice they gave to composers. It is significant that although male and female composers chose to ignore this advice, Barns and Verne-Bredt seem to have negotiated a freer form from 1905, whereas Susan Spain-Dunk and many of the male composers initially were more inclined to incorporate sonata qualities. The other chamber works by Maddison, Smyth and Owen also engage with sonata form, their use of the form generally being consistent with that of many other early twentieth-century composers.

Elements of the three non-phantasy works are perhaps unusual – Smyth's treatment of themes, Maddison's recurrence and, in a work for chamber ensemble usually assigned 'absolute music', Owen's use of reference and narrative – but they are different for each composer. So is their placing of climaxes. The evidence suggested that these were individual responses to the form rather than a collectively 'female' response.

Stylistically, then, the non-phantasy pieces are very different. Smyth, Maddison and Owen were in no sense a group with a collective identity. Barns, Verne-Bredt and Spain-Dunk, however, were from similar backgrounds; Barns and Spain-Dunk both studied at the RAM and would have known each other through the SWM. Verne-Bredt, through her sister Mathilde, associated with many of the same musicians as the other two. It can be argued that as a group they were more likely than Smyth, Maddison and Owen to have similar approaches to composition.

Of the composers in this study, only Spain-Dunk was a member of the SWM for a considerable period of time and was part of the inner circle of women organising the Society. It is evident, in the praise of her music by Scott and Eggar, that they considered her worth promoting. Both Smyth and Barns fell foul of the expectations of the SWM although perhaps, because of Smyth's standing as a composer, the SWM could not be overtly critical of either her music or her behaviour. From this perspective then the composers in this study did not see themselves as part of a collective of women.

However, there were two aspects of women's music to which the SWM contributed in this era especially and which produced repercussions much later in the twentieth century. Firstly there was the presentation of the debate on a female aesthetic; while many women composers were unwilling to engage in this, Scott and Eggar managed to highlight the issue within the press and to the members of the SWM. They took aspects of suffrage ideology and their own experiences as professional musicians in order to formulate their own agenda for contemporary music. It is noteworthy that Ethel Smyth and Virginia Woolf were having the same debate concerning women's literature, decades after the SWM had raised the issue within music.[1] In some respects the debate within women's music is more reminiscent of second-wave feminism than the aims of the suffrage movement.

Secondly the SWM's most significant contribution to chamber music was through their connection with Walter Willson Cobbett. The Cobbett competitions for the composition of phantasies had been established six years before the formation of the SWM but the relationship between Cobbett and the Society enabled Scott and Eggar to regularly voice their opinions. They gave encouragement as well as information to women musicians in general through their contributions to the journal *Chamber Music*. This meant a far wider audience was reached than merely their own members. Although the composers in this study were not vocal about their identities as women composers – Smyth being the notable exception – they composed within the context of the suffrage movement and the SWM's campaign. Indeed being a member of the SWM was a political statement. In any case, perhaps the greatest significance of the organisation is that it captured the spirit of the times, articulating the unspoken both for its own members and outsiders like Maddison and Owen.

Assessing how 'successful' the chamber works of these composers are is dependent on definitions of 'success'. Unsurprisingly, none of these works has a place in the musical canon; however, neither the works nor their composers have been completely invisible in music history.

As mentioned in the introduction, Paula Higgins argues that the assumed reasons for women's invisibility – lack of institutional training, lack of published work, lack of versatility in only composing for smaller forces, lack of professional status and lack of originality – need to be investigated further.[2] Against these

1 See Christopher Wiley, 'When a Woman Speaks the Truth about her Body'.

2 Higgins, 'Women in Music, Feminist Criticism and Guerilla Musicology', p. 189.

'assumptions', the women in this study, despite writing a diverse range of chamber music, can be judged as being perhaps surprisingly successful. Three had formal institutional training at the RAM; of those who did not, two went abroad for intensive individual lessons. All the works were published – apart from Owen's, produced while she was still at the RAM – and the works exhibit women composers not confining themselves to small works. Indeed Spain-Dunk, Smyth, Maddison, Owen and Barns had also written or went on to compose orchestral works or opera. While Spain-Dunk, Owen and Barns were also performers and Verne-Bredt did a considerable amount of teaching, it was not uncommon for professional composers to combine composition with these activities. Their presence as professional composers was not felt at this point, however, in the conservatoires.

The lack of originality is weighty criticism that has been levied against women composers and has been used as a reason to exclude them from the musical canon. Creative women, however, have had a difficult relationship with the concept of originality (linked with genius) as a value judgement. Citron suggests this is due to creative men needing to place a higher value on this attribute than women feel is necessary. She cites the concept of critic Harold Bloom, 'anxiety of influence' where '[t]he male needs to remove the onus of the (male) precursor's style and presence, and the only way to do so is to destroy, to kill that ontological weight'.[3] It could be posited, therefore, that the analyst should not expect to find this quality within music by women who value 'relationship and connectedness'.[4]

Christine Battersby argues that 'to see the significance of an individual creator it is necessary to situate her within a collective, or rather series of collectives, of tradition'.[5] In this sense the small sample of women in this research are viewed as part of the rich female musical world – but not yet a rich tradition – at the beginning of the twentieth century. They were not creatively isolated – as many had been in the previous centuries – and were visible in musical society, having their works played in both public and private arenas. Their music was part of recitals, salons and private music making. For the first time, their concerns were articulated and campaigned for publicly by a collective of women (SWM). Their chamber music is a product of their musical education, their place in society, and it reflects their identities as women who composed. Rather than producing a woman of 'genius' whose innovation led to a place in the mainstream canon, as a group they produced a body of work which advanced women's music, made it more visible and created opportunity for future generations.

3 Citron, *Gender and the Musical Canon*, p. 69.

4 Ibid.

5 Battersby, *Gender and Genius: Towards a Feminist Aesthetics*, p. 157.

Appendix 1
List of People Mentioned in the Text

The following is an annotated list of selected people mentioned in the text. It is not intended to provide exhaustive information but where appropriate includes references for further reading.

Aldridge, Amanda (1866–1956)
Aldridge was the daughter of black actor Ira Aldridge and Swedish opera singer Amanda Pauline von Brandt. She started composing under the pseudonym Montague Ring after training as a singer under Jenny Lind at the RCM. She became a renowned teacher and went on to publish many songs, often using lyrics from African American poets, as well as works for other instrumental combinations.

Backhouse, Rhoda (dates unknown)
Backhouse was a violinist and viola player specialising in chamber music. She had studied with Edith Knocker and Leopold Aver, performing her first London recital in 1917, the same year that she joined the SWM. She later formed her own string quartet the Backhouse Quartet.

Bantock, Granville (1868–1946)
Bantock was taught firstly by Gordon Saunders at Trinity College and then at the RAM by Frederick Corder. He was associated with using oriental influences in his works such as the symphonic poem collection *Curse of Kehama.* He was married to Helena Bantock and set some of her poetry. Bantock went on to organise the weekly orchestral concerts in New Brighton, programming works by many contemporary British composers including Parry, Stanford, Corder, German and Cowen. He then became director of the Midland Institute of Music supplementing his compositional activities.

Batten, Mabel (1856–1916)
Batten was from an aristocratic background and was one of the most highly regarded amateur lieder singers of her generation. She is perhaps best known for being the subject of a John Singer Sargent painting and for being the lover of the writer Radclyffe Hall. Although she was also painted by other artists including

Edward Poynter, Sargent's image of Batten singing with an exposed throat and closed eyes, remains in the public consciousness. Having married George Batten, Mabel had an affair with the poet Wilfred Scawen Blunt in the 1880s before meeting Radclyffe Hall in 1907. Hall and Batten continued their relationship until Batten's death in 1916. For further information on Sargent's paintings of Mabel Batten, Elsie Swinton and Ethel Smyth see Suzanne Raitt, 'The Singers of Sargent: Mabel Batten, Elsie Swinton and Ethel Smyth', *Women: A Cultural Review*, 3/1 (Spring, 1992): pp. 23–29.

Bax, Arnold (1883–1953)
Bax began his studies with Frederick Corder at the RAM in 1900, where his contemporaries were composers Montague Phillips, Eric Coates and York Bowen as well as pianists Myra Hess and Irene Scharrer. As a student he was inspired by Wagner and Strauss, and in 1904 he won the Charles Lucas Medal for his Symphonic Variations which were then also performed at the RCM. Bax travelled considerably in the early 1900s and had a keen interest in Ireland, which is reflected in his works. His music was widely played in his lifetime but declined after his death, his best-known work perhaps being the tone poem *Tintagel.* He was often criticised, however, by commentators such as Joseph Holbrooke for producing music that was too complex. He married in 1911, although he maintained a long-lasting relationship with the pianist Harriet Cohen, and he considered his creative highpoint to be during the years of the First World War. During the Second World War he found it increasingly difficult to produce music and instead wrote his memoirs entitled *Farewell My Youth.*

Bedford, Herbert (1867–1945)
While professionally Bedford was a portrait painter specialising in miniatures, he had received musical education at the GSM. His compositions included an unpublished opera *Kit Marlowe,* Symphony *The Optimist*, a musical setting of Act II from *Romeo and Juliet*, *Summer Dawn* for contralto and orchestra, symphonic poem *Saving the Wind*, other orchestral works and song settings. Bedford also published *An Essay on Modern Unaccompanied Song* in 1923 and a biography of Robert Schumann in 1925. In 1935 he was the first English composer to receive the Brahms medal in Hamburg and at the time of his death he was a representative on the Permanent Council for the International Co-operation of Composers. Married to Liza Lehmann, he was an Associate of the SWM and was a member of the SWM Composer Group.

Bilsand, Ethel (1892–1982)
Bilsand was a soprano, composer and pianist who studied composition at the RAM with John McEwen and singing with Agnes Larkcom. Bilsand later became

Professor of Singing at the same institution. Her successful career as a singer included Crystal Palace and Proms performances and she was signed by agents Ibbs and Tillett in the 1925/6 season. She had compositions performed as part of the SWM concerts in the 1913/14 season, which may have been one of the reasons why she wrote instrumental chamber music in this period, as an unpublished Quartette for violins, cello and piano, *Idyll and Harlequinade* for cello and piano (1913) and Three Suites for violin and piano (c.1910) have been recently discovered. For further information see http://refuge.wikispaces.com/Bilsland?f=print.

Bliss, Arthur (1891–1975)

After attending Rugby School and Cambridge University where he studied counterpoint and fugue with Charles Wood, Bliss entered the RCM in 1913 until the outbreak of war in August 1914. He was a contemporary of Herbert Howells, Eugene Goossens, Arthur Benjamin and Ivor Gurney, but was not enamoured by the teaching style of Charles Stanford. Bliss fought in the First World War, and after the end of hostilities to which he lost his brother Kennard, he started composing again including writing music for Nigel Playfair and Arnold Bennett's production of *As You Like It* at the Lyric Theatre. In the 1920s he became Director of Music at the BBC and was influential in programming music and re-considering the BBC's attitude to what should be broadcast. He wrote a wide range of symphonic music and opera including *The Olympians* in 1949.

Bridge, Frank (1879–1941)

Bridge was born in Brighton and was taught composition by Charles Stanford at the RCM. In the early twentieth century Bridge's chamber music was well played and successful in Cobbett competitions. He tended to write abstract music rather than encompass poetry, religion or mysticism as others were doing. The number of phantasies that Bridge wrote in the 1900s, can be argued to have had an effect on the structures of his other music such as delaying the return of the main theme until the final movement in multi-movement works. Later in the 1920s and 1930s Bridge embraced modernism, which appealed to a very different, and arguably smaller audience. Following his death in 1941 there was a decline in performances of his works, although his music is now being championed by musicologists and British music enthusiasts. For more information see Anthony Payne, *Frank Bridge: Radical and Conservative* (London, 1999).

Bright, Dora Estella (Mrs Knatchbull) (1863–1951)

Pianist and composer, Dora Bright was part of a group of young composers called the 'Party', having studied composition at the RAM with Ebenezer Prout. The group included composition students Ethel Boyce, Moir Clark, Edward German, A.J. Greenaway and William Scott, who attended concerts together, supporting each other in their early compositional activities. In 1888 Bright was the first woman to win the Charles Lucas medal for composition, which was later won by other women such as Susan Spain-Dunk. She established a piano career including a performance of her own Concerto in A minor at the Crystal Palace in 1891, but performed less frequently after her marriage to Captain Knatchbull in 1892. Her second piano concerto was performed in 1892 in Cologne and her Ballet music in London in 1907.

Bruckshaw, Kathleen (c.1877–1921)
From an Irish background, Bruckshaw made her piano début at the Crystal Palace under August Manns aged 12, although she may have been older. When Liszt pupil Bernard Stavenhagen heard her, she was offered free tuition at the Liszt classes in Weimar and staying for three years she gave performances with the Berlin Philharmonic and the Kain Orchestra in Munich. Having returned to London, Ferruccio Busoni heard her play and invited her to return to Weimar as he was now leading the Liszt classes. Her compositional development was encouraged through correspondence with the composer Edward MacDowell and following his death in 1905 she published a piano piece *In Remembrance* in his honour.

Bruckshaw had work performed as part of the SWM concerts in the 1913/14 season and was a member of the SWM Composer Group; her piano concerto was performed at the 1914 Proms under Henry Wood. During the First World War she renounced her German connections and composed *The Munitions Workers Song* for the opening ceremony of the Princesses Theatre in Crayford in 1916, which was performed by Brucksaw and Charles Mott. Married to mechanical engineer Seymour Darlington, she died after an illness at the age of 44. One of the few sources on Bruckshaw for further information is Valerie Chancellor, 'Kathleen Bruckshaw (1877?–1921): a Forgotten Pianist and Composer', *Musical Opinion*, 1488 (May/June 2012): pp. 34–35.

Chaminade, Cécile (1857–1944)
Born in Paris, Chaminade first studied piano with her mother. As her father would not allow her to enter the Conservatoire, she then continued to study piano and composition privately with Benjamin Godard among others. She made her professional piano début at the Salle Pleyel in 1877 and the following year gave the first recital of her own works. Having initially composed opera, symphonic works and ballet she confined herself to more profitable songs and piano works after her father's death in 1878. She developed huge followings of fans in England and America where hundreds of Chaminade clubs were formed to disseminate her music. In June 1892 she made her first visit to London, where she began to give annual recitals, her Organ Prelude was played at Queen Victoria's funeral in 1901 and from 1913 she returned to record piano rolls for the Æolian company. During her visit to London in June 1914 the SWM organised a concert in her honour as

she had agreed to become president 1913/14. In her later years the popularity of her music had declined considerably and she suffered ill health including having her left foot amputated due to decalcification caused by her extreme vegetarian diet. For more detailed information on Chaminade's life and works see Marcia J. Citron, *Cécile Chaminade: A Bio-Bibliography* (Westport, 1988).

Clarke, Rebecca (1886–1979)
Clarke was a founding member of the SWM in 1911, having studied violin firstly at the RAM until her father withdrew her in 1905 after her harmony tutor proposed to her, subsequently she went to the RCM. By 1912 she was employed by Henry Wood as part of the viola section of the Queen's Hall Orchestra and in the years after the First World War developed her chamber playing as well as composing. Her best-known works, Viola Sonata (1919) and Piano Trio (1921), were both written for the Berkshire Festival of Music competitions supported by American patron Elizabeth Sprague Coolidge. During the Second World War, Clarke moved permanently to the USA, where she worked as a nanny as well as continuing to compose. In 1944 she married James Friskin with whom she had been a student at the RCM. The Rebecca Clarke Society was founded to promote her music and research into her life see www.rebeccaclarke.org.

Cohen, Harriet (1895–1967)
Cohen became an international concert pianist, who specialised in the works of Bach as well as promoting contemporary British composers and had many pieces dedicated to her, including Vaughan Williams's Piano Concerto and much of Bax's piano music. She had studied at the RAM with Tobias Matthay and Frederick Corder but like Myra Hess ceased composing after graduating. Towards the end of her career she injured her right hand and for a number of years played with her left hand only before retiring in 1960. Valuable information on her life and London's musical society is contained in her memoirs *A Bundle of Time: The Memoirs of Harriet Cohen* (London, 1969).

Corder, Frederick (1852–1932)
Having trained at the RAM, Corder initially forged a career as a conductor and composer, supplementing these activities with translations of Wagner published with his wife. He is perhaps most influential, however, as a teacher becoming Professor of Composition at the RAM in 1888. He supported a generation of British composers including Arnold Bax, Granville Bantock and Morfydd Owen, who were taught in the German tradition. Corder went on to found the Society of British Composers in 1905 and published *A History of the Royal Academy of Music from 1822 to 1922* (London, 1922), which gives a detailed insight into the early years of the institution.

Dale, Benjamin (1885–1943)

Dale studied composition and organ at the RAM with Frederick Corder, Howard Jones, Herbert Lake and H.W. Richards. His compositions included an orchestral overture *The Tempest,* which was performed at the Queen's Hall in 1902, Piano Sonata in D minor which was played by both Myra Hess and Edwin York Bowen, *Romance and Finale* for viola and orchestra which was championed by Lionel Tertis and *Sextett* for six violas. Dale was appointed Professor at the RAM in 1909, however, during the First World War he was interned in Germany. On his return he continued to compose but also took positions as an examiner for the Associated Board and worked for the BBC Music Advisory Panel.

Darke, Harold (1888–1976)

Darke was a composer specialising in choral music who became a member of the SWM in 1914, having served on the committee of the RCM Union with Marion Scott. He was an organist, choral conductor, examiner, lecturer and adjudicator. There is an undated letter in the SWM archive from Katherine Eggar to SWM members informing them that the SWM choir would be reinstated with Darke as its conductor. As well as choral music, Darke's output included a symphony entitled 'Switzerland', Two Fantasies for string orchestra and a Fantasy for organ. In 1919 he founded the St Michael's Singers and was made CBE in 1966.

Davies, Fanny (1861–1934)

Davies was an international piano soloist, who had studied under Charles Hallé and Reinecke in Leipzig. She went on to study in Frankfurt and received piano lessons from Clara Schumann. She made her first public appearance as a child by playing the Beethoven *Funeral March* from memory at Birmingham Town Hall. Davies developed a wide repertoire through her career including performances of Brahms – whom she had known in Germany – Beethoven, Schumann and works by contemporary composers.

Daymond, Emily (1866–1949)

Daymond was a composer who was active in the SWM, having work played in the 1913/14 SWM concert season, as well as being an SWM Composer Group member. She had studied at the RCM with Hubert Parry and completed her undergraduate degree at Oxford in 1896 and her doctorate of music in 1901. She was the first woman to hold attain a PhD in music in the UK, although it was not awarded for 20 years. Later she was primarily involved in music education, teaching in the RCM Junior Department, and the Royal Holloway College for Women.

Dunhill, Thomas F. (1877–1946)

After studying first piano and then composition at the RCM between 1893 and 1901, Dunhill started to lecture, teach at Eton and tour for the ABRSM, as well as to continue to compose. He became influential as a critic and commentator in the press and in 1907 he founded the Thomas Dunhill Chamber Concerts in order to provide a second hearing of new works, which had already received a first performance. The concerts had a wide scope including works by British and non-British composers.

Eugénie, Empress, Maria Eugenia Ignacia Augusta de Montijo (1826–1920)

Having married Napoleon III in 1853 and becoming one of the most politically powerful women in France, Eugénie spent her later years in exile in Chiselhurst and then in Farnborough. She was a long-time friend of Queen Victoria having met her as a young woman on official state visits, and promoted Ethel Smyth's music to the Queen. Smyth was Eugénie's neighbour during her English exile and impressed her through both her music and her militant suffragette activities; Eugénie became a powerful advocate for Smyth's career.

Ewing, Alexander (1830–1895)

Alexander Ewing was a Scottish composer who had studied in Heidelberg and was an amateur musician, composer and served in the British army from 1855–1889.

Fox, Dorothy Kalitha (1894–1934)

There is little information on Fox, however she appears to have specialised in writing chamber music including Sonata for Viola and Piano (c.1925) and *Chant* Élégiaque (1922). She was in correspondence with Katherine Eggar concerning the return of a manuscript that she had sent to the SWM; Eggar also kept clippings of Fox's obituaries after her suicide in 1934.

Friskin, James (1886–1967)

Friskin was a pianist and composer who studied at the RCM with Dannreuther, Hartvigson and Stanford. His early chamber music had success in the Cobbett Phantasy competitions and until the First World War he taught at the Royal Normal College for the Blind. During the war he emigrated to America and went on to teach at the Julliard School. In the 1940s he was reunited with composer Rebecca Clarke.

Gates, Cecilia (dates unknown)
Gates was a second violinist who had studied with Sainton, Ludwig Straus and Whitehouse. She was only a member of the SWM for one season in 1917 however, she often played professionally with SWM members Beatrice Langley, May Mukle and Rhoda Backhouse. Gates was a member of the first all female string quartet as well as the Nora Clench Quartet and the Langley-Mukle Quartet. She established a reputation as a chamber musician, the composer Ernest Walker dedicated his Sonata in A minor for violin and piano to her.

German, Edward (1862–1936)
Having studied with Walter Hay in Shrewsbury and later at the RAM, Edward German became one of the foremost English composers of his generation. While at the RAM, he was a member of the group 'The Party' and went on to compose music for *Richard III* at the Globe in 1889 and for Henry Irving's production of *Henry VIII* at the Lyceum in 1891. From a musical family, German had two sisters who helped him copy the parts for his first operetta *The Two Poets* – later titled *The Rival Poets* – and were instrumental in encouraging him to approach Henry Irving. The very different trajectories of the musical activities of the siblings, highlights the different roles men and women were expected to play in the late nineteenth century. For further information see William H. Scott, *Edward German: An Intimate Biography* (London, 1932).

Gibson, Henry (1882–1954)
Henry Gibson was a musician and composer who had studied at the GSM and the RCM with Stanford and Walter Parratt. He went on to develop a career as a composer, organist and choirmaster, as well as acting as musical secretary for Thomas Beecham. Gibson's compositions included *Cornish Legend* for viola and piano and *Gaelic Pipe March*, which was performed at the Proms in 1934. He was married to composer Susan Spain-Dunk, their son Alan Gibson (1911–1999) returned to Folkestone where Spain-Dunk's family had originated and was the Vicar of Sandgate 1964–1976.

Goossens, Eugene (1893–1962)
The conductor of the Carl Rosa Opera Company Eugene Goossens (1867–1958) and singer Annie Cook (1860–1946) had five children, the eldest, Eugene, became one of the leading British conductors of the twentieth century. The Goossens family was a musical phenomenon and included harpists Marie and Sidonie, french horn player Adolphe and oboist Léon. Eugene attended the Muziek-Conservatorium in Bruges before returning to Liverpool and then studied composition at the RCM under Charles Stanford. He had worked with many of the women considered in this book, including playing second violin in the Langley-Mukle Quartet who

rehearsed in Percy Grainger's rooms and participated in presenting Grainger's works to London audiences. In the mid-1910s, Goossens was an active chamber music composer and his output included a Cobbett competition winning Phantasy Quartet, which was performed by the London String Quartet at the Æolian Hall in April 1916.

Sisters Marie and Sidonie both had lengthy careers as harpists in London's orchestras, and while Adolphe died in the First World War, Leon's life was supposedly saved while serving in the army when a bullet was deflected by a cigarette case he was wearing in his breast pocket. The cigarette case had been a present from Ethel Smyth to Eugene as a thank you for conducting one of her works. For further information see Carole Rosen, *The Goossens: A Musical Century* (London, 1993).

Grainger, Percy (1882–1961)
Grainger was born in Brighton (Melbourne), Australia and made his first public appearance as a pianist in 1894. A year later he entered the Hoch Conservatorium in Frankfurt to study composition with Iwan Knorr, where he became part of the Frankfurt Group, who included Balfour Gardiner, Norman O'Neill, Roger Quilter and Cyril Scott, as well as becoming friends with Danish composer Herman Sandby. Having relocated to London in 1901, his most prolific period of recital playing was from 1910. He started to publish compositions and a concert of his works was undertaken in 1912. At the outbreak of war, he emigrated to the USA with his mother, where he was finally appointed as an Army Band Music Instructor. After his mother's suicide in 1922 he married Ella Ström and travelled extensively including founding his own museum in Melbourne in 1935. In later life Grainger worked with scientist Burnett Cross to build musical machines. For more detailed information see Malcolm Gillies, David Pear and Mark Carrell (eds), *Self-Portrait of Percy Grainger* (Oxford, 2006).

Gurney, Ivor (1890–1937)
Gurney was a contemporary of Herbert Howells and Ivor Novello at Gloucester Cathedral, before transferring to the RAM, studying composition firstly with Stanford and then after the First World War with Vaughan Williams. Gurney served during the war suffering from shellshock, and was admitted to a series of mental health institutions eventually dying of tuberculosis in the City of London Mental Hospital in Dartford. He produced two volumes of poetry based on his wartime experiences, as well as writing a considerable number of songs during a creatively fruitful period between 1919 and 1922. His friends who included Marion Scott and Herbert Howells supported him in preparing items for publication as well as financially. After Gurney's death they organised his manuscripts and published volumes of his best songs through Oxford University Press.

Haas, Alma (1847–1932)

Haas was a pianist and teacher whose pupils included Liza Lehmann. She made her performance début at the age of 14 with Mendelssohn's Piano Concerto in G minor and went on to study in Berlin with Theodor Kullak. Her performance career stalled in 1872 when she married Ernst Haas, a Professor of Sanskrit at UCL. After her husband's death in 1882, however, she resumed giving recitals and was a noted interpreter of Beethoven. She taught piano at Bedford College, Kings College and was made Professor of the RCM in 1887. She became a member of the SWM and attended SWM Composer Group meetings.

Hall, Radclyffe (1880–1943)

Born Marguerite, Radclyffe Hall had a disrupted childhood with her father leaving the family just after she was born, followed by her violent mother remarrying the singer Albert Visetti who made sexual advances towards her in her teenage years. As a young woman Radclyffe Hall gained financial independence by inheriting her father's estate which allowed her to shun convention and develop her lesbian identity including changing her name to John. She had a series of volatile relationships with women including singer Agnes Nicholls, Mabel Batten, Batten's cousin Una Troubridge and Russian refugee Evguenia Souline. Radclyffe Hall is best known as the author of *The Well of Loneliness* which in 1928 was banned for containing graphic details of lesbian relationships despite legislation that would have made lesbianism illegal having been defeated in parliament in 1921. For further information see Diana Souhami, *The Trials of Radclyffe Hall* (London, 1999).

Halsey, Ernest (dates unknown)

Little is known about composer Halsey, however he appears to have been most prominent in the early twentieth century when *The Franklins Maid* was performed at the Proms in 1908 and *The Little Glove* in 1913. *Suite de Ballet* was performed by Dan Godfrey in Bournemouth, during the 1906/7 season.

Hamaton, Adela (dates unknown)

Hamaton was a composer who was actively involved with the SWM by giving employment advice to members and having her own work played as part of the SWM 1913/14 concert season. In 1926 she became the principal of Middlesex College of Music and after her retirement in 1931 she founded the London Musical Club. The Club at 21 Holland Park, was designed as cheap accommodation for struggling music students or those visiting London for auditions. The combination of space for living and instrumental practice proved to be popular and attracted musicians from around the world.

Hartog, Cécile (1857–1940)
Born in London, Hartog was from a Jewish background, and studied piano and composition privately as well as with Frederick Cowen at the RAM. As a composer she published mainly piano pieces and songs but also wrote music for plays. Her setting of Browning's *The Year's at the Spring* was performed at the Proms in 1909. She was also a member of the SWM Composer Group, having work played in the SWM 1913/14 concert season.

Hayward, Marjorie (1885–1953)
Hayward was a violinist who had studied at the RAM and then with Czech violinist Otaker Ševčík. She became Professor of Violin at the RAM and specialised in chamber music, leading her own string quartet as well as the Pro Musica String Quartet and performing with the English Ensemble. In 1924 Hayward became the leader of the Virtuoso Quartet, which had been established by The Gramophone Company (HMV) for the purpose of producing recordings.

Henkel, Lily (1860–1936)
Born in Nottingham, Henkel studied piano in Karlsruhe and later for two years with Clara Schumann in Frankfurt, where she became a close friend of fellow pupil Mathilde Verne. On returning to England, Henkel performed with Sarasate at the Nottingham Orchestral and Philharmonic Drawing Room Concerts as well as the Promenade concerts, the Queen's Hall and St James's Hall. She was a chamber music specialist and in 1910 formed the Henkel Piano Quartet. The Quartet in various guises performed regularly until 1927; *The Times* reported in January 1911 that for the first concert the Quartet consisted of Mme Lily Henkel, M.M. Alfred Hobday, Fritz Hirt and Ivor James. They performed Piano Quartets in G minor by Brahms and Mozart and the Phantasy Quartet in F♯ minor by Frank Bridge.

Herzogenberg, Heinrich von (1843–1900) and Elisabet (Lisl) (1847–1892)
In 1868 pianist and organist Elisabet moved from Vienna to Dresden to marry composer Heinrich von Herzogenberg. Heinrich had studied composition at the Vienna Conservatoire where he had first met Brahms (who had taught Elisabet) and the Herzogenbergs became part of a musical circle in Leipzig where they developed close friendships with not only Brahms but also Clara Schumann and a young Ethel Smyth. In 1885 Heinrich became Professor of Composition at the Hochschule in Berlin until 1889 when his ill health necessitated an absence, before retiring completely just before his death in 1900. Elisabet died eight years previously from a heart condition aged 45.

Hess, Myra (1890–1965)

Hess received the Ada Lewis scholarship at the age of 12, to study with Tobias Matthay at the RAM. She made her début when she was 17, under Beecham at the Queen's Hall playing the 4th concertos by Beethoven and Saint-Saëns. She had a close relationship with her cousin, the pianist Irene Scharrer who was also a Matthay student at the same time as Hess. The cousins formed a piano duo and Hess went on to develop an international career both as a piano soloist and as a chamber musician. She is best remembered for instigating the lunchtime concerts at the National Gallery during the Second World War, receiving the DBE in 1941 for her services. Although she had a wide performance repertoire she did not make many recordings, preferring live performance.

Holbrooke, Joseph (1878–1958)

Holbrooke was a composer as well as pianist and conductor but was perhaps most influential as an advocate for British composers. He published widely on the British composition including his candid volume *Contemporary British Composers* (London: Cecil Palmer, 1925). Holbrooke's patron Lord Howard de Walden assisted in gaining performances not only of Holbrooke's works but also for composers that Holbrooke wished to support. Holbrooke was able to write for large forces such as the opera trilogy *The Cauldron on Annwn* with a libretto by Lord Walden, who published as T.E. Ellis, however, he also wrote smaller scale instrumental pieces as well as opera and orchestral music. Performances of his works declined at the end of his life but articles on his music began to appear again in the 1990s.

Holland, Ruby (dates unknown)

Ruby Holland was a member of the SWM and took part in composition activities. The British Library hold published piano works by her from 1918 onwards but her dates of birth and death are unknown. Another Ruby Holland (1914–2006) was also a composer but appears not to be related to the Ruby Holland discussed here.

Holmés, Augusta (1847–1903)

Of Irish background, Holmés spent her childhood in France studying piano and organ privately after being encouraged by her godfather poet Alfred de Vigny. She became part of Franck's musical circle in Paris, although it is unclear whether she was taught composition by him or indeed what the nature was of their relationship. She went on to have a long-term relationship with writer Catulle Mendès having a family of five children. As a composer Holmés was one of the few women that Ethel Smyth had contact with. Holmés and Smyth had similar interest in writing opera and orchestral music, however only one of Holmés's operas *La Montagne Noire* was staged in Paris in 1895. For further information see Karen Henson, 'In the House of Disillusion: Augusta Holmés and La Montagne Noir', *Cambridge Opera Journal*, ix/3 (1997): pp. 233–62.

Horne, Elsie (dates unknown)
Pianist Elsie Horne became a stalwart member of the SWM in 1912 and took part in many composition activities, including becoming a member of the SWM Composer Group. Her work was played at the first public SWM concert at the Queen's Small Hall in 1912 and she went on to organise a concert at the SWM headquarters in 1915, which included her own works and was reviewed in the *Musical Times*. She became president of the SWM in 1933 and after her death a memorial prize was established in her honour.

Horne, Marie (dates unknown)
Singer Marie Horne was the sister of Elsie and was also involved in the SWM as a composer, joining with her sister in 1912. She had work played in the 1912 Queen's Small Hall SWM concert and during the 1913/14 SWM concert season. In addition she wrote an opera *The Belle of Brittany* jointly with composer Howard Talbot in 1908.

Howell, Dorothy (1898–1982)
As a young woman Howell shot to fame after her orchestral piece *Lamia* was premiered by Henry Wood at the Proms in 1919, and she was pursued back to her home town of Stourbridge by press desperate to interview a 'girl' composer. Having studied at convent schools in Birmingham, Bonn and Clapham, she became a piano student of Percy Waller and Tobias Matthay, and a composition student of J.B. McEwen at the RAM at the age of 15. The success of *Lamia* was followed by *Danse Grotesque* for orchestra being performed at Buckingham Palace in November 1919 and performances of the ballet *Koong Shee* (1921), Cobbett prize winning Phantasy for violin and piano (1921), Piano Concerto (1923) and orchestral piece *The Rock* (1928) at the Last Night of the Proms.

In 1924, Howell became Professor of Harmony and Composition at the RAM, also teaching at the Tobias Matthay Pianoforte School and the Birmingham School of Music among others. After serving in the Women's Land Army in the Second World War, she found getting her works accepted for publication increasingly difficult and ceased composing for larger ensemble.

Howells, Herbert (1892–1983)
Howells was born in Gloucestershire and received his early musical education at Gloucester Cathedral by becoming an articled pupil of Herbert Brewer alongside Ivor Gurney and Ivor Novello. One of his seminal musical experiences in this

period was hearing *A Theme of Thomas Tallis* by Vaughan Williams at the 1910 Gloucester Festival. In 1912 Howells followed Ivor Gurney to study at the RCM with Stanford, where his contemporaries included Arthur Bliss, Arthur Benjamin and Eugene Goossens. Howells went on to win the 1917 Cobbett competition for a phantasy string quartet however, much of his output of both chamber and orchestral music was removed by the composer, as he became hyper-sensitive to criticism of his works.

Hurlstone, William Yeates (1876–1906)
As the winner of the first Cobbett competition, Hurlstone showed early promise as a composer, particularly of chamber music, which included a Cello Sonata, Piano Quartet and a Piano Concerto. He had studied at the RCM with Charles Stanford who continued to support his compositional activities. Hurlstone was part of the early twentieth-century set of composers including Thomas Dunhill, Frank Bridge and Percy Grainger. At the time of his early death he had been appointed as Professor of Counterpoint at the RCM, and there was a sense of grief in the British musical community at his loss. For further information see Katharine Hurlstone (ed.), *William Hurlstone, Musician: Memories and Records by his Friends* (London, 1949).

Ireland, John (1879–1962)
Ireland destroyed much of his early chamber music and did not publish significantly until he was 29 years old. He fell between the 'Parry' group of composers and the later modernists, and although he was part of musical society, he did not achieve as many performances of his works as other contemporaries. A friend of composer Thomas Dunhill and critic Edwin Evans, he had a reputation for being a difficult man and had periods where he battled alcoholism. Despite this he had a successful career as a pianist and organist, editor, examiner for the Associated Board and professor at the RCM. He was keenly interested in literature especially the work of author Arthur Machen, and this permeated his music. He chose to write in smaller forms which were often linked thematically. For further information see Lewis Foreman (ed.), *The John Ireland Companion* (Woodbridge, 2011).

Johnstone, Lucie (dates unknown)
Johnstone was a song composer and contralto who, published under the pseudonym Lewis Carey. She was a regular member of the SWM Composer Group, and became a prolific ballad song-writer. Her songs were performed at the Ballad Concerts at the Royal Albert Hall in 1915.

Jones, Ernest (1879–1958)

Jones was the foremost follower of Freud's psychoanalytical methods in the UK. He founded the British Psycho-Analytical Society and *The International Journal of Psycho-Analysis*, as well as being involved of the rescue of and resettlement of Jews in the 1930s. After completing medical training in London in the 1890s, his psychoanalytical practice became successful during the First World War when his patients included D.H. Lawrence. Jones is reported as being a difficult man by colleagues and his early medical career stalled due to a series of complaints relating to inappropriate sexual behaviour towards children in his care. After living with Loe Kann his common law wife, he married the composer Morfydd Owen in 1917, who died in mysterious circumstances in 1918. He went on to marry Katharina Jokl in 1919, having four children together. For further information on Jones see Brenda Maddox, *Freud's Wizard: The Enigma of Ernest Jones* (London: John Murray, 2006).

Joseph, Jane (1894–1929)

Joseph is generally remembered as the amanuensis for Gustav Holst, however, during her short life she became a published composer of choral, orchestral and piano works. She had been a pupil of Holst's at St Paul's School and after studying at Cambridge she returned to London to assist Holst in his compositional work as well as at Morley College. After joining the SWM in 1919, she was also part of the team that instigated the Kensington Musical competition festival in 1922 and the Kensington Choral Society in 1925. Her unpublished works include a String Quartet and Oboe Quartet.

Klean, Bluebell (dates unknown)

Little is known about composer Bluebell Klean who had work played as part of the SWM 1913/14 concert season. From the programme of the Bournemouth Symphony Orchestra concert on 13 December 1917, when her Piano Concerto in E minor was played, we learn that she received her musical education in England and her other compositions include a Quintet in C minor and a Piano Trio in F, as well as numerous songs. McCann Collection, British Concert Programmes, RAM, London. See also http://landofllostcontent.blogspot.com/2009/08/bluebell-klean-composer-concertpianist.html

Lambert, Agnes H. (1860–1929)

Lambert was a composer, having songs performed at the Proms in 1908 and 1909. She then became a member of the SWM Composer Group and had work played as part of the SWM 1913/14 concert series.

Langley, Beatrice (1872–1958)

Langley was a solo and chamber violinist, forming the Langley-Mukle Quartet with cellist May Mukle. She was educated privately with Joseph Ludwig and Wilhemj, making her début at the Crystal Palace Saturday Concerts. Similarly to Mukle she toured the USA and other British colonies. She was married to journalist and author Basil Tozer, and was an active member of the SWM when in London.

Lara, Adelina de (1872–1961)

De Lara was a pianist and composer who had trained the Frankfurt Conservatoire with Iwan Knorr and Clara Schumann. Her career spanned 75 years from her début in 1891 at St James's Hall, until her farewell recital at the Wigmore Hall in 1954. She particularly specialised in Robert Schumann's music and was an advocate for Clara Schumann's style of playing. De Lara remained active throughout her career as a performer, teacher, writer and broadcaster. Although she never attained considerable recognition as a composer she wrote a number of piano pieces, songs and a Piano Concerto. Her autobiography *Finale* was published in 1955.

Long, Kathleen (1896–1968)

Long studied piano at the RCM with Herbert Sharpe and then taught at the same institution for 44 years. She became known as chamber musician, interpreter of Mozart and contemporary British composers. She formed piano quartet *The English Ensemble* and played in particular with the violinist Antonio Brosa.

Macfarren, George (1813–1887)

Macfarren studied first with his father and Charles Lucas before being admitted to the RAM in 1829 to study composition under Cipriani Potter. Macfarren then taught at the RAM becoming its principal in 1875. He was very much part of London's musical society helping to form the Society of British Musicians in 1834 as well as the Handel Society in 1844. He aspired to be an opera composer, his output included *King Charles II* and *Robin Hood* but later in life produced a greater amount of chamber music. He lost his sight in 1860 but continued to compose, teach and write.

Mackenzie, Alexander (1847–1935)

Mackenzie was a conductor and composer who, was influential for a generation of music students when he became Principal of the RAM in 1888. He was involved in the reorganisation of the institution to make it competitive with the newer RCM. In his lifetime Mackenzie enjoyed considerable success as a composer, producing a wide range of orchestral, choral and chamber works and as such was at the centre of British musical society. His influence reached further by appointments including President of the International Musical Society, President of the Royal College of Organists, organising international congresses of contemporary music in Vienna and London, and receiving a knighthood in 1895.

Macpherson, Stewart (1865–1941)
Macpherson was educated at the RAM and became Professor of Composition there in 1887. He held many institutional and examiner posts including being a member of the Board of Studies for the University of London, External Examiner for Music at the National University of Ireland and Chairman of the Music Teacher's Association. He had an influence stretching beyond his immediate pupils through his published student handbooks such as *Practical Harmony* (1894), *Practical Counterpoint* (1900), *Rudiments of Music* (1903) and *Music and Its Appreciation* (1910).

Maitland, John Fuller (1856–1936)
Having studied piano with Dannreuther and also performing as a harpsichord player, Fuller Maitland made his career as critic and music journalist with the *Pall Mall Gazette* and the *Manchester Guardian.* He had an interest in English Folk Song, helping to found the Folk Song Society in 1898 and contributing to a volume on English song with Lucy Broadwood.

Marshall, M.E. (dates unknown)
M.E. Marshall is likely to be M. Ethel M. Marshall who was pianist and taught at Withington Girls School in Manchester. She studied with Fraülein Hoffmann, Frank Merrick and later at Manchester University. She joined the SWM in 1915 and took part in a concert for younger SWM composers in 1920, also having *Baby Seed Song* performed at the Proms in the same year.

Mely, Marie (Comtesse Vanden Heuvel)
Mely was a singer and teacher, who also had her compositions played as part of the SWM 1913/14 concert season.

Moger, Gladys (dates unknown)
Moger was a singer educated at the RCM and also spent time in Paris. Joining the SWM in 1917, she went on to teach singing at Tunbridge Wells High School, Queen's College, Abbey School in Reading and High School Putney. In addition she taught music history, class singing, conducting, harmony and musical appreciation. She married the concert agent Philip Ashbrooke. Moger knew musicologist Edward Dent and collaborated on a booklet with him on music education in 1918.

Mukle, May (1880–1963)

Mukle was one of the foremost cellists of her generation, performing in public for the first time at the age of ten. She was the daughter of orchestrion maker Leopold Mukle and often performed with her sister Anne. Having studied at the RAM, Mukle toured extensively in Australia, Canada, USA and South Africa. She described herself as a chamber music specialist, playing in the Langley-Mukle Quartet and other ensembles including performances for the SWM.

O'Neill, Adine (1875–1947) and Norman (1875–1934)

Adine O'Neill is presently best remembered for being the wife of composer Norman O'Neill, however Adine was a well-known pianist having been a soloist for the Queen's Hall Promenade Concerts and recording for the BBC. She became the principal teacher of piano at St Paul's Girls School in the same department as Gustav Holst. She was active in the SWM and became President between 1921 and 1923 as the Society moved towards campaigning for more women to be included in British orchestras.

Norman O'Neill had started theory and composition lessons with his neighbour Arthur Somervell and also had support from John Fuller-Maitland and accompanist Henry Bird. He then transferred to the Frankfurt Hoch Conservatorium, where he was taught by Iwan Knorr at the suggestion of Joseph Joachim. O'Neill was part of a group of British composers who became known as the Frankfurt group.

While in Frankfurt studying piano with Clara Schumann, Adine studied harmony with Norman and they married in 1899. They continued their careers in London, where Norman's compositional output included instrumental chamber music and songs as well as theatre music, and Adine played for the Foundations of Music series for the BBC including recordings of Mozart, Haydn and French composers. They often gave joint chamber music concerts where Adine would perform Norman's works. For further information see Derek Hudson, *Norman O'Neill: A Life of Music* (London, 1945).

Parry, C. Hubert H. (1848–1918)

Parry was a composer and scholar who had a lasting impact on British composers not least through his position as principal of the RCM, a position he was appointed to in 1895 having previously been Professor of Music History. He had studied at Oxford and was employed for a number of years as an underwriter at Lloyds, although during his employment he continued to study piano with Dannreuther, through who he became a devotee to the music of Wagner. Parry benefited from the support of George Grove who gave him the position of sub-editor for the first edition of the *Dictionary of Music and Musicians*, as well as employing him when the RCM opened in 1883. Although Parry is known for large-scale choral works, his earlier output included a considerable amount of instrumental chamber music including the Piano Trio in E Minor (1877), Nonet for wind instruments (1877) and Piano Quartet (1879). For further information see Jeremy C. Dibble, *C. Hubert H. Parry: his Life and Music* (Oxford, 1992).

Phillips, Charles (1865–?)

Phillips was a singer who studied at the RAM with Edwin Holland and Signor Moretti in Milan. He launched his career in 1892 at the St James's Hall and went on to have a professional concert career as well as building a large teaching practice, becoming Professor of Singing at the RAM. Until 1913 he was married to composer Ethel Barns and together they organised and performed in the Barns Phillips Concert Series.

Polignac, Princesse de (Winnaretta Singer) (1865–1943)

Descended from the Singer family who made their fortune producing sewing machines, Winnaretta was born in New York, but travelled to Paris, London, Devon and finally returned to Paris after the death of her father in 1875. Winnaretta had a lesbian identity, and her first marriage to Prince Louis de Scey-Montbéliard was annulled, after which she entered a mutually understanding and creatively supportive marriage with Prince Edmond de Polignac, who was a composer. She went on to have numerous affairs with women in Parisian society including Ethel Smyth and author Violet Trefusis.

With her husband, Winnaretta established a musical salon where she acted as a patron for contemporary music for composers such as Ravel, Fauré and Debussy as well as women such as Ethel Smyth and Adela Maddison. After Edmund died, Winnaretta increased the amount of money she applied to the arts and started commissioning new works by younger French composers including Satie, Milhaud and Poulenc. She was also involved in charitable work concerned with public housing conditions in Paris, working with Marie Curie to establish radiology units in the First World War, and after her death the Foundation Singer-Polignac continued to distribute funds to science and the arts. For more detailed information see Sylva Kahan, *Music's Modern Muse: A Life of Winnaretta Singer, Princesse de Polignac* (Rochester, 2003).

Prout, Ebenezer (1835–1909)

Prout was a music theorist, organist, pianist and composer who despite mainly being self taught in music went on to teach at the National Training School of Music, at the RAM from 1879 and the GSM from 1884. His influence extended not only to his pupils at these institutions but to generations of music students through his series of treatises on harmony, counterpoint, canon, fugue, musical forms and the orchestra published over ten years between 1889 and 1899. He later also published an edition of Handel's *Messiah* in 1902 and other editions of both Bach and Handel. He had competitive success with his early instrumental chamber music including String Quartet in E, Piano Quartet in E and Piano Quintet in G, however, his larger scale orchestral, choral and organ works along with the rest of his output are rarely played.

Ronald, Landon (1873–1938)
Ronald is primarily considered to be one of the foremost British conductors of his generation conducting, among others the New Symphony Orchestra, the Scottish Orchestra, the Birmingham Symphony Orchestra and the New Birmingham Symphony Orchestra. He had trained at the RCM under Stanford and Parry and was also a pianist and composer, writing ballet, orchestral and stage music, his song *Down in the Forest* is perhaps his best known work.

Sainton, Prosper (1813–1890)
Sainton was a French violinist who having studied in Toulouse and the Paris Conservatoire, moved to London in 1845. Here he was active chamber music player as well as leading the orchestra of the Philharmonic Society, the Royal Italian Opera at Covent Garden and the orchestra of Her Majesty's Theatre. His violin compositions were often performed by his pupils to show off their technique and his output included a large number of fantasies.

Saumarez Smith, Mabel (1873–1931)
Saumarez Smith was the daughter of William Saumarez Smith the Anglican Bishop of Sydney and Primate of Australia. Mabel was the second daughter of a large family and became a composer who was active in London in the early years of the SWM. She was a member of the SWM Composer Group, composing mainly songs, and had work played in the SWM 1913/14 concert season.

Sauret, Emile (1852–1920)
Sauret was a violinist and composer, who studied in France with De Bériot and Vieuxtemps developing his international career as a solo violinist in childhood. He was Professor of Violin at the RAM in London and in Stockholm, as well as for a short time at the GSM. Sauret's compositions were mainly for violin including violin concertos, Etudes and *Gradus and Parnassum* which, became standard works for violin students in the twentieth century.

Scharrer, Irene (1889–1971)
Scharrer was a pianist, studying first with her mother and then with Tobias Matthay at the RAM. Unlike her friends and fellow pianists Myra Hess and Harriet Cohen, she was briefly a member of the SWM in 1912. Scharrer had made her début

at St James's Hall in 1901 in a programme that included Mendelssohn's *Rondo Capriccioso* and Chopin's *Rondo in E Flat* and she went on to build a substantial career as a concert pianist specialising in nineteenth-century romantic music. She played for the Landon Ronald Symphony Concerts, the Richter-Hallé Concerts in Manchester and the Nikitsch Concerts at the Gewandhaus in Leipzig. She recorded frequently and one of her best-known recordings was Henry Litolff's *Concerto Symphonique no. 4* in 1933 conducted by Henry Wood. Scharrer was a visitor to philanthropist Frank Schuster's house on the Thames in the nineteen-teens, where Elgar is reported to have promised her the first performance of his piano concerto. The British Library holds an extensive collection of Scharrer recordings.

Schlesinger, Kathleen (1862–1953)
Active SWM member Schlesinger was born in Co. Down in Ireland before completing her education throughout Europe. She went on to become an early ethnomusicologist her many publications included *The Significance of Musical Instruments in the Evolution of Music* (1929) and *The Greek Aulos* (1939). In the mid-1910s she was in demand as a lecturer on folk music and the evolution of musical instruments including lectures at the British Museum, Victoria and Albert Museum, University of London and for the SWM. In 1914 she started a fellowship in Music Archaeology at Liverpool University and in 1916 met the Australian composer and fellow SWM member Elsie Hamilton. Schlesinger and Hamilton were both part of Rudolph Steiner's Anthroposophy movement and formed a close working collaboration to the extent that Hamilton produced music using Schlesinger's Harmonia a new language of music based on her work on Ancient Greek music systems. For further information see http://www.nakedlight.co.uk/pdf/articles/KS%20and%20EH%20biog.pdf.

Scholes, Percy (1877–1958)
Scholes was a music scholar, writer, journalist and broadcaster, who in 1918 founded *The Music Student Magazine*, which later became *Music Teacher*. He had a particular interest in promoting British composers by dedicating a special issue to Stanford, Mackenzie, Elgar, Bantock and Holst, as well as writing numerous articles on younger composers. Scholes went on to found the Home Music Study Union, which produced graded pieces for home learning and provided reading recommendations for improving historical and theoretical musical knowledge. Scholes embraced broadcasting in its early inception including recording technology. Among his published works were *The Listener's Guide to Music* (1919), *The Beginner's Guide to Harmony* (1922), *Everybody's Guide to Recorded Music* (1926) and his best-known work *The Oxford Companion to Music* (1938). His later positions included Music Editor for *The Radio Times*.

Schuster, Leo Francis Howard (Frank) (1852–1927)

Schuster was from a rich Jewish family and inherited money from his father's banking business. He was an eminent patron to composers, especially Elgar to who he left £7,000 in his will. Schuster particularly promoted contemporary music describing himself as having a 'conscientious curiosity' and hosted musical events at his houses in Westminster and Thames-at-Bray. His musical evenings became elaborate, culminating in the first performance of Elgar's Violin Concerto in 1910, when the dinner menu was themed according to the three movements of the work. In the 1920s, Schuster's financial situation made it necessary to sell his Westminster property and reduce his musical activities.

Scott, Cyril (1879–1970)

After a brief period of study in Frankfurt and then Liverpool in his early teens, Scott returned to the Frankfurt Hoch Conservatorium to study with Iwan Knorr and became part of the Frankfurt Group. His other friends included poet Stefan George who inspired Scott to write, as well as the stained glass window designer Melchior Lechter. He had early success with orchestral works being performed in Liverpool, Manchester, at the Proms in London and in Germany, but in the early 1900s he became a successful piano and song composer publishing with Elkin. In Britain his name was associated with short popular works, whereas in Germany he managed to gain performances of his operas such as *The Alchemist.* His eccentric behaviour and dress, as well as his interest in occultism have overshadowed his musical and literary output, with few performances of his works since his death.

Stanford, Charles Villiers (1852–1924)

Born in Dublin, Stanford's family were very much part of musical society and at age eight the composer had a march played as part of the pantomime at the Theatre Royal, Dublin. In 1862 he continued his performance and compositional education in London before studying at Cambridge. He later went to Leipzig to further develop with Reinecke and in Berlin with Keil. In addition to a professorship at Cambridge, in 1885 Stanford was appointed Professor at the Royal College of Music. A prolific composer whose output includes large-scale choral and orchestral works, performances of Stanford's pieces declined in his later years. Stanford was considered to be part of the 'Parry' group, which included Alexander Mackenzie, Hubert Parry and Frederick Cowen; its members developed their careers in the late nineteenth century and were influential in the education of British composers in the early twentieth century.

Swepstone, Edith (1885–1930)

Swepstone is an elusive composer but there is documentation showing 14 of her orchestral works were performed by Dan Godfrey with the Bournemouth

Municipal Orchestra and that she lectured at the City of London School. She also published settings of Robert Louis Stevenson for children in 1935. She had studied at the GSM but her music has not been located in manuscript form and is likely to have been destroyed.

Tovey, Donald Francis (1875–1940)

Tovey was tutored in piano playing by Sophie Weisse and subsequently gained the Nettleship Scholarship to study at Oxford. Having graduated he became a freelance musician, performing widely as a piano soloist and chamber musician in Austria, Germany and Britain. In this period he also began to compose, lecture, write essays and contribute to the *Encyclopaedia Britannica.* In 1914 he was elected Reid Chair of Music at Edinburgh University where he remained until his death in 1940.

During his time at Edinburgh, Tovey formed the Reid Orchestra, which gave a series of regular concerts but was not used as a vehicle for his own works. His compositions were, however, performed in London at the St James's and Chelsea Concerts and through the patron Edward Speyer at the Classical Concerts Society. Although his Piano Concerto was broadcast by the BBC after he received a knighthood in 1935, Tovey's career was very much split between being a pianist/scholar and a composer. His compositional output was not acknowledged to the same extent as his performing and scholarly writing and he did not complete another large work after the First World War.

Trefusis, Mary Lady (1869–1927)

Lady Mary Trefusis (neé Lady Lygon) was the daughter of the sixth Earl of Beauchamp, the wife of Henry Walter Hepburn-Stuart-Forbes-Trefusis and lady in waiting to Queen Mary. She was a patron of music – Elgar's 13th Enigma Variation is likely represent Trefusis – she also directed numerous choirs and was involved in the folk dance movement working with Cecil Sharp, and in 1904 formed the Association of Competitive Festivals with Mary Wakefield. The main character of the opera *The Rebel Maid* (1956) by Montague Phillips was also called Lady Mary Trefusis and was sung by Phillips's wife Clara Butterworth.

Verne, Adela (1877–1952)

Adela Verne was the youngest of the Verne family of musicians and received her piano education from her elder sister Mathilde, becoming an international pianist. She made her performance début aged 14 and toured widely until after the First World War, when she moved to the USA. On her return to England she continued to perform and also composed *Queen Elizabeth's March* for the Grenadier Guards in 1938. Her son John Vallier (1920–1991) was a piano soloist and composer of piano music.

Verne, Mathilde (1865/68?–1936)
The elder sister of Alice and Adela, Mathilde Verne studied piano with Franklin Taylor and later Clara Schumann. She made her public début aged nine, playing the Hummel Concertino with orchestra. She went on to play for London and provincial concert series, as well as touring Germany and the USA. She is best remembered as a piano teacher, opening the Mathilde Verne Piano School in 1909, and discovering the child prodigy Solomon when he was seven years old.

Visetti, Albert (1846–1928)
As a composer, singer and conductor, Visetti was an active male associate of the SWM in its early years. He came from an Italian/English background, however, having studied in Milan, he became a British citizen and settled in London in 1871. He acted as a musical advisor to Adelina Patti writing *La Diva Waltz Song* for her. He went on to become Professor of Singing at the GSM and the RCM, among his pupils were Louise Kirkby-Lunn and Agnes Nicholls. He lectured and published extensively including an Italian translation of Hullah's *History of Modern Music*. His compositional output comprised songs and opera such as *Les Trois Mousquetaires* performed at the Teatro Carrano in Milan. He was known to embellish details of his past claiming to have spent time in the court of Napolean III and receiving a knighthood from the King of Italy.

Walthew, Richard (1872–1951)
Walthew was a composer who studied first at the GSM and then at the RCM. He became Musical Director of the Passmore Edwards Settlement in 1899 and went on to become the Conductor of the University of London Musical Society and the opera class of the GSM. His compositions included many songs and chamber music.

Warner, H. Waldo (1874–1945)
Warner was a violist, violinist and composer leading the viola section of the New Symphony Orchestra from 1907. He had studied at the GSM and became Professor of Viola there in 1893. Although he wrote opera and songs he was best known as a chamber music composer, his work *Three Elfin Dances* was performed at the Proms in 1917 and repeated in 1924.

Warwick, Countess Frances Evelyn (Daisy) Maynard (1861–1938)
Frances Maynard was a wealthy heiress who married Francis Greville heir to the Earl of Warwick. She was part of the Edwardian house party set and was the lover of Edward VII before Alice Keppel, remaining close friends with him until his death. She became interested in Socialism, standing as a Labour candidate for

Warwick and Lemington in the 1923 election. Her daughter Mercy married the Theatre Director Basil Dean who knew Eugene Goossens and Gustav Holst. The group were hosted by Frances at her estate at Easton in Essex. Interested in music, the Countess of Warwick was seen at the premiere of Ethel Smyth's opera *Victory* in 1902 with her lover Joe Laycock. For further information see Sushila Anand, *Daisy: The Life and Loves of the Countess of Warwick* (London, 2008).

White, Harold R. (dates unknown)
Little is known about Harold R. White other than he was a composer whose overture *Shylock* was performed at the Proms in 1907 and he published a volume entitled *Stories from Operas.* There is another composer Harold Felix White who appears not to have been the same person and explains the R. initial used in White's name.

Wood, Haydn (1882–1959)
Wood was a composer and violinist who studied at the RCM. He had early success with his winning Phantasie for string quartet but he is primarily known for writing light orchestral works, musical comedy and a large output of ballads. For more detailed information on his works see Philip L. Scowcroft, *British Light Music: A Personal Gallery of Twentieth-Century Composers* (London, 1997).

Wood, Henry J. (1869–1944)
Wood had studied at the RAM with Ebenezer Prout, Charles Steggall and Walter Macfarren and went on to achieve lasting fame as a conductor, his name being synonymous with the Proms concerts. His work with women musicians was a source of great pride and his decision to include female players in the Queen's Hall Orchestra as early as 1913 is often cited as an example of his progressive stance, he was, however, also a powerful advocate for women composers. Women who had works played at the Proms included Dora Bright, Amy Horrocks, Dorothy Howell, Poldowski, Ethel Smyth and Susan Spain-Dunk. Much has been written on Wood's life since the first biography by Rosa Newmarch in 1904, for more detailed information see Arthur Jacobs, *Henry J. Wood: Maker of the Proms* (London, 1995).

York Bowen, Edwin (1884–1961)
York Bowen learnt piano from his mother, progressing to the North Metropolitan College of Music (where he met fellow composer Benjamin Dale, whose father was the principal), the Blackheath Conservatoire, the junior division of Trinity College of Music and aged 14 years entered the RAM. He spent seven years at the institution, studying piano with Tobias Matthay and composition with Frederick

Corder. In the early 1900s, York Bowen was part of the musical scene in London appearing as a pianist at the Proms, performing his Piano Concerto at a Philharmonic Society concert in 1906, as well as a piano sonata in B minor at the St James's Hall. He also worked closely with viola player Lionel Tertis, who premiered York Bowen's Viola Concerto in 1908. In 1910 he performed his own and John Ireland's Phantasy Trios written for Cobbett competitions with SWM members Beatrice Langley and May Mukle. He married the actor Sylvia Dalton, who re-trained as a lieder singer and the couple performed recitals together. York Bowen served in the Scots Guards in the First World War and 1937 formed a long-lasting piano duo with Harry Isaacs. He was a prolific composer, including 51 chamber works, but few remained in print after his death. For further information see Monica Watson, *York Bowen: A Centenary Tribute* (London: Thames Publishing, 1984).

Appendix 2
SWM Members 1911–1920

A

Miss Evelyn Aldridge 1912–1914
Miss Louise Alexander 1915–1917
Miss Gertrude Denis Allen 1917–1920
Miss Mary L.C. Allen 1917–1920
Miss Gwendoline Allport (singer at RCM left 1910) 1912–1913
Madame Amy d'Anville 1913–1914
Madame Augaude 1912–1913
Mrs Aves 1919–1920
Mrs Florence Aylward (SWM composer group member/organiser/popular song writer 1862–1950) 1916–1920

B

Miss Rhoda Backhouse (see Appendix 1) 1916–1920
Miss Dora Bagwell 1913–1915
Mrs Bailey 1919–1920
Miss Cicely Bailey 1912–1915
Miss Elsa Barnard 1912–1918
Miss Ethel Barns (composer/violinist RAM, works performed in SWM concert 1913–1914) 1911–1914
Miss Pauline Barrett 1911–1913
Mrs Barwick 1916–1917
Miss Margaret Barwick 1916–1920
Miss Mabel Bartlett (pianist) 1912–1914
Miss May Bartlett (celleist) 1912–1913
Madame Alexia Bassia 1912–1913
Miss Honoura Batchelor 1913–1915
Mrs Philip Belben 1915–1917
Miss Emily Belcher 1912–1913
Miss Olive Bell (died 1914, violist) 1911–1913
Miss Lilian Belletti 1919–1920
Miss Theresa Beney (SWM composer group member/published choral composer) 1912–1920
Miss Dora Bernhardt (work performed in SWM concert 1913–1914) 1913–1920
Miss E.E. Bilsand (See Appendix 1) 1913–1915

Miss Janie Blake (singer/sub professor RAM) 1915–1920
Mrs Bland (Helena?) (composer) 1912–1913
Miss Gertrude Blower 1913–1915
Mrs Sidney Bostock 1911–1913
Miss Daveron Bowen 1917–1920
Miss Gertrude Bowley 1915–1917
Mrs Bowman (Madame Gertrude Allin) (singer and pupil of Charles Phillips) 1913–1919
Miss Denise Bower 1915–1920
Miss Sybil Boyson (Mrs Lecky) 1912–1918
Miss Marie Brema (opera singer/SWM president) 1913–1920
Miss Irene Brettell 1918–1920
Miss M.A. Brightman 1915–1919
Miss V. de Broë 1913–1914
Miss Kathleen Bruckshaw (see Appendix 1) 1911–1920
Miss F. Brunton 1915–1920
Miss C.S. Burns 1912–1914
Miss Louise Burns (Mrs Swanson) (singer, works performed in SWM concert 1913–1914) 1912–1914
Miss Laura Bush 1911–1920
Miss Clara Butterworth (actress/singer, married to composer Montague Phillips) 1915–1920

C

Miss Jessie Cameron (active in British Legion Women's Section) 1914–1920
Madame Alice Campbell (possibly Lady Angela Mary Alice Campbell, involved in women's rights) 1917–1920
Miss E.A. Capel-Cure (possibly Agnes Capel Cure, antiques collector) 1912–1913
Madame San Carolo (singer) 1912–1914 and 1915–1920
Miss G.A. Chalk 1917–1920
Madame Chaminade (see Appendix 1) 1913–1920
Miss Lillie Chipp 1913–1914
Miss Agnes Christa 1912–1919
Miss Charlotte Clarke 1919–1920
Miss Fanny Beatrice Clarke 1912–1914
Miss Gertrude Kelly Clarke 1913–1914
Miss Rebecca Clarke (see Appendix 1) 1911
Miss Frances Hefford Cocking 1913–1919
Miss Lilian Cogan 1917–1920
Mrs Herbert Cohen (wealthy patron of artists) 1914–1919
Miss Dorothy Collins 1919–1920
Miss Mary Congreve Pridgeon 1912–1914
Miss M.E. Cook 1916–1918

Miss Julia Cook-Watson (composer, works performed in SWM concert 1913–1914) 1911–1914
Mrs Cooper 1917–1920
Miss Elsie Cooper (Mrs King) (pianist/sub professor RAM) 1918–1920
Miss Gertrude Cotter (pianist/sub professor RAM) 1914–1917
Miss Muriel Couper 1914–1915
Miss Ella Crosby-Heath 1913–1914
Mrs Curwen (developed Tonic Sol-fa system/married to John Curwen) 1915–1920

D

Miss Louise Dale (Mrs Hamilton Earle) (composer/singer) 1917–1920
Miss M. Dalzell 1913–1915
Miss A. Beatrix Darnell (RCM student) 1911–1913 and 1914–1920
Miss Frances Davidson (works performed in SWM concert 1913–1914) 1911–1914
Miss Kathleen Davies 1913–1914
Miss Mary Davies MusD (singer/RAM student, b.1885) 1915–1920
Miss Fanny Davies (see Appendix 1) 1916–1920
Mrs Eleanor Davies (Mrs Samuel Hart, died 1913) 1911
Miss Theodora Davies 1912–1920
Mrs Frank Dawes 1912–1920
Miss Emily Daymond MusD (see Appendix 1) 1911–1920
Miss Olive Mary Dean 1913–1914
Madame Livia Doria Devine 1911
Madame Amy Dewhurst (singer) 1912–1914
Miss Emma Dhai 1919–1920
Madame Adelina Dinelli 1915–1920
Miss Elsa Dinelli 1916–1920
Miss Helene Dolmetsch (cellist/viol de gamba player, b.1880) 1913–1914
Mrs Donaldson 1913–1920
Madame Dorini 1913–1914
Miss Celia Doubleday (performed in a string trio with her sisters Leila and May Doubleday) 1913–1914
Miss Leila Doubleday 1914–1917
Miss May Doubleday 1913–1920
Mrs Halliday Douglas 1911–1920
Mrs Driscoll 1917–1919
Miss Elsie Dunham 1916–1920
Miss Bertha Dunn 1917–1920

E

Miss Caroline Earle 1918–1920
Miss Marion Eastern 1913–1917

Miss Gertrude Eaton (singer/SWM founder and president) 1911–1920
Miss Marjorie Edes 1919–1920
Miss F.W. Edkins 1916–1920
Mrs Richard Eggar (mother of Katherine) 1912–1920
Miss Katherine Eggar (composer/pianist/SWM founder and president/Composer Group Leader and concert organiser) 1911–1920
Miss Edith Elsworth (SWM Composer Group member) 1915–1920
Miss Fanny Emerson 1913–1914
Miss Hilda Erskine 1913–1915
Miss Lena Ess 1915–1916
Miss F. Von Etlinger (singer) 1913–1914
Miss M. Evans 1913–1914
Miss Katherine M. Everett (RCM student) 1912–1916 and 1919–1920

F

Mrs Faber (pianist) 1912–1913
Miss Ella Faber (works performed in SWM concert 1913–1914) 1912–1914
Mrs R. Farebrother 1916–1918
Miss Rose Feilman 1912–1913
Miss Stella Fife 1911–1920
Miss Eveline Fife 1914–1920
Miss W.E. Fish 1916–1919
Miss C. Fitch (pianist) 1912–1914
Miss A. Fitzherbert 1919–1920
Miss Kate Flinn 1917–1920
Miss Evangeline Florence (singer, received honorary degree at 1907 Eisteddfod) 1911–1920
Miss Rose Foilman 1913–1914
Miss B.E. Formby 1913–1915
Miss E.C. Foskett 1913–1920
Miss Sybil Fountain 1917–1920
Miss Miligan Fox 1912–1915
Mrs E.W. French (Miss Marjorie Richardson) 1919–1920
Mrs Fyffe 1915–1920
Miss Marion A. Fyffe 1911–1915

G

Miss Cecilia Gates (see Appendix 1) 1917–1918
Miss Gertrude Geere 1912–1919
Mrs Arthur Gibson 1912–1920
Miss Ella Mabel Gibson 1915–1919
Miss Isobel Gilles 1912–1920

Mrs Glen Broder 1918–1920
Miss Ethel Goldney-Chitty 1912–1914
Madame Amina Goodwin (pianist/SWM Composer Group member/founded The London Trio) 1913–1920
Miss Helen Gough (2nd violinist in The Helen Egerton Quartet) 1912–1917
Miss Muriel Gough 1912–1913
Miss Fanny Graeff 1919–1920
Miss Kerr Grainger (sometimes seen as Miss Grainger Kerr) (contralto specialising in modern music) 1917–1920
Miss Margery Granger 1912–1914
Miss Mina Gratton (SWM Composer Group member, works performed in SWM concert 1913–1914) 1912–1918
Miss P. Lee Graves 1918–1920
Miss Thelma Green (SWM Composer Group member) 1918–1920
Miss Broadley Greene 1912–1914
Miss Elsie Gresholz 1913–1914
Miss H.M. Grieveson (SWM Composer Group member) 1917–1920
Miss Jessie Grimson (violinist, founded The Jessie Grimson Quartet) 1912–1917
Miss Elsie Grosholz 1912–1913
Miss Maude Estlin Grundy 1912–1914
Miss Louisa Gunn 1917–1920
Miss Marjorie Gunn (violinist) 1919–1920

H

Madame Alma Haas (see Appendix 1) 1911–1920
Miss Vera Hale-Smith 1918–1920
Mrs Edward Haley (pianist) 1915–1920
Miss Olga Haley (singer) 1915–1920
Miss Elsie Hall (Australian, taught Constant Lambert) 1911
Mrs Derek Hallett 1916–1920
Miss Adela Hamaton (see Appendix 1) 1911–1920
Miss Elsie Hamilton (SWM composer) 1915–1920
Miss Edith Hands (RAM student) 1912–1915
Mrs Julius Hannes 1912–1914 and 1915–1919
Mrs Gladys Hansard 1914–1915
Miss Edith Hanson (cellist in The Kendall Quartet) 1913–1914
Miss Maude Hardy (Mrs Henderson) 1912–1914
Miss Alice Hare (conductor/singer) 1912–1917
Miss Kathleen Harries 1912–1914
Miss Dorothy Harris (SWM Composer Group member) 1915–1920
Miss Louisa Grace Hart 1915–1919
Miss Marion Hart 1916–1917
Miss Cecile Hartog (see Appendix 1) 1911–1920

Miss Maud Harvey 1911
Miss Hastings-Wright 1913–1914
Miss Caroline Hatchard (opera and concert soprano/RAM student) 1915–1919
Miss Isobel Hearne 1911–1915
Miss Ella Crosby-Heath 1914–1919
Mrs H. Hemsley 1912–1915
Mrs Henderson (Miss Clarice Harvey) 1912–1920
Madame Lily Henkel (see Appendix 1) 1911–1916 and 1918–1920
Mrs Fraser Henry 1914–1916
Miss Graily Hewitt 1914–1915
Madame Edith Heymann 1913–1914
Miss F. Heyermanns 1912–1914
Miss Fanny Heywood 1912–1914
Miss N.U. Ward Higgs 1914–1916
Miss Annie Hill 1912–1914
Miss Cecilia Hill (secretary of Herts and North Middlesex Music Festival) 1913–1920
Miss Mabel Hills 1913–1920
Miss G.U. Hislop (Gladys) (member of RCM Union Committee 1910) 1912–1914
Miss Pattie Hoe 1912–1915
Miss M.F.G. Hogan 1917–1919
Miss Truda Hogan 1912–1916
Miss Alice Holder 1913–1919
Miss Nellie M. Holand 1917–1920
Miss Ruby Holland (pianist/SWM Composer Group member) 1916–1920
Miss Dorothea Hollins (composer) 1912–1915
Miss Ethel Horne 1912–1914
Mrs Hooghinkel-Leoni 1912–1920
Madame Elsie Horne (see Appendix 1) 1912–1920
Madame Marie Horne (see Appendix 1) 1912–1915
Miss Pattie Hornsby (Mrs Chorley) (SWM Composer Group member) 1911 and 1913–1920
Miss Winifred Houghton 1919–1920
Miss Evelyn Hunter 1912–1920
Mrs Hunter 1915–1917
Mrs Hutchinson (soprano/teacher, student at RAM with Agnes Larkcom, b.1851) 1917–1920

J

Mrs A.M. Jackson 1915–1920
Miss E.L. John 1916–1920
Miss Lucie Johnstone (see Appendix 1) 1912–1919
Miss Muriel Johnstone (Mrs McCullagh) 1912–1919
Miss Frances C. Jones (SWM Composer Group member) 1912–1920

Miss Gurney Jones (1913–1914)
Miss Jane Joseph (composer/assistant to Gustav Holst) 1919–1920
Madame Jeanne Jouve (singer) 1917–1920
Miss Marion Juckles 1918–1920

K

Miss Grace Keeble 1913–1917
Miss Mary Keen 1919–1920
Miss Eva Kelsey 1912–1914
Miss Constance Keyl (Mrs Andreae) 1913–1914
Miss Elsie King (singer/SWM Composer Group member) 1915–1918
Miss Winifred Kingsford 1918–1920
Miss Bluebell Klean (see Appendix 1) 1913–1917
Miss Fannie Kreuz 1912–1914
Miss Henrietta Kruger 1911–1913

L

Mrs Agnes Lambert (see Appendix 1) 1912–1920
Mrs Alfred Lampson 1912–1914
Mrs E.R. Lancaster 1917–1920
Madame Beatrice Langley (see Appendix 1) 1911–1918
Miss Edith Langsford (SWM Composer Group member, works performed in SWM concert 1913–1914) 1913–1920
Madame Adeline de Lara (see Appendix 1) 1912–1914
Madame Agnes Larkcom (composer/singing professor at RAM) 1911–1920
Madame Liza Lehmann (composer/singer/SWM president/SWM Composer Group member, works performed in SWM concert 1913–1914, died 1918) 1911–1917
Miss Marguerite Le Manns 1912–1915
Miss Amy Le Marchant 1913–1914
Miss Adelina Leon (violinist/cellist) 1917–1918
Miss Daisy Levetus (SWM Composer Group Member) 1912–1920
Mrs Scott Lindsay 1919–1920
Miss Evelyn Longman 1913–1914
Miss Amy Lott 1912–1914
Miss Maud Lucas (cellist in The Lucas String Quartet) 1913–1915
Miss Miran Lucas (violinist in The Lucas String Quartet) 1913–1919
Miss Patience Lucas (violist in The Queen's Hall Ladies Quartet) 1913–1915

M

Mrs George Macmillan 1913–1920
Miss Landseer Mackenzie 1914–1917

Miss Charlotte McCleod 1919–1920
Miss Annabel McDonald (singer) 1915–1920
Miss Amy McDowell (singer/teacher) 1911–1920
Miss Florence MacNaughton (singer/student at RCM) 1912–1914
Miss Elsie MacSwinney 1914–1916
Miss Kathleen McQuitty (pianist/professor at RCM) 1917–1920
Miss Jeanie Mair (Mrs Thain) 1912–1914
Mrs Rutherford Maitland (SWM Composer Group member) 1913–1920
Miss F. Vere Manooch (singer) 1912–1913
Miss Amy Marchant 1914–1915
Mrs Marshall (SWM Composer Group member) 1915–1920
Miss Georgia Mathieson 1913–1915
Madame Matthaei (married to pianist/teacher Tobias Matthay/Matthaei) 1911–1919
Miss May 1911
Miss Maud Melliar (oboist) 1911–1919
Madame Marie Mely (Comtesse Van Heuval) (see Appendix 1) 1912–1914
Miss Gena Milne (cellist) 1919–1920
Miss Helen Milne 1918–1920
Miss H. Milvar 1917–1920
Madame Zara Minidieu 1918–1920
Miss Janet Mitchell 1919–1920
Miss Annie Mixer 1919–1920
Miss Gladys Moger (see Appendix 1) 1917–1920
Miss Martha Möller 1912–1920
Miss Hilda Moon (SWM librarian) 1912–1918
Miss Dorothy Morgan 1912–1915
Miss Eva Morton 1912–1913
Miss Mabel Moss (pianist/SWM Composer Group member) 1915–1918
Miss Minnie Mouillot 1912–1913
Miss Anne Mukle (pianist) 1911–1920
Miss May Mukle (see Appendix 1) 1911–1920

N

Madame Deszö Nemès 1912–1920
Madame Blanche Newcombe 1914–1917
Miss Claire Newton (composer of popular songs) 1912–1913
Miss Violet Nicholson (composer of guitar and mandolin music) 1913–1914
Mrs Norris 1917–1920

O

Miss G Oldham 1916–1917
Mrs Norman O'Neill (see Appendix 1) 1912–1920

Mrs Gladys O'Rourke (American soprano?) 1912–1918
Mrs Orde (SWM Composer Group member) 1914–1918
Miss Valentine Orde (cellist in The Wayfaring Quartet) 1914–1917
Miss Phoebe Otway (SWM Composer Group member) 1911–1919
Madame Eugene Oudin (née Louise Parker) (opera singer/professor at RCM/SWM Composer Group member, works performed in SWM concert 1913–1914) 1912–1914
Miss Muriel Overton (composer of popular songs/SWM composer) 1912–1920
Mrs Outhwaite 1918–1920

P

Miss Marcia Padbury 1915–1917
Miss A.K. Estelle Pattenden 1917–1920
Miss Annie Peck (composer) 1915–1920
Miss Margaret Pedler (novelist/studied piano and singing at RAM/SWM Composer Group member) 1912–1915
Mrs Pedler (SWM composer) 1917–1920
Miss Caroline Percival (works performed in SWM concert 1913–1914) 1911 and 1913–1915
Miss Perkins 1911
Miss Florence Pertz (pianist) 1913–1914
Miss Frances Pertz 1915–1920
Miss Alice Pirie 1912–1917
Miss Dorothy Platt 1913–1920
Madame Eva Plouffer-Stropes 1913–1915
Miss Lilian Polkinghorne 1914–1917
Miss C. Pridham 1919–1920
Mrs Stansfield Prior 1912–1920
Miss Isobel Purdon (violinist) 1913–1914
Miss Dorothy Pyke (composer of popular songs, works performed in SWM concert 1913–1914) 1912–1915

R

Miss Iris Rainbow 1911–1914
Mrs Stepney Rawson (author Maud Stepney Rawson?) 1911
Miss Adelaide Reed 1914–1915
Miss Edith Reed (carol translator) 1917–1920
Miss Esmé Reid (Mrs Edwards) (SWM Composer Group member) 1914–1920
Mrs Ernest Rendall 1912–1919
Miss Theresa del Riego (composer, works performed in SWM concert 1913–1914) 1912–1914
Miss Kathleen Richards (pianist/SWM Composer Group member) 1915–1920

Miss Lilian Risque 1917–1920
Madame Florence Hill Rivington (composer/violinist) 1919–1920
Miss Kathleen Robinson (SWM Composer Group member) 1912–1920
Miss Dorothy Rogers 1919–1920
Miss Helen Rootham (writer/musician/governess to Edith Sitwell) 1913–1914
Miss L.J. Russell 1917–1919
Miss Marjorie Russell 1919–1920

S

Miss Helen Sanders 1912–1914
Miss Amy Sargent (singer) 1913–1920
Miss Mabel Saumarez-Smith (see Appendix 1) 1911–1920
Miss Ella Savage 1915–1920
Miss M. Savory 1916–1917
Miss Irene Scharrer (see Appendix 1) 1912–1913
Miss Kathleen Schlesinger (see Appendix 1) 1913–1920
Miss Constance Schultz 1913–1914
Miss Marion Scott (violinist/composer/writer/SWM founder and president/SWM Composer Group member, works performed in SWM concert 1913–1914) 1911– 1920
Mrs Keith Seth-Smith 1914–1916
Miss Eleanor Shaw 1912–1920
Mrs Sheldon (SWM Composer Group member) 1917–1920
Miss Annie Constance Shinner 1913–1920
Miss Annie Sich 1912–1920
Miss Ethel Carre Smith (SWM Composer Group member) 1911–1920
Miss Gladys Smith 1917–1920
Miss K. Villeneuve Smith 1912–1920
Miss Elizabeth Smithson 1915–1920
Miss Ethel Smyth (composer) 1911–1914
Miss Barbara Smythe 1914–1920
Miss Muriel Soames 1911
Madame Burgess Soar 1916–1919
Madame Harriet Solly (violinist, studied at RCM) 1911–1914
Miss C. Somerset 1916–1920
Miss Pitt Soper 1911 and 1917–1920
Miss Susan Spain-Dunk (Mrs Henry Gibson) (composer) 1914–1920
Miss Margaret Sparrow 1913–1917
Miss Joan Spink (violinist/composer/pianist/critic) 1918–1920
Mrs Stamm 1914–1915
Mrs Edward Stannard 1912–1914 and 1915–1920
Miss Steeves 1915–1919
Miss A. Cheetham Strode (SWM composer) 1915–1920

T

Miss Georgina Tanner 1918–1920
Miss Florence Thomas 1919–1920
Miss Rhoda Thomas 1912–1915
Mrs Kathleen Thorn (SWM composer) 1915–1920
Mrs Oliver Thorn 1913–1914
Madame Hilda Thornton (Mrs Whitacker) 1919–1920
Mrs Ernest Thring (string player) 1912–1914
Mrs Ticknell 1914–1920
Miss Annetta Tidbury 1913–1914
Mrs Titman 1916–1920
Miss Joan M. Tipper (SWM composer) 1917–1920
Miss Helen Torrens (SWM composer) 1914–1920
Miss Cicely Trask (The book *Chats on Violins* by Olga Racster was dedicated to Cicely Trask, 1905) 1912–1917
Miss Harriet Trask 1912–1914
Lady Mary Trefusis (Lady Mary Lyon) (see Appendix 1) 1917–1920
Mrs Boswell Tucker (possibly related to author Herbert Boswell Tucker) 1912–1920
Miss Dorothy Tucker 1917–1920
Miss Olive Turner (SWM Composer Group member) 1917–1920

U

Miss Pattie Templeton Upton (SWM composer) 1912–1914 and 1915–1920

V

Miss Ethel L. Voynich (writer/SWM Composer Group member, friends with Marion Scott and Ivor Gurney) 1912–1920
Miss Winifred Vincent 1912–1913
Mrs Vuilliamy 1919–1920

W

Mrs Ethel Waddy 1918–1919
Miss D. Walenn (possibly related to cellist Herbert Walenn) 1916–1920
Miss E.M. Walker (possibly American soprano Edyth Walker) 1916–1917
Miss Marjorie Walker 1915–1920
Mrs Walton 1919–1920
Miss Doris Walton 1919–1920
Miss Kathleen Waring 1912–1914
Miss Gertrude E. Watson (composer of popular songs) 1915–1917

Miss Rosabel Watson (double bassist/conductor/founder of the Æolian Ladies Orchestra) 1911–1919
Miss Margaret Way 1913–1914
Mrs Edith Westbrook (SWM composer) 1915–1920
Miss Olive Westbrook (Mrs Corder) 1915–1919
Miss Annie Weston 1912–1920
Mrs Renshaw Westray 1912–1920
Mrs Seymour Whatley 1912–1913
Miss E.H. Wheelhouse 1912–1914
Mrs Humphrey Wilkins 1918–1919
Miss Dora Wilson (singer) 1913–1914
Miss Gladys Wilson 1912–1914 and 1915–1920
Miss Mary Wilson (singer/professor at RAM) 1917–1920
Mrs Purcell Wilson 1917–1920
Miss Dora White (SWM Composer Group member, works performed in SWM concert 1913–1914) 1913–1920
Miss Edith White 1912–1914
Miss Maude Valerie White 1912–1920
Mrs Whitman 1913–1920
Miss E.F. Wood 1917–1920
Miss Gertrude Malcolm Wood 1915–1920
Mrs Violet Gordon Woodhouse (harpsichordist) 1911–1915
Miss F.C. Woodright 1916–1917
Miss Vivian Worth (singer) 1919–1920
Mrs Clare Wright 1917–1920
Mrs Hastings Wright 1914–1915

Y

Mrs Hilda Young 1915–1916

Z

Miss Ethel Zillhardt-Ullhorne (cellist/SWM Composer Group member) 1912–1920

Appendix 3
Extracts from Katherine Eggar, Address to the SWM Inaugural Meeting, Saturday 15 July 1911, SWM Archive, RCM

There is no other society of women musicians, you may say that is an argument in favour of starting one. Perhaps in the minds of some there is a lurking fear that we are a suffragist society in disguise; our only connection with the suffragist movement is a similarity of ideals. In both political and musical life, there is a great deal of wire pulling and party policy; one does not need to know much about musical dealings in general, to know this.

The suffragists saw there was a great deal in political matters which needs purifying and they believed that would do a great deal to effect reform. We see a great deal that is corrupt in artistic life, we believe that most women desire a higher ideal in musical transactions, but they have been unable to fight against the monster of commercialism which rules the musical world. This perhaps one great reason for our forming a musical society, that through it, musical life may be purified, and public opinion reformed.

We want to get women to sharpen their wits, to criticise things that are happening. I think one of the greatest reproaches against musicians is that they are so thoughtless, that is the 'bane' of musical beings, they are not 'brainy' in the best sense.

Secondly we believe that the benefits of co-operation might be very great, we hope that those of expertise will be willing to help the in-experienced and to advise them; we hope to have on our council women who have proved themselves to be leaders.

Thirdly, we hope that the society will be the means of bringing composers and executants into touch with one another: how many a composer has given up composing simply because she never gets a hearing. This brings one to speak of our connection with the Women's Institute. By affiliating ourselves with the Women's Institute we shall have the use of its premises, for the purpose of concerts, and there would be the advantage of the secretarial office. It is a most tremendous asset for a society about starting, to have no difficulty with regard to its premises. These are practical advantages to women musicians.

The next object is rather more indefinite, it needs a little more imagination, but it is none the less important. We who have invited you to come here to-day do not want to be content with making things as they are just a little more tolerable. We do not accept music as it is as final. We all of us feel and talk vaguely about the wonders of music, but what are we really making of it in our daily lives? It should be a moral factor in our education, such as the Greeks taught. Have we any real knowledge of the harm music can do? Can we prove what is bad music? Have we any knowledge of the physical effects produced by sound? If we had any real conviction of the Sacredness of Art, should we permit the artificialities of our pleasant concert giving and music making? I believe that we all in our heart of hearts can imagine what music can be, but it ought to be something very different from what we make it. Each of us comes into the world with everything more or less arranged for us, so that we take around us for granted and conclude that things seen are eternal. It needs a Bernard Shaw to make us begin to think that things may be merely temporal conventions. The conventions of music must be challenged. Women are already challenging conventions in all kinds of ways. Everywhere we see them refusing to accept artificialities for realities. Surely this is bound sooner or later to bring a great impulse into art. It is the worker, the toiler, the philanthropist in women that has been roused; the artist of the future is not yet here. Is not the time come for that torch to kindle the flame on a new alter to art? Does not the world need a music that has not yet come? May it not be that need shall be met by women?

There is one branch of creative Art in which woman has not excelled: in painting, in literature she has attained but not in musical composition. It was the conviction that the time had come for women to develop as composers that led Miss Scott to the forming of a society of women musicians. We believe in a great future for women composers, but that future can only be great as we put our trust in the invisible, or the inaudible; we shall only write great music by seeking the life behind all forms. We must help women to believe in their possibilities as composers.

In conclusion, we want women to join us who will take an active share in vitalising the artistic conception. Life must not be lived by a standard of ideals. Let me say with the poet ‘Hitch your wagon to a star’.

Appendix 4
Male Associates of the SWM 1911–1920

A

Mr Melchior Amberg 1915–1916
Mr Edgar Archer (performer) 1912–1914

B

Mr Herbert Bedford (see Appendix 1) 1912–1920 (on active service 1915–1918)
Captain Arthur Bliss (see Appendix 1) 1915–1920 (on active service 1915–1918)
Mr Oskar Borsdorf (horn player/popular song composer) 1912–1914
Mr Orton Bradley (pianist/teacher, MA Oxford) 1915–1920 (on active service 1916–1917)
Captain K.R. Bull (SWM Composer Group member) 1915–1919 (on active service 1916–1918)

C

Mr Gerald Clamp 1918–1920
Mr Reginald Clarke (pianist) 1912–1916
Mr W.W. Cobbett (patron of music) 1912–1920

D

Mr Harold Darke (see Appendix 1) 1914–1920
Mr Charles Deacon 1912–1913
Mr Denis-Browne (died in action) 1913–1914
Mr Edward Dent (musicologist) 1918–1920
Mr Thomas Dunhill (see Appendix 1) 1911–1920
Mr Spencer Dyke (violinist/professor at RAM/member of Wessley Quartet) 1912–1914

E

Mr H.M. Ellercamp (SWM Composer Group member) 1915–1920

F

Mr J.H. Foulds (SWM Composer Group member) 1915–1920

G

Captain van Someren Godfrey 1915–1920 (on active service1916–1918)
Mr Teasdale Griffiths (composer) 1919–1920

Mr Ernest Groome 1913–1914 and 1915–1918 (on active service 1915–1918)
Mr Ivor Gurney (see Appendix 1) 1912–1914 and 1915–1918 (on active service 1915–1918)

H
Mr O.G. Herford 1919–1920
Mr St John Horne (SWM Composer Group member) 1915–1919
Mr E.W. Howard 1919–1920
Mr Riddell Hunter (composer) 1912–1914

L
Mr Craig Sellar Lang (composer/editor/SWM Composer Group member) 1913–1914 and 1915–1919
Mr Faulkner Lee 1912–1914 and 1915–1919 (on active service 1915–1918)
Mr Mewburn Levien (baritone/teacher) 1915–1920

M
Mr Somerled Macdonald 1912–1920

N
Mr Montagu Nathan (composer) 1912–1919
Mr Ernest Newton (critic/composer of popular songs, studied at Cambridge) 1912–1913
Mr Norman Notley (baritone/teacher) 1919–1920

P
Mr Hugh Peyton (composer) 1912–1913
Mr Charles Phillips (see Appendix 1) 1912–1914

R
Dr Cyril Rootham (composer/conductor/organist, MA and MusDoc from Cambridge) 1913–1920
Mr Sydney Rosenbloom (composer) 1918–1920

S
Mr H. Sayer 1912–1914
Mr Percy Scholes (see Appendix 1) 1915–1920
Mr Sydney Scott (father of Marion Scott) 1912–1920
Mr George Shapiro (conductor/pianist, born in Russia) 1913–1918
Mr Sydney Shimmin (composer, studied at RAM) 1912–1914 and 1915–1918 (on active service 1915–1918)
Mr Morton Stephenson (composer) 1912–1913

V

Mr Russell Vincent 1913–1914
Mr R.F. Virgoe 1913–1914 and 1915–1918 (on active service 1915–1918)
Mr Albert Visetti (see Appendix 1) 1912–1920

W

Mr Leonard Willmore 1915–1918
Mr Arthur Williams 1915–1920
Mr Percy Whitehead (singer/composer) 1917–1920

Appendix 5
Instrumental Chamber Music (Trios, Quartets, Quintets, Sextets) by Women Composers c.1905–1920[1]

Bech	Bechstein Concerts Programmes Archive
BL	British Library
BMIC	British Music Information Centre
BMS 20	The British Music Society Annual 1920
BMS 22	The British Music Society Catalogue of Composers 1922
Everitt	William Everitt, British Piano Trios, Quartets and Quintets, 1850–1950
MCA	Morley College Archive
McCann	McCann Concert Programmes Collection, Royal Academy of Music
RAM	Royal Academy of Music
RAMC	Royal Academy of Music Concert Archive
RCM	Royal College of Music
SPC	South Park Concert Series

Marian Arkwright (1863–1922)
Quintet piano, oboe, clarinet, horn, bassoon. BMS 20
Trio piano, oboe, horn. BMS 20
Scherzo and Variations piano, clarinet, bassoon. BMS 20
Trio piano, oboe, viola. BMS 20

Mary Barber
Piano Quartet. BMS 22

Ethel Barns (1873–1948)
Adagio, Trio in F minor violin, viola and piano op.10 (1909). London: Schott and Co. BL†

[1] This list includes work with music scores extant but also works whose existence is known only because it is included in the British Music Society Annual and Catalogue.†= score extant

Fantasie, 2 violins and piano (1911). London: Schott and Co.†
Sonata, G minor op. 24, violin and piano (1911). BL London: Schott and Co.†
Suite, violin, cello, piano. BMS 22 and BL MS†
Trio no.1 violin, viola and piano. BMS 20
Trio no.2, violin, viola and piano. BMS 20

Ethel Bilsand
Serenade, string quartet and piano. Date unknown, KEE and MMS in CM
String Quartet in B minor, MS RAMC

Kathleen Bruckshaw (1877–1921)
Piano Quintet. Date unknown
Piano Quartet. BMS 20

Gyula Buxhorn (female?)
Canto Religioso, violin or cello, piano, organ (harmonium) and bass ad lib. London: Schott, 1908. †

Dulcie Cohen
Trios, violin, viola, piano. BMS 22

Harriet Cohen (1896–1967)
Miniature Trio, piano, violin, cello. MS RAMC

Ruby Davy (1883–1949)
Piano Trio. BMS 22
Piano Quartet. BMS 22

Katharine Eggar (1874–1961)
Wolfram's Dirge, 1v pf vc (1906), 1920. Brighton: J and W Chester RAM†
My Soul is an Enchanted Boat 1v str qrt. Date unknown
Piano Quintet (?1907). BMS 20
Trio G minor, piano, violin, cello. BMS 20
Sonata C minor, cello and piano. BMS 20

Dorothy Erhardt

Quintet D major piano and strings: Adagio; allegro/presto scherzo/adagio ma non troppo/allegro moderato (alla breve). London: J and W Chester, 1917

Rosalind Ellicott (1887–1924)

String Trio. Date unknown

Adela Hamaton

Piano Quartet. Date unknown, KEE and MMS in CM

Cécile Hartog

Piano Quartet. Date unknown but probably pre 1905 (KEE and MMS in CM)
Quartet A major, piano, violin, viola, cello. MS BMS 20

Helene Heale

Polacca, 3 violins and piano. Augener, BMS 20

Ruby Holland

Trio one Movement, violin, viola, piano. MS, BMS 20

Jane Joseph (1894–1929)

String Quartet. Date unknown
Quartet, oboe, violin, viola, cello. Date unknown
2 Piano Trios. Dates unknown
Allegretto, woodwind sextet. Date unknown

Bluebell Klean

Piano Quintet, strings and piano. Date unknown but probably between 1910 and 1913, KEE and MMS in CM
Piano Trio. Date unknown, McCann

Adela Maddison (1866–1929)

Piano Quintet, 1916. London: J Curwen and sons 1925†

M.E. Marshall
2 String Quartets. Dates unknown
Dance Phantasy Trio. Instrumentation and dates unknown
Piano Trio. BMS 22

Fiona McCleary
String Quartet. Date unknown

Margaret D. Meredith
Quintet, piano, cello, violin, flute and clarinet. Date unknown, KEE and MMS in CM, Manuscript, BMS 20

Morfydd Owen (1891–1918)
Pianoforte Trio 1912
Pianoforte Trio The Cathedral at Liège/The Cathedral at Rheims. Unpublished. Written under pseudonym, Lenavanmo, 1915. Cardiff University Library†

Oliveria Louisa Prescott 1843–1919
Quartet A minor. BMS 20
Quartet C minor. BMS 20
Quartet G major. BMS 20

Clara Kathleen Rogers (1844–1931) settled in Boston 1873
Chamber Music Selections [String Quartet D Minor op.5, Sonata in G Major op.23 violin and piano, *Reverie* violin and piano]. Middleton, Wis.: A-R Editions, c.2001†

Marion Scott (1877–1953)
Piano Trio. Manuscript, BMS 20
Incidental Music to the Song of Kalashnikov string quartet. Manuscript, BMS 20

Doris Shopland
Trio, piano, violin, cello. MS RAMC

Ethel Smyth (1858–1944)
String Quartet, E minor, 1912 (1914). Leipzig: Universal Editions, BL†

Concerto for violin, horn and orchestra arranged by the composer for violin horn (or viola/cello) and piano. London: J. Curwen and sons, 1928. BL manuscript BL†

Susan Spain-Dunk (1880–1963)

Phantasy Quartet, D minor, 2 violins, viola, cello, Goodwin and Tabb 1915. RAM/BMS 20†

Phantasy, A minor (Cobbett Prize) piano trio. Date unknown, KEE and MMS in CM, BMS 20

Sextet, E minor op. 55. Date unknown, SPC

Trio, 2 violins and piano. BMS 20

Phantasy Quartet, E minor. BMS 20

Edith Swepstone (1885–1930)

Piano Quintet, E minor. Date unknown, SPC performed 1906–7

Quintet, D major, horn and string quartet. Date unknown, SPC

Quintet, E♭ major, wind and piano. Date unknown, SPC

Lyrical Cycle, string quartet. Date unknown, SPC

Piano Trios, in D minor, G minor, and A minor. Dates unknown, SPC

Piano Quartet, A minor. Performed 1912–13 season SPC Meadmore 23

Josephine Emily Troup (d.1912)

Romanza in C, string quartet. BMS 20

Alice Verne-Bredt (1868–1958)

Phantasy, piano quartet. 1908 performed 26/2/1914 Æolian Hall

Phantasy, piano trio, 1908 (1910). London: Schott and co. BL, KEE and MMS in CM†

Phantasy, piano quintet. Date unknown, KEE and MMS in CM

Dora White

Nocturne, piano quintet. BMS 20

Appendix 6
Catalogue of Phantasies Written/Published between 1905 and 1920

1905

William Yeates Hurlstone (1876–1906) Phantasy Quartet string quartet wins 1st prize in 1st Cobbett competition, London: Novello (1905) pub [1906].

Frank Bridge Phantasy Quartet string quartet wins 2nd prize in 1st Cobbett competition.

1906

York Bowen (1884–1961) Phantasie Trio piano trio with cello or viola op.24 supposedly published Ascherberg, Hopwood and Crew. MS in RAM, viola part only, 1906?

John Ireland (1879–1962) Phantasie in A minor piano trio, London; Novello and co. (1906) pub [1908].

1907

Alfred H. Barley (1872–?) Trio Fantasie op.11 Piano trio London: Charles Avison, 1907.

Harry Waldo Warner (1874–1945) Phantasie Trio in B minor 1907.

Frank Bridge (1879–1941) Phantasie String Trio (1907).

1908

Frank Bridge (1879–1941) Phantasie in C minor H.79 piano trio London: Novello (1908) pub [1909].

Thomas F. Dunhill (1877–1946) Phantasy Trio in C minor piano trio op.26 unpublished manuscript private collection 1908?

James Friskin (1886–1967) Phantasie in E minor piano trio London: Novello (1908) pub [1909].

Susan Spain-Dunk (1880–1962) Phantasy Trio 1908 unpublished.

Alice Verne-Bredt (1868–1958) Phantasie Trio in one movement piano trio London: Schott (1908) pub [1910].
Alice Verne-Bredt (1868–1958) Phantasie piano quartet (1908) unpublished.

1909

H.V. Jervis-Read Phantasy Trio in B minor piano trio op.10 no.2 London: Novello 1909.

1910

Frank Bridge (1879–1941) Phantasy piano quartet in F♯ minor H.94 (1910) London: Goodwin and Tabb [1911] no. 1 in Cobbett series and London: Augener [1920].
James Friskin (1886–1967) Phantasy in F minor piano quintet London: Stainer and Bell (1910) pub [1912] no. 2 in Cobbett series.

1912

Ethel Barns (1873–1948) Fantasie op.26 2 violins and piano London: Schott (1912) pub [1912] no.4 in Cobbett series.
Thomas F. Dunhill (1877–1946) Phantasy-Trio 2 violins and piano in E♭ major op.36 London: Stainer and Bell (1912) pub [1912] no.6 in Cobbett series.
Richard Henry Walthew (1872–1951) Phantasy quintet violin, viola, cello, bass and piano London: Stainer and Bell (1912) pub [1912] commissioned by the Worshipful Company of Musicians.

1915

Susan Spain-Dunk (1880–1962) Phantasy Quartet D minor string quartet London: Goodwin and Tabb 1915.

1916

Gustav Holst *Phantasy* String Quartet unpublished/withdrawn 1916.

1917

James Cliffe Forrester (1860–1941) Trio folk-song Phantasy piano trio London: Novello received 1st prize 1917 Cobbett competition pub [1918].

1920

Sir A.H. Crossfield Phantasy Trio in D piano trio London: Stainer and Bell, 1920.

No Dates

Alan Gray Phantasy in B♭ piano trio unpublished Cambridge University Library no date.
Harry A. Keyser (b.1871) Fantasie-Trio in A minor no date in BMS 1920.
Frederick Nicholls (b.1871) Fantasie Trio piano trio op.43 no date in BMS 1920.
Alice Verne-Bredt (1868–1958) Phantasy Quintet piano quintet no date.

Appendix 7
Judging Panel for 1914–1915 Cobbett Competition

List of judges for the 1914–1915 Cobbett String Quartet Competition played by the Egerton Quartet (Helen Egerton, Helen Gough†, Winifred Jones and Gwendoline Griffiths, who were also judges) as printed in *Chamber Music*, 15 (July, 1915).

Rebecca Clarke†
Winifred Christie
Katherine Eggar†
Cecilia Gates†
Jessie Grimson†
Susan S. Gibson†
Marjorie Hayward
Lily Henkel†
Mrs Alfred Hobday
Mrs E. Homan
Beatrice Langley†
A. León†
Marion Scott†
Lady Woodrow
S. Petre

Horace M. Abel
A.J. Clement
C.A. Crabbe
Désiré Defauw
T.F. Dunhill†
Spencer Dyke†
Warwick Evans
Nicholas Gatty
Eugene Goossens
Edgar Homan
Alfred Hobday
Joseph Jungen
M. Lenson
Jan Mulder
E. Younge

Percy A. Scholes†
Felix Salmond
John Saunders
Emile Sauret
Albert Sammons
Dr T.L. Southgate
Oscar Street
Richard Walthew
Hans Wessley
Waldo Warner
W.E. Whitehouse
C. Woodhouse
J. Van der Straeten
H.T. Trust

†= SWM member anytime between 1911 and 1920.

Bibliography

Manuscript Sources

Author's collection, Alice Verne Bredt, *2 Letters from T. C. Fenwick, Clerk, Musicians Company 1907 concerning Cobbett Phantasy Competition.* Bodleian Library, Oxford, Deneke Papers, uncatalogued.

———, Oxford Ladies Musical Society MS Top Oxon e. 473, 474, 475, MS Eng d.3370, MS Top Oxon L.613, 614, MS Eng.Lett c.621, MS Top Oxon. C.612 f675.1–256, MS 257–500 (ult).

British Library London, Ethel Barns Manuscripts, ADD 63058–9, 63634–9.

———, Ethel Mary Smyth Archive, ADD 46857, ADD 68893, ADD 419196, Eq. 3306 and ADD 45934.

———, O'Neill Correspondence (Papers of Adine and Norman O'Neill) Add 71456–72 MS MUS 931–2.

———, Rensburg Collection MS MUS 308. Dorothy Howell Trust, Bewdley, Dorothy Howell Collection, uncatalogued.

Kirlees Archive, Huddersfield, Frances Hefford Cocking Papers, KC508/2, KC508/3 KC508/4, KC508/9, KC508/11, KC508/29, KC508/30, and KC508/32.

Lancaster Family Collection, London, Mabel Batten and Cara Lancaster Archive.

National Library of Wales, Bangor, Eliot Crawshay Williams correspondence with Morfydd Owen and press cuttings, G25–48.

———, Kitty Idwal Jones correspondence with Morfydd Owen 13/1–15 and diary notes relating to Morfydd Owen.

Royal Academy of Music, London, Ethel Barns Student Record.

———, McCann Collection, British Programmes 1900–1920 and letters.

———, Susan Spain-Dunk, Student Record.

Royal Albert Hall Archive, London, Royal Albert Hall database of performances 1910–1920.

Royal College of Music, London, Herbert Norman Howells papers.

———, Marion Scott Collection.

———, Society of Women Musicians Archive.

Wigmore Hall Archive, London, Bechstein Hall Programmes 1910–1920.

Printed Primary Sources

Morley College Magazine, 1905–1920

The Overture: A Monthly Musical Journal (The Royal Academy of Music Student Magazine), vols 1–4, 1890–1894.

Royal Academy of Music Concert Programmes, 1900–1920.
Royal College of Music Union Magazine, 1910–1920

Secondary Sources

Abbate, Carolyn, *Unsung Voices: Opera and Musical Narrative in the Nineteenth Century* (Princeton, New Jersey: Princeton University Press, 1991).

Allan, Jean Mary, 'Ewing, Alexander', *Grove Music Online*, Oxford Music Online, <www.oxfordmusiconline.com> [Accessed 18 April 2009].

Almén Byron, *A Theory of Musical Narrative* (Bloomington and Indianapolis: Indiana University Press, 2008).

Anand, Sushila, *Daisy: The Life and Loves of the Countess of Warwick* (London: Portrait, 2008).

Antcliffe, Herbert, 'The Recent Rise of Chamber Music in England', MQ, 7 (1920): 12–23.

Ash Arndt, Jessie, 'Musicians Gain Prestige', *Christian Science Monitor* (2 Nov 1960): 6.

Bailey, Alison, Ethel Bilsand, http://refuge.wikispaces.com/Bilsland?f=print [accessed 30 June 2010].

Bailey, Joanna, 'Gender as Style: Feminist Aesthetics and Postmodernism', *Contemporary Music Review*, 17/1 (1998): 105–13.

Baillie, Isobel, *Never Sing Louder Than Lovely* (London: Hutchinson, 1983).

Banfield, Stephen, *Sensibility and English Song: Critical Studies of the Early 20th Century* (Cambridge: Cambridge University Press, 1985).

———, 'Rebecca Clarke', in Julie A. Sadie and Rhian Samuel (eds), *New Grove Dictionary of Women Composers* (London: Macmillan, 1994): 119.

———, 'Lehmann, Liza', Grove Music Online, Oxford Music Online, <www.oxfordmusiconline.com> [accessed 2 June 2009].

Bantock, Myrrha, *Granville Bantock: A Personal Portrait* (London: J.M. Dent and Sons Ltd, 1972).

Barkin, Elaine and Lydia Hamessley (eds), *Audible Traces: Gender, Identity and Music* (Zurich: Cariofoli Verlagshaus, 1999).

Barthes, Roland, 'The Death of an Author', in *Image-Music-Text: Essays Selected and Translated by Stephen Heath* (London: Fontana, 1977), pp. 142–8.

Bashford, Christina, 'Learning to Listen: Audiences for Chamber Music in Early-Victorian London', *Journal of Victorian Culture*, 4/1 (Spring, 1999): 25–51.

———, 'Chamber Music', NGDMM, 15 (2001): 434–48.

Battersby, Christine, *Gender and Genius: Towards a Feminist Aesthetics* (London: Women's Press, 1989).

Bayliss, Stanley, 'Broadcast Music', MT, 98/1373 (July, 1957): 375–6.

Beddoe, Deidre, *Back to Home and Duty: Women Between the Wars 1918–1939* (London: Pandora, 1989).

Beecham, Thomas, *A Mingled Chime: Leaves from an Autobiography* (London: Hutchinson, 1979, first pub. 1944).

Benson, John, *The Rise of Consumer Society in Britain 1880–1980* (London, New York: Longman, 1994).

Berger, Melvin, *A Guide to Chamber Music* (London: Robert Hale, 1985).

Bergeron, Katherine and Philip V. Bohlman (eds), *Disciplining Music: Musicology and Its Canons* (Chicago and London: University of Chicago Press, 1992).

Bernstein, Jane, '"Shout Shout Up With Your Song!" Dame Ethel Smyth and the Changing Role of the British Woman Composer', in Jane Bowers and Judith Tick (eds), *Women Making Music* (New York: Macmillan Press, 1986).

Bird, John, *Percy Grainger* (Oxford: Oxford University Press, 1999).

Bishop, James, *The Illustrated London News: A Social History of Edwardian Britain* (London: Angus and Robertson, 1977).

Blevins, Pamela, *Ivor Gurney and Marion Scott: Song of Pain and Beauty* (Woodbridge: Boydell Press, 2008).

Bliss, Arthur, *As I Remember* (London: Faber and Faber, 1970).

Blom, Eric and Peter Platt, 'Marion Scott', in Stanley Sadie (ed.), *New Grove Dictionary of Music and Musicians*, 23 (London: Macmillan, 2001): 3–4.

———, 'Scott, Marion M', *Grove Music Online*, Oxford Music Online, <www.oxfordmusiconline.com> [accessed 14 October 2009].

Bowers, Jane and Judith Tick (eds) *Women Making Music: The Western Art Tradition 1150–1950* (Urbana: University of Illinois Press, 1986).

Boyd, Malcolm, *Grace Williams* (Cardiff: University of Wales Press, 1980).

Brittain, Vera, *Testament of Youth* (London: Virago, 1978, first pub. 1933).

———, *The Women at Oxford: A Fragment of History* (New York: Macmillian, 1960).

Burnham, Scott, 'A. B. Marx and the Gendering of Sonata Form', in Ian Bent (ed.), *Music Theory in the Age of Romanticism* (Cambridge: Cambridge University Press, 1996).

Burrell, Diana, 'Review', *BBC Music Magazine*, 6/9 (May 1998): 92–3.

Butler, Judith, *Gender Trouble: Feminism and the Subversion of Identity* (London, New York: Routledge, 1990).

———, *Bodies that Matter: On Discursive Limits of "Sex"* (New York, London: Routledge, 1993).

B.V., 'Chamber Music', MT, 66/992 (October, 1925): 909.

Caffrey, Kate, *The Edwardian Lady: Edwardian High Society 1900–1914* (London: Gordon and Cremonesi, 1979).

Cannadine, David, *The Decline and Fall of the British Aristocracy* (New Haven, London: Yale University Press, 1990).

Canning, Kathleen, *Gender History in Practice: Historical Perspectives on Bodies, Class and Citizenship* (Ithaca NY: Cornell University Press, 2006).

Carey, Hugh, *Duet for Two Voices: An Informal Biography of Edward J. Dent Compiled from his Letters to Clive Carey* (Cambridge: Cambridge University Press, 1979).

Chadwick, Whitney and Isabelle de Courtivron, *Significant Others Creativity and Intimate Partnership* (London: Thames and Hudson, 1993).

Chancellor, Valerie, 'Kathleen Bruckshaw (1877?–1921): a Forgotten Pianist and Composer', *Musical Opinion*, 1488 (May/June 2012), pp. 34–35.

Citron, Marcia J., *Cécile Chaminade: A Bio-Bibliography* (Westport: Greenwood Press, 1988).

———, 'Feminist Approaches to Musicology', in Susan C. Cook and Judy S. Tso (eds), *Cecilia Reclaimed: Feminist Perspectives on Gender and Music* (Illinois: University of Illinois Press, 1994).

———, *Gender and the Musical Canon* (Illinois: University of Illinois Press (1993, 2000).

Clément, Catherine, *Opera or the Undoing of Women* (London: I.B. Tauris, 1997).

Cobbett, Walter Willson, 'British Chamber Music', MT, 52/818 (April, 1911): 242–3.

———, 'A Foreword', *Chamber Music: A Supplement to the Music Student*, 1 (June, 1913): 1–2.

———, 'Duo Repertory: Some Comments', *Chamber Music: A Supplement to the Music Student*, 1 (June, 1913): 7–9.

———, 'A Chamber Music Causerie', *Chamber Music: A Supplement to the Music Student*, 2 (August, 1913): 13–16.

———, 'Some War-time Reflections', *Chamber Music: A Supplement to the Music Student*, 11 (November, 1914): 17–18.

———, 'The Beginning of Chamber Music', *Chamber Music: A Supplement to the Music Student*, 13 (March, 1915): 49–50.

———, 'Obiter Dicta', *Chamber Music: A Supplement to the Music Student*, 20 (May, 1916): 57.

———, 'More Plain Words', MT, 59/900 (February, 1918): 62–5.

———, 'Chamber Music Life', in Walter Willson Cobbett (ed.), *Cobbett's Cyclopedic Survey of Chamber Music* (2 vols, London: Oxford University Press, 1929).

———, 'Cobbett Competitions', in Walter Willson Cobbett (ed.), *Cobbett's Cyclopedic Survey of Chamber Music* (2 vols, London: Oxford University Press, 1929).

———, 'Ethel Barns', in W.W. Cobbett (ed.), *Cobbett's Cyclopedic Survey of Chamber Music* (2 vols, London: Oxford University Press, 1930).

———, 'Phantasy' in W.W. Cobbett (ed.), *Cobbett's Cyclopedic Survey of Chamber Music* (2 vols, London: Oxford University Press, 1930).

———, 'Society of Women Musicians' in W.W. Cobbett (ed.), *Cobbett's Cyclopedic Survey of Chamber Music* (2 vols, London: Oxford University Press, 1930).

———, 'Women Composers' in W.W. Cobbett (ed.), *Cobbett's Cyclopedic Survey of Chamber Music* (2 vols, London: Oxford University Press, 1930).

Cohen, Harriet, *A Bundle of Time: The Memoirs of Harriet Cohen* (London: Faber and Faber, 1969).

Cook, Susan C., and Tsou, Judy S. (eds), *Cecilia Reclaimed: Feminist Perspectives on Gender and Music* (Illinois: University of Illinois Press, 1994).

Cooper, Sarah (ed.), *Girls! Girls! Girls! Essays on Women and Music* (London: Cassell, 1995).

Coover, James, *Music Publishing Copyright and Piracy in Victorian England. A Twenty-Five Year Chronicle, 1881–1906 from the Pages of the Musical Opinion and Music Trade Review and Other English Music Journals of the Period* (London and New York: Mansell Publishing Ltd, 1985).

Corder, Frederick, *A History of the Royal Academy of Music from 1822 to 1922* (London: F. Corder, 1922).

Crawshay-Williams, Eliot, 'Morfydd Owen', *Wales*, 4 (1958): 50–56.

Curtis, Liane, 'Rebecca Clarke and Sonata Form: Questions of Gender and Genre', MQ, 81/ 3 (1997): 393–429.

———, 'Rebecca Clarke', *Grove Music Online*, Oxford Music Online, <www.oxfordmusiconline.com> [accessed 2 June 2009].

Dale, Catherine, *Music Analysis in Britain in the Nineteenth and Early Twentieth Centuries* (Aldershot: Ashgate, 2003).

Dale, Kathleen, 'Ethel Smyth's Prentice Work', ML, 30/4 (October, 1949): 329–36.

Davidoff, Leonore, *World's Between: Historical Perspectives on Gender and Class* (Cambridge: Polity Press, 1995).

Davies, Rhian, *Yr Eneth Ddisglair Annwyl (Never so Pure a Sight): Morfydd Owen (1891–1918): A Life in Pictures* (Llandyssyl, Dyfed: Gower Press, 1994).

———, 'A Refined and Beautiful Talent: Morfydd Llwyn Owen (1891–1918)' (unpub. PhD Diss. University of Wales, Bangor, 1999).

De Beauvoir, Simone, *The Second Sex*, ed. and trans H.M. Parshley (Harmondsworth: Penguin, 1972).

DeNora, Tia, 'Review of Feminine Endings', *Contemporary Sociology*, 22/1 (1993): 116–7.

Dibble, Jeremy, C., *C. Hubert H. Parry: His Life and Music* (Oxford: Clarendon Press, 1992).

Douglas-Home, Jessica, *Violet Gordon Woodhouse* (London: The Harvill Press, 1996).

Dowson, Jane, 'Older Sisters are Very Sobering Things: Contemporary Women Poets and the Female Affiliation Complex', *Feminist Review*, 62 (1999): 6–20.

Draper, Muriel, *Music at Midnight* (London: William Heinemann Ltd., 1929).

Drake Brockman, M., 'Women Composers', in W.W. Cobbett (ed.), *Cobbett's Cycopedic Survey* (2 vols, London: Oxford University Press, 1929).

Dunhill, David, *Thomas Dunhill: Maker of Music* (London: Thames Publishing, 1997).

Dunhill, Thomas F., *Chamber Music A Treatise for Students* (London: Macmillan and Co. and Stainer and Bell, 1913).

———, 'British Chamber Music', in W.W. Cobbett (ed.) *Cobbett's Cycopedic Survey* (2 vols, London: Oxford University Press, 1929).

Eagleton, Mary (ed.), *Feminist Literary Theory: A Reader* (Oxford: Basil Blackwell, 1986).

———, 'Introduction' in Mary Eagleton (ed.), *Feminist Literary Theory: A Reader* (Oxford: Basil Blackwell, 1986).

Ebel, Otto, *Women Composers: A Biographical Handbook of Woman's Work in Music* (New York: Chandler-Ebel Music, 1913).

Eggar, Katherine, 'Ethel Barns' in W.W. Cobbett (ed.), *Cobbett's Cyclopedic Survey of Chamber Music* (2 vols, London: Oxford University Press, 1929).

Eggar, Katherine Emily and Scott, Marion Margaret, 'Women's Doings in Chamber Music: Chamber Music Clubs', *Chamber Music: A Supplement to the Music Student*, 1 (June, 1913): 10.

———, 'Women's Doings in Chamber Music: Concert Organisation', *Chamber Music: A Supplement to the Music Student*, 2 (August, 1913): 27–8.

———, 'Women's Doings in Chamber Music: Women in the String Quartet', *Chamber Music: A Supplement to the Music Student*, 3 (October, 1913): 12– 15.

———, 'Women's Doings in Chamber Music: Women in European Chamber Music', *Chamber Music: A Supplement to the Music Student*, 4 (December, 1913): 30–32.

———, 'Women's Doings in Chamber Music: The Strings Club', *Chamber Music: A Supplement to the Music Student*, 5 (January, 1914): 41–2.

———, 'Women's Doings in Chamber Music: Women as Composers of Chamber Music', *Chamber Music: A Supplement to the Music Student*, 7 (March, 1914): 59–60.

———, 'Women's Doings in Chamber Music: Women as Composers of Chamber Music Second Paper', *Chamber Music: A Supplement to the Music Student*, 8 (May, 1914): 75–6.

———, 'Women's Doings in Chamber Music: Women as Composers of Chamber Music Third Paper', *Chamber Music: A Supplement to the Music Student*, 9 (July, 1914): 97–8.

———, 'Women's Doings in Chamber Music: Women Musicians and the Leipzig Exhibition', *Chamber Music: A Supplement to the Music Student*, 10 (November, 1914): 29–31.

Ehrlich, Cyril, *The Music Profession in Britain since the Eighteenth Century: A Social History* (Oxford: Clarendon, 1985).

Ellis, Katharine, 'Female Pianists and Their Male Critics in Nineteenth-Century Paris', *Journal of the American Musicological Society*, 50/2&3 (1997): 353–85.

Englesberg, Barbara, 'The Life and Works of Ethel Barns, British Violinist-Composer 1873–1948' (Upub. PhD Diss., Boston University, 1987).

Feldman, Shoshana, 'Women and Madness: The Critical Phalacy', in Mary Eagleton (ed.), *Feminist Literary Theory: A Reader* (Oxford: Basil Blackwell, 1986).

Felski, Rita, *Literature after Feminism* (Chicago, London: University of Chicago Press, 2003).

Fend, Michael and Michel Noiray (eds), *Musical Education in Europe 1770–1914: Compositional, Institutional and Political Challenges* (Berlin: Berliner Wissenschafts-Verlag, 2005).

Fenton, David, 'Piano Quartet', *Grove Music Online*, Oxford Music Online, <www.oxfordmusiconline.com> [accessed 14 October 2009].

_______. 'Piano Quintet', *Grove Music Online*, Oxford Music Online, <www.oxfordmusiconline.com> [accessed 14 October 2009].

Field, Christopher D.S. et al, 'Fantasia', *Grove Music Online*, Oxford Music Online, <www.oxfordmusiconline.com> [accessed 3 May 2009].

Fifield, Christopher, *Ibbs and Tillett: The Rise and Fall of a Musical Empire* (Aldershot: Ashgate, 2005).

Foreman, Lewis, *Bax: A Composer and his Times* (London, Berkeley: Scholar Press, 1983).

_______, 'Edith Swepstone', *Grove Music Online*, Oxford Music Online, <www.oxfordmusiconline.com> [accessed 20 May 2010].

_______ (ed.), *The John Ireland Companion* (Woodbridge: Boydell Press, 2011).

Foreman, Lewis and Susan Foreman, *London: A Musical Gazetteer* (New Haven: Yale University Press, 2005).

Forrester, Viviane, 'What Women's Eyes See' in Mary Eagleton (ed.), *Feminist Literary Theory: A Reader* (Oxford: Basil Blackwood, 1986).

Forster, Edward M., *Howard's End* (London: Edward Arnold, 1910).

Foucault, Michel, 'What is an Author?', in Paul Rabonow (ed.), *The Foucault Reader: An Introduction to Foucault's Thought* (London: Penguin Books, 1984), pp. 101–20.

F.S.H., 'Bournemouth Festival', MT, 68/1012 (June, 1927): 552.

Fuller, Sophie, *Pandora Guide to Women Composers: Britain and the United States* (London: Pandora, 1994).

———, 'Women Composers During the British Musical Renaissance 1880–1918' (Unpub., PhD Diss., Kings College University of London, 1998).

———, 'Devoted Attention: Looking for Lesbian Musicians in Fin-de-Siècle Britain', in Sophie Fuller and Lloyd Whitesell (eds), *Queer Episodes in Music and Modern Identity* (Urbana: Univeristy of Illinois Press, 2002).

———, 'Dora Bright', in Sylvia Glickman and Martha Furman Schleifer (eds), *Women Composers Through the Ages* (Newhaven, Conn: G.K. Hall and Co, 2003).

———, 'Barns, Ethel.' *Grove Music Online*, Oxford Music Online, <www.oxfordmusionline.com> [accessed 2 June 2009].

———, 'Bright, Dora', *Grove Music Online*, Oxford Music Online, <www.oxfordmusiconline.com> [accessed 2 June 2009].

———, 'Eggar, Katherine Emily', *Grove Music Online*, Oxford Music Online, <www.oxfordmusiconline.com> [accessed 14 October 2009].

———, 'Smyth, Dame Ethel (Mary)', *Grove Music Online*, Oxford Music Online, <www.oxfordmusiconline.com> [accessed 14 October 2009].

Gibson, Lorna, *Beyond Jerusalem: Music in the Women's Institute 1919–1969* (Aldershot: Ashgate, 2008).

Gillett, Paula, 'Ambivalent Friendships: Music Lovers and Amateurs and Professional Musicians in the Late Nineteenth Century', in Christina Bashford and Liane Langley (eds), *Music and British Culture 1785–1914* (Oxford: Oxford University Press, 2000).

———, *Musical Women in England, 1870–1914: Encroaching on all Man's Privileges* (Basingstoke: Macmillan, 2000).

Gillies, Malcolm, Pear, David and Carrell, Mark (eds), *Self-Portrait of Percy Grainger* (Oxford: Oxford University Press, 2006).

Glickman, Sylvia and Martha Furman Schleifer, *Women Composers: Music Through the Ages* (Newhaven Conn: G. K. Hall and Co, 2003).

Goossens, Marie, *Life on a Harp String* (London: Thorne Printing and Publishing Co., 1987).

Gould, Carol C. (ed.), *Key Concepts in Critical Theory: Gender* (Atlantic Highlands New Jersey: Humanities Press, 1997).

Grayzel, Susan R., *Women and the First World War* (Harlow: Longman, 2002).

Greer, David, *A Numerous and Fashionable Audience: The Story of Elsie Swinton* (London: Thames Publishing, 1977).

Greer, Germaine, *The Whole Woman* (London: Anchor, 1999).

Gregory, Gill, *The Sound of Turquoise* (London: Kingston University Press, 2009).

———, 'Dr Hazel Chodak-Gregory', < http://hle.org.uk/history.html> [Accessed 8 January 2011].

Haldane, Charlotte, *Music My Love! One Listener's Autobiography* (London: Arthur Baker Ltd., 1936).

Hall, Catherine, *White, Male and Middle Class: Explorations in Feminism and History* (Cambridge: Polity Press, 1992).

Halstead, Jill, *The Woman Composer: Creativity and the Gendered Politics of Musical Composition* (Aldershot: Ashgate Publishing Ltd., 1997).

Hardy, Lisa, *The British Piano Sonata 1870–1945* (Woodbridge: Boydell Press, 2001).

Harrison, Beatrice, *The Cello and the Nightingale* (London: John Murray Publishers Ltd., 1985).

Harrison, Wendy Cealy and John Hood-Williams, *Beyond Sex and Gender* (London, Thousand Oaks, New Dehli: Sage Publications, 2002).

Hawkins, Frank V., *A Hundred Years of Chamber Music* (London: South Place Ethical Society, 1987).

Henson, Karen, 'In the House of Disillusion: Augusta Holmés and La Montagne Noir', *Cambridge Opera Journal*, ix/3 (1997): pp. 233–62.

Herschel Baron, John, *Intimate Music A History of the Idea of Chamber Music* (Stuyvesant: Pendragon Press, 1998).

Higgins, Paula, 'Women in Music, Feminist Criticism, and Guerilla Musicology: Reflections on Recent Polemics', *19th Century Music*, 27/2 (Fall, 1993): 174–192.

Hisama, Ellie M., *Gendering Musical Modernism: The Music of Ruth Crawford, Marion Bauer, and Miriam Gideon* (Cambridge: Cambridge University Press, 2001).

Hodges, Betsi., 'W.W. Cobbett's Phantasy: A Legacy of Chamber Music in the British Musical Renaissance' (unpub., DMA Diss., University of North Carolina at Greensboro, 2008).

Holbrooke, Joseph, *Contemporary British Composers* (London: Cecil Palmer, 1925).

Holst, Imogen, *Gustav Holst: A Biography* (London, New York, Toronto: Oxford University Press, 1969).

Hudson, Derek, *Norman O'Neill: A Life of Music* (London: Quality Press Ltd., 1945).

Hughes, Meirion, *The English Musical Renaissance 1840–1940: Constructing a National Music* (Manchester: Manchester University Press, 2001).

Hull, Robert, 'On Simplicity in Music', MT, 67/1005 (November 1926): 996–7.

Hurlstone, Katharine (ed.), *William Hurlstone, Musician: Memories and Records by his Friends* (London: Cary and Co., 1949).

Hyde, Derek, *New Found Voices: Women in Nineteenth-Century English Music* (Ash: Tritone Music Publications, 1991).

Jacobs, Arthur, *Henry J. Wood Maker of the Proms* (London: Menthuen, 1994).

Jaggar, Alison M., 'Human Biology in Feminist Theory: Sexual Equality reconsidered', in Carol C. Gould (ed.), *Key Concepts in Critical Theory* (Atlantic Highlands New Jersey: Humanities Press, 1997).

Jones, Bethan, 'Letter of 30th May 1976', *Welsh Music*, 3 (Summer, 1976): 100.

Jones, Kitty I., 'The Enigma of Morfydd Owen', *Welsh Music*, 5/1 (1975-6): 8–21.

Jones, Leslie, 'Seventy Years of Composing: An Interview with Vivian Fine', CMR, 16/1 (1997): 21–6.

Jung, Carl G., 'Psychological Types' in Constance Lang (ed.) *Collected Papers on the Psychology of Phantasy* (London: Baillière, Tindall and Cox, 1920).

Kahan, Sylvia, *Music's Modern Muse: A Life of Winaretta Singer Princesse de Polignac* (Rochester: University of Rochester Press, 2003).

King, A.T., 'Woes of a Woman Composer: Dame Ethel Smyth', *Musical Courier*, 89 (1924): 11.

Kington, Beryl, 'Thomas F. Dunhill and Sibelius 7', *Journal of the British Music Society*, 18 (1996): 54–65.

———, 'Dunhill, Thomas F.', *Grove Music Online*, Oxford Music Online, <www.oxfordmusiconline.com> [accessed 14 October 2009].

Kolneder, Walter, *Anton Webern: An Introduction to his Works*, Humphrey Searle (trans.) (Westport Connecticut: Greenwood Press, 1982).

Lehmann, Liza, *The Life of Liza Lehmann* (London: T Fisher Unwin, 1919).

Leppert, Richard, *Music and Image: Domesticity, Ideology and Socio-cultural Formation in Eighteenth Century England* (Cambridge: Cambridge University Press, 1988).

———, *The Sight of Sound: Music, Representation, and the History of the Body* (Berkeley, London: University of California Press, 1993).

Lewis, Jane, *Women in England 1870–1950: Sexual Divisions and Social Change* (Brighton: Wheatsheaf, 1984).

Liddell, Nona, 'Jessie Grimson: Me and My Teacher', *The Strad* (July 2007): 37.

Lim, Lemy, 'The Reception of Women Pianists 1950–1960' (unpub PhD diss. City University, 2011).

Long, Constance E., *Collected Papers on the Psychology of Phantasy* (London: Baillière, Tindall and Cox, 1920).

Lockwood, Annea et al., 'In Response', PNM, 20/1&2 (Autumn 1981–Summer 1982): 288–329.

Lutyens, Elisabeth, *A Goldfish Bowl* (London: Cassell, 1972).

McAlpin, Colin, 'Britain: Her Music', MT, 57/884 (October, 1916): 445–7.

McCalla, James, *Twentieth-Century Chamber Music* (New York, London: Routledge, 2000).

Macarthur, Sally, *Feminist Aesthetics in Music* (Westport, Connecticut and London: Greenwood Press, 2002).

———, *Towards a Twenty-first-century Feminist Politics of Music* (Farnham: Ashgate, 2010).

McClary, Susan, *Feminine Endings: Music, Gender, Sexuality* (Minneapolis: University of Minnesota Press, 1991).

———, 'Reshaping a Discipline: Musicology and Feminism in the 1990s', *Feminist Studies*, 19/2 (Summer, 1993): 399–423.

———, 'Paradigm Dissonances: Music Theory, Cultural Studies, Feminist Criticism', PNM, 32 (1994): 68–85.

Macdonald, Hugh, *Skryabin* (New York, Melbourne: Oxford University Press, 1978).

McDowell, Linda and Rosemary Pringle (eds), *Defining Women Social Institutions and Gender Divisions* (Cambridge: Polity Press, 1992).

———, 'Introduction', in Linda McDowell and Rosemary Pringle (eds), *Defining Women Social Institutions and Gender Divisions* (Cambridge: Polity Press, 1992).

McEwan, Ian, 'Hello Would You Like a Free Book?', *The Guardian Online*, 19 September 2005 <www.guardian.co.uk/books/2005/sep/20/fiction.features11> [accessed 18 October 2009].

McKenna, Marian C., *Myra Hess: A Portrait* (London: Hamish Hamilton, 1976).

Macpherson, Stewart, *Form in Music with Special Reference to the Designs of Instrumental Music* (London: Joseph Williams, 1908).

Maddox, Brenda, *Freud's Wizard: The Enigma of Ernest Jones* (London: John Murray, 2006).

Marcus, Jane, 'Virginia Woolf and her Violin: Mothering, Madness and Music' in Ruth Perry and M. Watson Brownley (eds), *Mothering the Mind: Twelve Studies of Writers and their Silent Partners* (New York: Holmes and Meier, 1984).

Marwick, Arthur, *The Deluge: British Society and the First World War* (New York: W.W. Norton, 1965).

———, *Women at War* (London: Fontana, 1977).

Marx, A.B., *Die Lehre von der Musikalschen Komposition, Praktisch – Theoretisch*. 2nd edn (4 vols, Leipzig: Breitkopf and Härtel, 1841–1851).

Mason, Michael, *The Making of Victorian Sexuality* (Oxford: Oxford University Press, 1994).

Mathias, Rhiannon, *Lutyens, Maconchy, Williams and Twentieth-century Music: A Blest Trio of Sirens* (Farnham: Ashgate, 2012).

Musgrave, Michael, *The Musical Life of the Crystal Palace* (Cambridge: Cambridge University Press, 1995).

n.a., 'Correspondence to the Editor', *The Overture*, 4/1 (March, 1893): 16.

———, 'Songs of the Century: no. 1 The Youthful Composers Pæan of Joy', *The Overture*, 4/1 (March, 1893): 7.

———, 'George Alfred Gibson', MT, 41/ 686 (April, 1900): 225–28.

———, 'Front Matter', MT, 46/749 (July, 1905): 430.

———, 'Front Matter', MT, 46/754 (December, 1905): 791.

———, 'Patron's Fund Concert', MT, 47/755 (January, 1906): 44.

———, 'Prize Phantasies', MT, 47/761 (July, 1906): 489.

———, 'London Concerts', MT, 48/769 (March, 1907): 181.

———, 'Foreign Notes', MT, 51/804 (February, 1910): 114–16.

———, 'The Society of Women Musicians', MT, 52/822 (August, 1911): 536.

———, 'Organizing a "Society of Women Musicians" in London', *The New York Times*, October 22, 1911.

———, 'London Concerts', MT, 52/826 (December, 1911): 805–807.

———, 'Chamber Music', MT, 53/829 (March, 1912): 181.

———, 'Other Recitals', MT, 53/829 (March 1912): 181–2.

———, 'The Musical Works of Dr. Ethel Smyth: Foreign Appreciation', MT, 54/840 (February, 1913): 104.

———, 'Occasional Notes', MT, 54/845 (July 1913): 444.

———, 'Occasional Notes', MT, 55/855 (May 1914): 305.

———, 'London Concerts', MT, 56/864 (February, 1915): 108.

———, 'London Concerts', MT, 56,/8 (June 1915): 364.

———, 'Society of Women Musicians', MT, 57/883, (September, 1916): 419.

———, *Etiquette for Ladies: A Guide to the Observances of Good Society* (London: Ward, Lock and Co., 1923).

———, 'The Folkestone Festival', MT, 71/1053 (November, 1930): 1035.

———, 'Trinity College of Music', MT, 72/1066 (December, 1931): 1128.

———, 'A Woman Composer', *The Sydney Morning Herald* (21 March 1932): 3.

———, 'Royal Academy of Music', MT, 72/1058 (April, 1932): 357–8.

———, 'The Truth About Man', in *The Lady's Realm A Selection from the Monthly Issues: November 1904 to April 1905* (London: Arrow Books, 1972).

Nectoux, Jean, *Gabriel Fauré: A Musical Life, Roger Nichols* (trans.) (Cambridge: Cambridge University Press, 1991).

Neuls-Bates, Carol, *Women in Music* (New York: Harper and Row, 1982).

Newman, Ernest, *Essays from the World of Music*, ed. Felix Aprahamian (London: John Calder, 1976).

Newton, Judith L., Mary P. Ryan and Judith R. Walkowitz (eds), *Sex and Class in Women's History* (London: Routledge and Kegan Paul, 1983).

Nicholson, Virginia, *Singled Out: How Two Million Women Survived Without Men After the First World War* (London: Viking Press, 2007).

O'Brien, Mary, *The Politics of Reproduction* (London and Boston: Routledge & Kegan Paul, 1981).

Orledge, Robert, *Gabriel Fauré* (London: Eulenburg, 1979).

Ortner, Sherry B., 'Is Female to Male as Nature is to Culture?', in Carol C. Gould (ed.) *Key Concepts in Critical Theory* (Atlantic Highlands New Jersey: Humanities Press, 1997).

Osbourne, Peter and Lynne Segal (eds), 'Extracts from Gender as Peformance: An Interview with Judith Butler, London 1993', in *Radical Philosophy* <http://www.theory.org.uk/but-int1.htm> [Accessed 30 August 2008].

Palmer, Christopher, *Herbert Howells: A Celebration* (London: Thames Publishing, 1996).

Parrott, Ian, *Cyril Scott and his Piano Music* (London: Thames Publishing, 1991).

Parry, C. Hubert H., *The Art of Music*, 5th edn (London: Kegan Paul, Trench, Trübner and Co., 1894).

Payne, Anthony, *Frank Bridge: Radical and Conservative* (London: Thames Publishing, 1999).

Pendle, Karin (ed.), *Women and Music: A History*, 2nd edn (Bloomington: Indiana University Press, 2001).

Perris, Arnold, *Music as Propaganda Art to Persuade and Control* (Westport, Conn.: Greenwood Press, 1985).

Perris, G.H., *New York Times* (21 September 1914), *New York Times* Online Archive, < http://query.nytimes.com/mem/archivefree/pdf?res=9F07E4D7113FE633A25752C2A96F9C946596D6CF> [Accessed 2 June 2009].

Prout, Ebenezer, *Musical Form*, 4th edn (London: Augener, 1893).

———, *Applied Forms: A Sequel to 'Musical Form'* (London: Augener Ltd., 1895).

Purvis, June (ed.), *Women's History. Britain 1850–1945: An Introduction* (London, New York: Routledge, 1995).

Raitt, Suzanne, 'The Singers of Sargent: Mabel Batten, Elsie Swinton and Ethel Smyth', *Women: A Cultural Review*, 3/1 (Spring, 1992): pp. 23–9.

Raynor, Henry, *Music and Society Since 1815* (London: Barrie and Jenkins, 1976).

Reich, Nancy B., *Clara Schumann: The Artist and the Woman* (Ithaca and London: Cornell University Press, 2001).

Riley, Denise, 'Does Sex have a History? 'Women' and Feminism', *New Formations*, 1 (Spring 1987): 35–45.

Ritterman, Janet, 'The Royal College of Music 1883–1899 Pianists and their Contribution to the Forming of a National Conservatory', in Michael Fend and Michel Noiray (eds), *Musical Education in Europe 1770–1914* (2 vols, Berlin: Berliner Wissenschafts-Verlag, 2005).

Robinson, Suzanne, 'Smyth the Anarchist: Fin-de-Siècle Radicalism in The Wreckers', *Cambridge Opera Journal*, 20/2 (2009): 149–79.

Rogers, Clara K., *Memories of a Musical Career* (Private Distribution: Plimpton Press, 1932).

Rolley, Katrina, 'Cutting a Dash: The Dress of Radclyffe Hall and Una Troubridge', *Feminist Review*, 35 (1990): 54–66.

Rosen, Carole, *The Goossens: A Musical Century* (London: André Deutsch Ltd., 1993).

Rosen, Charles, *Sonata Forms*, rev. edn (London, New York: W.W. Norton and Co., 1988).

St John, Christopher, *Ethel Smyth: A Biography* (London,: Longmans, Green and Co., 1959).

Samuel, Rhian, 'Women's Music: A Twentieth-Century Perspective', in Julie. A. Sadie and Rhian Samuel (eds), *The New Grove Dictionary of Women Composers* (London: Macmillan, 1994).

Saxe Wyndham, Henry and Geoffrey L'Epine (eds), *Who's Who in Music A Biographical Record of Contemporary Musicians* (London: Sir Isaac Pitman and Sons Ltd, 1913).

———, *Who's Who in Music A Biographical Record of Contemporary Musicians*, 2nd edn (London: Sir Isaac Pitman and Sons Ltd, 1915).

Scher, Steven P. (ed.), *Music and Text: Critical Inquiries* (Cambridge: Cambridge University Press, 1992).

Schmitz, Robert, *The Piano Works of Claude Debussy* (Westport: Greenwood Press, 1950).

P.A.S (Scholes, Percy), 'The Society of Women Musicians: A Model for Men', *Music Student* (May, 1918): 335.

Scholes, Percy A., *The Mirror of Music 1844–1944: A Century of Musical Life in Britain as Reflected in the Musical Times* (London: Novello and Co. and Oxford University Press, 1947).

Scott, Cyril, The Philosophy of Modernism and its Connection to Music (London: Kegan Paul, Trench, Trübner and Co., 1917).

———, 'Suggestions for a More Logical Sonata Form', MMR, xlvi (1 May 1917): 104–5.

Scott, Derek B., *The Singing Bourgeois: Songs of the Victorian Drawing Room and Parlour* (London: Open University Press, 1989).

———. *From the Erotic to the Demonic: on Critical Musicology* (New York: Oxford University Press, 2003).

Scott, Joan W., 'Deconstructing Equality-versus-Difference: or, The Uses of Post-Structuralist Theory for Feminism', in Linda McDowell and Rosemary Pringle (eds) *Defining Women Social Institutions and Gender Divisions* (Cambridge: Polity Press, 1992).

Scott, Marion M., *Beethoven* (London: J.M. Dent and Sons, 1934).

Scott, William H., *Edward German: An Intimate Biography* (London: Chappell and Co., 1932).

Scowcroft, Philip, L., *British Light Music: A Personal Gallery of Twentieth-Century Composers* (London: Thames, 1997).

Segal, Hanna, *Dream Phantasy and Art* (London and New York: Tavistock/Routledge, 1991).

Shead, Richard, *Constant Lambert* (London: Simon Publications, 1973).

Shepherd, John, *Music as Social Text* (Cambridge: Polity Press, 1991).

Showalter, Elaine, *A Literature of Their Own: British Women Novelists from Brontë to Lessing* (London: Virago, 1978).

———, *Sexual Anarchy: Gender and Culture at the Fin de Siècle* (London: Bloomsbury, 1991).

Simpson, Barbara Penketh, 'History', *Society of Women Artists*, <www.society-women-artists.org.uk/history.html> [accessed 20 May 2009].

Smart, Carol (ed.), *Regulating Womanhood: Historical Essays on Marriage, Motherhood and Sexuality* (London, New York: Routledge, 1992).

Smyth, Ethel M., 'Dr Ethel Smyth Argues for Fair Sex Rights in Music at Concert', *Musical America*, 33/10 (1921): 3–23.

———, *Streaks of Life* (New York: Longmans, Green and Co., 1924).

———, *A Final Burning of Boats Etc.* (New York: Longmans, Green and Co., 1928).

———, *Female Pipings in Eden* (London: Peter Davies Ltd., 1933).

———, *Beecham and Pharoah* (London: Chapman and Hall, 1935).

———, *As Time Went On…* (London: Longmans, Green and Co., 1936).

———, *The Memoirs of Ethel Smyth*, Ronald Crichton (intr. and abbr.) (Harmondsworth: Viking, 1987).

Solie, Ruth A., *Music in Other Words: Victorian Conversations* (Berkeley, Los Angeles: University of California Press, 2004).

Souhami, Diana, *The Trials of Radclyffe Hall* (London: Virago, 1999).

Specht, Richard., 'Dr Ethel Smyth', MT, 53/829 (March, 1912): 168.

Spicer, Paul, *Herbert Howells* (Bridgend: Poetry Wales Press Ltd., 1998).

Stanford, Charles V., *Musical Composition A Short Treatise for Students* (London: Macmillan and Co., 1911, 1930).

Stradling, Robert and Meirion Hughes, *The English Musical Renaissance 1860–1940 Construction and Deconstruction* (London, New York: Routledge, 1993).

Stratton, Stephen S., 'Woman in Relation to Musical Art', *Proceedings of the Musical Association, 9th Session, 1882–1883* (May 1882): 115–46.

Stuckenschmidt, Hans H., *Arnold Schoenberg*, E. Temple Roberts (trans.) (Westport Connecticut: Greenwood Press, 1979).

Suppan, Wolfgang, 'Wind Quintet', *Grove Music Online*, Oxford Music Online, <www.oxfordmusiconline.com> [accessed 14 October 2009].

Swan, Alfred J., *Scriabin* (New York: Da Capo Press, 1923, 1969).

Swinburne, J., 'Women and Music', *Proceedings of the Musical Association, 46th Session, 1919–1920* (January, 1920): 21–42.

Thiele, Beverly, 'Vanishing Acts in Social and Political Thought: Tricks of the Trade', in Linda McDowell and Rosemary Pringle (eds), *Defining Women Social Institutions and Gender Distortions* (Cambridge: Polity Press, 1992).

Thomas, Gill, *Life on all Fronts: Women in the First World War* (Cambridge: Cambridge University Press, 1989).

Thomson, David, *England in the Twentieth Century: (1914–1979)*, Geoffrey Warner (rev.) (Harmondsworth: Penguin Books Ltd., 1981).

Tick, Judith, 'Passed Away is the Piano Girl: Changes in American Musical Life, 1870–1900', in Jane Bowers and Judith Tick (eds) *Women Making Music: The Western Art Tradition, 1150–1950* (London and Basingstoke: Macmillan Press, 1986).

———, *Ruth Crawford Seeger: A Composer's Search for American Music* (New York: Oxford University Press, 1997).

Tickner, Lisa, *The Spectacle of Women: Imagery of the Suffragette Campaign 1907–1914* (London: Chatto and Windus, 1987).

Tilmouth, Michael, 'Chamber Music', in Stanley Sadie (ed.) *New Grove Dictionary of Music and Musicians* (London: Macmillan Publishers Ltd., 1980).

———, and Basil Smallman, 'Piano Trio', *Grove Music Online*, Oxford Music Online, <www.oxfordmusiconline.com> [accessed 14 October 2009].

Tovey, Donald, *The Classics of Music: Talks, Essays, and Other Writings Previously Uncollected*, Michael Tilmouth (ed.), David Kimbell and Roger Savage (completed) (Oxford: Oxford Univerity Press, 2001).

Verne, Mathilde, *Chords of Remembrance* (London: Hutchinson and Co., 1936).

Walker, Ernest, 'The Modern British Phantasy', *Chamber Music*, 17 (November, 1915): 17–26.

Walker, Paul M., 'Fugue: The Romantic Era', *Grove Music Online*, Oxford Music Online, <www.oxfordmusiconline.com> [accessed 14 October 2009].

Wallach Scott, J., *Gender and the Politics of History* (New York: Colombia University Press, 1988).

Walthew, R.H., 'A New Book on Chamber Music', *Chamber Music: A Supplement to the Music Student*, 2 (August 1913): 25–6.

———,'String Quartets', *Proceedings of the Musical Association, 42nd Session* 1915–1916 (June, 1916): 145–62.

Warwick, Frances Countess of., *A Woman and the War* (London: Chapman and Hall, 1916).

———, *Afterthoughts* (London: Cassell and Company, 1931).

Watkins, Glenn, *Proof Through the Night: Music and the Great War* (California: University of California Press, 2002).

Watson, Janet S.K., *Music and the Middle Class: The Social Structure of Concert Life in London, Paris and Vienna* (New York: Holmes and Meier, 1975).

———, *Fighting Different Wars: Experience, Memory and the First World War in Britain* (Cambridge: Cambridge University Press, 2004).

Watson, Monica, *York Bowen: A Centenary Tribute* (London: Thames Publishing, 1984).

Weber, William, 'Concerts at Four Conservatoires in the 1880s: A Comparative Analysis', in Michael Fend and Michel Noiray (eds), *Musical Education in Europe 1770–1914* (2 vols, Berlin: Berliner Wissenschafts-Verlag, 2005).

Webster, James, 'Sonata Form', *Grove Music Online*, Oxford Music Online, <www.oxfordmusiconline.com> [accessed 14 October 2009].

Weininger, Otto, *Sex and Character* (New York: A.L. Burt, 1906).

Wessely, Othmar and Bernd Wiechert, 'Heinrich Freiherr von Herzogenberg', *Grove Music Online*, Oxford Music Online, <www.oxfordmusic.com>. [accessed 2 June 2009].

White, Maude Valerie, *Friends and Memories* (London: Edward Arnold, 1914).

———, *My Indian Summer* (London: Grayson and Grayson, 1932).

Wickham, Anna, *Writings of Anna Wickham, Free Woman and Poet*, R.D. Smith (ed.) (London: Virago, 1984).

Wiley, Christopher, '"When a Woman Speaks the Truth About her Body": Ethel Smyth, Virginia Woolf, and the Challenge of Lesbian Auto/Biography', ML, 85/3 (August 2004): 388–414.

———, 'Re-writing Composer's Lives: Critical Historiography and Musical Biography' (Unpub. PhD Diss, Royal Holloway University of London, 2008).

Wilson, Andrew Norman, *After the Victorians 1901–1953* (London: Hutchinson, 2005).

Wood, Elizabeth, 'Women, Music and Ethel Smyth: A Pathway in the Politics of Music', *Massachusetts Review*, 24/1 (Spring 1983): 125–39.

———, 'Performing Rights: A Sonography of Women's Suffrage', *Musical Quarterly*, 79/4 (1995): 606–43.

Woodgate, Gordon K., *The Oxford Chamber Music Society A Brief History* (Oxford: Oxford Chamber Music Society, 1997).

Woolf. Virginia, *A Room of One's Own* (London: Hogarth Press, 1991).

Young, Percy M., *A History of British Music* (London: Ernest Benn Lyd, 1967).

Music Sources

Barns, Ethel, *Adagio* (London: Schott and Co., 1909).
———, *Fantasie* (London: B. Schott's Söhne, 1912).
Bridge, Frank, *Phantasie in C Minor* (London: Augener, 1907).
Dunhill, Thomas F., *Phantasy-Trio* (London: Stainer and Bell, 1912).
———, *Phantasy in F Major* (London: J. B. Cramer and Co., 1923).
Fauré, Gabriel, *Quartet No. 1* (New York: International Music Company, 1956).
Fine, Vivian, *Meeting For Equal Rights 1866* (Vivian Fine Estate, 1975).
Hurlstone, William Y., *Phantasie* (London: Novello and Co. for The Worshipful Company of Musicians, 1906).
———, *Trio in G* (London: Charles Avison, 1907).
Ireland, John, *Piano Trio No. 2 in One Movement* (London: Stainer and Bell, 1918).
Maddsion, Adela, *Quintet* (London: Curwen, 1916).
Owen, Morfydd (Lenavanmo), Piano Trio 'Cathedral at Rhiems', 'Cathedral at Liége' (Unpublished, 1915).
Smyth, Ethel, *String Quartet in E Minor* (London: Universal Edition, 1914).
Spain-Dunk, Susan, *Phantasy Quartet in D Minor* (London: Goodwin and Tabb, 1915).
Verne-Bredt, Alice, *Phantasie* (London: Schott and Co., 1910).
Walthew, Richard, *Phantasy* (London: Stainer and Bell, 1912).

Recorded Sources

Archaeus Quartet, *Smyth, Beach and Spain-Dunk* (Lorelt, LNT114, 2003).
Banfield, Stephen, *Light English Composers* (Sound Recording Radio 3, National Sound Archive, H5440/21:02:59", 1995).
Evans, Nancy, *Leaders of National Life interviewed by Rebecca Abrams* (Sound Recording, National Sound Archive, C408/018/01-05, 1991).
The Fibonacci Sequence, *Edward Elgar: Three Movements from Piano Trio, Frank Bridge: Piano Quartet in C Minor, Adela Maddison: Piano Quintet* (Dutton Epoch, CDLX7220, 2009).
Radio 4, *Women's Hour Feature on Adela Maddison* (11 April 2007).
Sheffield, G. and A. Lyle (producers), *Music Weekly Walter Wilson Cobbett* (Sound Recording BBC Radio 3, National Sound Archive, 1987).
Summerhayes Piano Trio, *English Romantic Trios* (Meridian Records, CDE84478, 2005)

Index